CORVETTE

CHEVROLET'S SUPERCAR

RANDY LEFFINGWELL

motorbooks

25 24 23 22 21   2 3 4 5

ISBN: 978-0-7603-6850-3

Digital edition published in 2021
eISBN: 978-0-7603-6851-0

The Library of Congress has cataloged the previous edition as follows:

Leffingwell, Randy, 1948- author.
   [Corvette (2015)]
   Corvette : seven generations of American high performance /
by Randy Leffingwell.
      pages cm
   ISBN 978-0-7603-4663-1 (hc w/jacket)
   1. Corvette automobile. I. Title.
   TL215.C6L44 2015
   629.222'2—dc23
                        2014031322

Acquiring Editor: Darwin Holmstrom
Page Design and Layout: Simon Larkin
Cover Design and Additional Layout: Cindy Samargia Laun

FRONT COVER: The stunning 2020 Stingray. David Newhardt
Photo © 2020, courtesy GM Media Archives

BACK COVER: Take a black Corvette Grand Sport, put it in a black studio, and add light. The result is spectacular. *Photo © 2020, courtesy GM Media Archives*

FRONTIS: 1953 Corvette Roadster.
Randy Leffingwell

TITLE PAGE: A glimpse into the 1963 split-window.
Randy Leffingwell

Printed in China

DEDICATION

For the late Anatole "Tony" Lapine (1930–2012), who made design history on two continents. His touch, imagination, direction, and administration turned the vehicles he developed not only into important automobiles, but also into significant design language.

ACKNOWLEDGMENTS

Thanks first to Peggy Kelly, Global Asset Manager, GM Media Archive and Licensing Trademark, Detroit. In addition, my thanks go to Gene Reamer, Manager, Trademark Licensing Consumer Products, General Motors; Peggy Vezina, Event Coordinator, GM Heritage Center, Sterling Heights, Michigan, for access to the collection.

Indianapolis Motor Speedway Hall of Fame Museum Director Ellen Bireley has supported and encouraged my projects for many years, and I am grateful to her and to Indianapolis Motor Speedway President Doug Boles.

Great thanks to my friend Ed Baumgarten, the talented, tireless chief photographer at Mid America Motorworks (Effingham, Illinois), and "head cheerleader" Mike Yager, who opened their impressive photo archives of the extensive Corvette collection. I am grateful to Wendell Strode, Executive Director at the National Corvette Museum (Bowling Green, Kentucky), as well as Katie Frassinelli, Marketing and Communications Manager, and Tammy Bryant, Corvette Store Manager/Buyer. I also wish to thank Lance Miller and Bill Miller III, co-owners at Carlisle events, home of Corvettes at Carlisle (Carlisle, Pennsylvania), and to Chris Hahn, director of Creative Services and Technology.

Ken Lingenfelter, Lingenfelter Motor Sports (Brighton, Michigan), offered me the chance to photograph four cars for this book from his important collection. I am very grateful. I also want to thank long-time friend Nathan Sheets (Ken's Marketing Manager) for the invitation to come shoot. My thanks as well to Kaki Bandfield, Administrative Assistant, for help keeping the history straight.

In addition, I want to acknowledge generous help from Kevin Adams, Tom Armstong, Peter Brock, Reeves Callaway, John Carefoot, Dave Ferguson, Eric Gustafson, the late David Hmura, Roger Judski, Kevin Mackay, Jim Mangione, Rich Mason, Dana Mecum, Peter Mullin, Sam Murtaugh, Leonard and Jonathan "Hoss" Nagel, Leslie Tuttle, and Harry Yeaggy.

Last but not least, my deep thanks to David Newhardt (Nashville, Tennessee), for access to his wonderful Corvette files.

Thank you all,
Randy Leffingwell,
Santa Barbara, California

CONTENTS

INTRODUCTION

THE STATE OF THE SPORTS CAR ART

The Corvette occupies a unique spot in automobile history. It is a true sports car from an American manufacturer that has been in continuous production for more than 65 years. Other sports car makers have been in business as long or longer—Jaguar, Ferrari, Aston Martin, Porsche—but these have evolved from one model to the next, changing descriptions and designations. Although General Motors made headlines in 2019 with a switch to the mid-engine format for the new eighth-generation Stingray, it hasn't strayed much further from its formula. It hasn't gone from V-8 to V-12 and back. It hasn't gone from two front seats to four seats, or from an air-cooled flat four or a flat six to a water-cooled four.

From 1953 to the present day, Corvette has defined the American sports car. Not what it can be. What it is.

Carroll Shelby leapt onto the field in the early 1960s with a hybrid blend of British sports car and American V-8. He called it the Cobra. Dodge introduced its Viper in the 1990s, but its V-10 acknowledged that the front-engine V-8 belonged to the Corvette. Vipers and Cobras skirmished with Corvettes on two-lane back country roads, drag strips, and international road circuits in the United States and abroad, but when the dust settled, the two-seat, front-engine, rear-drive Corvette usually triumphed.

But what was it like in the early 1950s? For many auto enthusiasts, it was the early 1940s all over again. Used car lots offered 1930s Duesenberg two-seaters for $500. These were the former treasures of industrialists or movie actors gone broke or grown bored. On the East and West Coasts, those same individuals had fancied and imported French Talbot-Lagos

and Bugattis and prewar English sports cars such as MG PA and PB models and Jaguar's precursor SS100s. All of these could be found going for dimes on the original dollars in classified ads in newspapers and early enthusiast magazines.

For those who could afford new cars, there were dreams to be bought. Ferrari, founded in 1948, already had become the exclusive playmate of playboys, jewel thieves, royals, and celebrities. Enzo Ferrari sold Italian style for five figures ahead of the decimal. The same investment bought most Americans a two-bedroom house. For half a house, buyers could own an equally Italian Maserati or an English Aston Martin. For half *that* figure, still a princely sum, Americans could buy the latest, sleekest Jaguar, the XK120, a model whose designation evocatively revealed its top speed. It was front engined—an inline six—with two seats and rear-wheel drive.

And so was the first Corvette. To that extent, Chevrolet's sports car, the brainchild of General Motors' flamboyant vice-president of styling, Harley J. Earl, and corporation chairman Alfred P. Sloan, represents one of the country's first efforts to bring an element of European culture to American buyers.

It was an uphill battle. By the early 1950s, racing in the United States fell into several distinct categories. Since 1911, open-wheeled, single-seat, cigar-shaped cars had been hurtling around an oval track at Indianapolis and other venues across the nation. Sanctioned by the Automobile Association of America (AAA) Contest Board, open-wheel racing resumed at Indy in 1946 following the war. While the competing cars bore no resemblance to any car available to average buyers, the Indianapolis 500 event captivated audiences because of its speed, its noise, and its excitement. With the inauguration of Indy race television coverage in 1949, long before most Americans had televisions in their homes, the open-wheel series cemented its place among American enthusiasts in the same way open-wheel Formula One races had in Europe.

The same year racing returned to Indy, a Florida mechanic named Bill France quit his job to further his competition career in American stock cars. Spurned by the AAA Contest Board when he asked them to sanction his first event, France gathered some friends and founded the National Association for Stock Car Automobile Racing—NASCAR. He established a series of speed events on the sand at Daytona Beach. After wealthy individuals and well-supported private and factory-sponsored teams had completed their runs, France opened the course to spectators, each of whom paid a small fee to see what their own cars could do. If they topped 100 miles per hour on a two-way average, France made them members of NASCAR's Century Club. With new Chevrolets, Fords, and Plymouths selling for around $800, every session brought legions of wannabe racers to Daytona Beach to watch, learn, and try for themselves.

On the West Coast, two other versions of speed trials took hold. The hot rod culture, born before World War I by people hoping to put life into their Model Ts, grew between the wars and spread across the country. It took particular hold in California. There, the climate offered year-round racing with top speed, as always, the goal. But some wondered about absolute top speed, and those devotees headed to the state's dry lake beds where the Southern California Timing Association, SCTA, established between the wars, organized events run on nearly limitless sand. As speeds rose, the far horizons closed in, and the annual competition moved to the Utah salt flats where distances were measured in dozens of miles.

Chevrolet had several serious boasts with its 1953 Corvette. Fiberglass reduced the car's weight—the man is holding the floorpan, the largest single piece of the new car. What's more, fiberglass molds took a fraction of the time and cost of producing dies for steel bodies. *GM Media Archives*

The 1953 series production Corvette was almost everything Harley Earl and Ed Cole wanted in their dream car. They felt it answered their critics who demanded an all-American sports car. *GM Media Archives*

For those obsessed with brutal acceleration, a group of Los Angeles racers founded the National Hot Rod Association, NHRA, in 1951. This group devoted itself initially to getting speed-crazed youngsters to stop drag racing each other on city streets. Hot rodders helped establish the nation's first dedicated drag raceway in Goleta, California, in 1948.

For road-racing enthusiasts, the Automobile Racing Club of America (ARCA), the major organizer and sanctioning body for racing between the wars, disappeared in late 1941. A handful of former members founded the Sports Car Club of America (SCCA) in early 1944, its goal being "to further the preservation of sports cars, to act as an authentic source of information thereupon, and to provide events for these cars and their owners." Racing historian Albert Bochroch has characterized the SCCA's events from 1944 through 1948 as vintage car meets. However, that's primarily because few new sports cars were available or affordable.

The hot rod philosophy of exchanging one engine for another and adding homemade or store-bought performance enhancement parts carried over to road racers; those who weren't competing in decade-old Stutz or Packard two-seaters or French or English imports were swapping American engines into them. This led to generations of cars such as Briggs Cunningham's Buick-powered Mercedes-Benz SS-bodied roadster, Marmon-powered Duesenbergs, Cadillac, Ford, and Mercury V-8s under the hoods of English Allards. These cars competed through towns and villages such as Watkins Glen, New York, starting in October 1948. NASCAR opened its door, welcoming sports cars at Broward County Speedway in February 1949. When cities balked, friendly military commanders opened air force bases and marine air corps stations. Near the drag strip in Goleta, Santa Barbara's air base and surrounding hills hosted its first races and trials in August 1949. Towns such as Elkhart Lake, Wisconsin, and Pebble Beach, near Carmel, California, joined military bases from Sebring, Florida, to Santa Ana, California, becoming home to races and fans for several years.

Two Americans made serious efforts to build their own sports cars to race themselves and to sell to others. Both Briggs Cunningham in Palm Beach, Florida, and Sterling Edwards in San Francisco, California, manufactured and competed in cars they designed and had mechanics engineer and assemble. Cunningham and Edwards used engines and running gear from other manufacturers. After several years of trying, Briggs and Sterling gave up. It took everything they had, and they learned that much more was needed.

To conceive, design, engineer, test, launch, and support a sports car and a racing program took the means and resources of a large corporation. That required the imagination and vision of a small group of powerful, influential men that began with Harley Earl and Alfred Sloan and a project they called the "Opel."

1 IN THE BEGINNING

THE BIRTH OF THE CORVETTE

There was nothing humble about these beginnings. The car was Harley Earl's creation. As one of the most influential and significant automotive stylists of the twentieth century, Earl altered the perspectives and tastes of car designers and buyers throughout the world. When he got an idea, even Alfred P. Sloan, chairman of General Motors and the only man Harley answered to for his work, got up and took notice.

It was the early 1950s and Earl wanted to build a sports car. Decades earlier, Chairman Sloan had famously commented that the purpose and function of General Motors was to "build a car for every purse and purpose." GM had sedans, convertibles, station wagons, and pickup trucks. It manufactured buses and locomotives. But it offered no sports car.

The concept of an American sports car was not new; Mercer Raceabouts and other examples had appeared in the 1910s. These cars had just two seats and a sporting nature. In the 1920s, Earl had been in the midst of this market, designing custom bodies for Hollywood celebrities out of Don Lee's Cadillac dealership in Los Angeles.

Earl possessed an uncommon ability to measure the car buyer's pulse and quicken it. Once word got out that Earl was inside GM, talented designers from around the country and Europe hurried to join his department. At first his kingdom was called "Art and Colour," adopting the English spelling; when GM named him a vice president in 1940, he rechristened it "Styling."

Left: Chevrolet wasted no time hauling this 1953 pre-production prototype around the country for advertising and promotional photos. The front fender spear barbs hung down on these prototypes, and Chevrolet placed the "Corvette" name on the nose. *GM Media Archives*

Top: With the exception of trim details, these early 1953 pre-production cars gave a clear picture of what the series cars looked like; however, Chevrolet added a full-length chrome side molding to production versions. *GM Media Archives*

Bottom: This was where America's fascination with the Corvette began. Harley Earl's Design Center staff assembled this prototype, EX-122, for the 1953 Motorama debut at the Waldorf-Astoria hotel in New York City. *GM Media Archive*

Earl and select members of his team routinely attended major auto races and international car shows. They returned home with inspiration, sketches, photos, and notes. Ideas sparked concepts and assignments went out to his "fellahs," as he called his staff. One such project, code-named Opel, grew from many sources.

One of the origins was the competition. Many of the sporting vehicles that competed in racing could best be described as hybrid cars, or hyphenates. They generally came from an English, a French, an Italian, or a German manufacturer and often were implanted with another manufacturer's engines and running gear.

One maker, Jaguar, whose sensuous forms, elegant appointments, and exciting engine sound first appeared in 1948, had introduced England's first entirely new sports car after World War II. In many ways, it inspired Earl to imagine what was possible for GM's customers. But there were other influences acting upon GM's Styling chief.

COMPETITIVE NATURE

It is human nature to compete. Given four wheels and some kind of motive power, the question arises: Who is faster? Some racers ran against a clock, competing in events in which car and driver crossed a given distance faster than all others. Others ran against each other, and that form of competition began as soon as there were four-wheeled, and even three-wheeled, automobiles. Possibly even two.

Racing, especially in the early days, appeared in newspapers; the winners—driver and car—often were mentioned in the first sentence of the story. Such was the marketing purpose of racing. The other equally important function was to test and prove the company's engineering. While that motive seldom appeared in print, successful engineering was what got cars to the finish line first. Routine car development, Corvette Generation One to Two, for example, might take years. Yet improvements gained through racing, big and small, take place from one race to the next.

Earl had friends who raced, and one of them, Briggs Cunningham, chided him for GM's failure to manufacture an automobile suitable for racing. Cunningham spoke from practical experience; he had taken a Cadillac coupe to France to compete in the 24 Hours of Le Mans in 1950. He also had assembled his own car, a massive ungainly roadster with a Cadillac engine. It took huge amounts of work to make each car a racer. Cunningham undertook to manufacture his

Opposite: Following the approval of Harlow Curtice and Ed Cole in June 1952, Harley Earl got his Design Center staff scrambling to meet the January 1953 Motorama deadline. Assembling the handmade prototype required many hands in this early December 1952 photo. *GM Media Archive*

Below, left: Once EX-122 left New York, it embarked on a 10-city road tour with other GM production models and "dream cars." Everywhere it went, it drew a crowd. *GM Media Archive*

Below, right: Prototype fiberglass body panels that the Design Center staff produced were paper thin and translucent. Technicians had months of experience handling the lightweight material by the time they began fabricating the first Corvettes. *GM Media Archive*

own sports cars and returned to Le Mans in 1951 with four of them. But eventually the costs and complexities wore him out.

One of Earl's acquaintances did his best to encourage racing. Air Force General Curtis LeMay understood that pilots and mechanics were bored after combat ended. During weekend liberties, stateside fliers, soldiers, and sailors grew restless. Some who had ridden motorcycles during the war created and organized weekend rides and races. Others, stationed in England, France, Italy, and Germany, had seen smaller cars with better handling. Though they couldn't afford to bring home Triumphs, Renaults, Fiats, or Porsches, they found workable alternatives. Some were 10-year-old French or English cars; others were cars they modified to let off their steam. LeMay owned a Cadillac-engined Allard. He opened Air Force bases and encouraged Marine commandants to offer their air stations to racers on the weekends to keep GIs entertained and on the base.

Anyone who rode a motorcycle or fixed a tank, drove a staff car or serviced an airplane knew there were ways to make anything go faster. An industry in America, born before the war but mothballed for the duration, re-emerged and went into high gear manufacturing speed equipment. The hot-rod culture that emerged among four-cylinder Model T and Model A enthusiasts before World War I resurfaced to service flathead V-8 engines between the wars. In the late 1940s, it expanded exponentially as speed-hungry Yanks felt an itch growing beneath their skin: I need to be faster than you.

Harley J. Earl, a clever, perceptive, and visionary man, sensed the itch. He believed he had in his mind the vehicle that could scratch it. He had plenty of help inside GM. Buick's general manager Harlow Curtice, a rapidly rising star within the corporation, had become an early admirer of Earl's work and his impact on sales. With Styling's assistance, Curtice had turned around his struggling division. He appreciated Earl's loyalty—Harley's first personal concept car, the Y-Job in

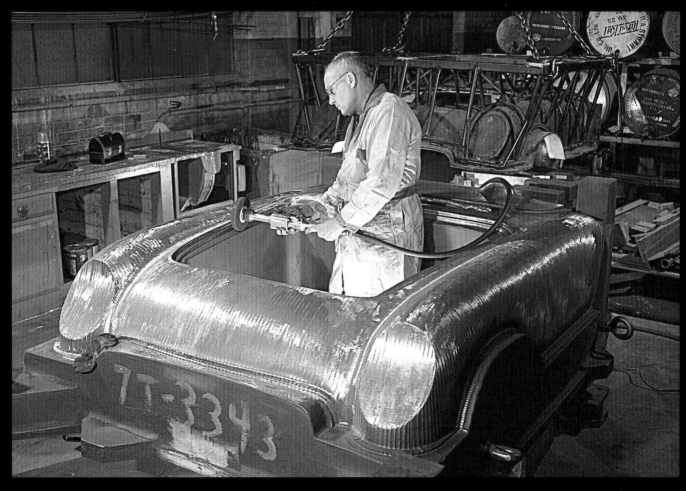

Above: Harley Earl poses next to his 1951
Le Sabre concept car, the epitome of his
design philosophy of "long, low, and
wide." The top of the windshield is below
Earl's belt. *GM Media Archive*

Right: The 1939 Y-Job launched many
automotive innovations, including an
automatic transmission, retractable
headlights, and a power roof. GM series
production cars still mounted headlights in
individual pods on each front fender. *GM
Media Archive*

Harley Earl

Harley J. Earl was born November 22, 1893, in Hollywood, California. His father, J. W., a coachbuilder, designed, fabricated, and assembled custom carriages for the wealthy families of Los Angeles. By the time Harley turned 15 in 1908, his father had reorganized his business as J. W. Earl Automobile Works. The film industry had settled on Southern California as its home, and J. W. Earl capitalized on their need for service vehicles, custom cars, and equipment and camera trucks. Harley worked evenings, weekends, and summers for his father, learning the business and the art. He began industrial design studies at Stanford University, but his time away from home frustrated him. In Los Angeles, his father was working on airplane fuselages for the Glenn L. Martin Company, a Southern California aircraft pioneer.

By 1918, Earl Automobile Works occupied its own three-story block-long building just south of downtown Los Angeles. That year, the firm displayed its first complete automobiles at the L.A. Auto Show with bodies designed by Harley. Soon after, Harley left Stanford to help his father run the business, where he specialized in servicing the company's celebrity clientele. Earl learned from his entertainment clients the importance of a vibrant color palette in satisfying singers who sought to outdo their bandleaders and movie actors who commissioned automobiles to stroke their own egos.

Earl Automobile Works had a benevolent patron. Don Lee was the West Coast distributor for Cadillac's automobiles and parts. He owned a dealership in downtown Los Angeles at Seventh and Bixel, and, more important, he also owned Beverly Hills agency Hillcrest Cadillac on Wilshire Boulevard, an elegantly decorated facility that catered to movie stars and moviemakers. He understood the power of promotion.

In 1919, Lee bought Earl Automobile Works and asked Harley to remain as manager and chief designer. Lee renamed his new acquisition Don Lee Coach and Body Works and, under Lee, "Hollywood Harley" Earl continued to provide unique cars to a discriminating and influential clientele. Newspapers, fan magazines, and movie newsreels covered the activities of this crowd, and their cars showed up in print and on the screen.

In Detroit, General Motors chairman Alfred Sloan paid attention to product appearance. He asked his division vice presidents if GM's cars were as advanced in their appearance as they were mechanically. Sloan believed they could do better.

Cadillac's division manager Lawrence P. Fisher agreed with Sloan. As the two prepared to launch Cadillac's second vehicle line in 1923, the LaSalle, Fisher went to Los Angeles. He watched as Earl and his modelers formed scale models of cars in clay. This allowed Earl the creative freedom to experiment with lines, shapes, and light reflections and make mistakes before committing to full-scale manufacture. Earl's hoods flowed into windshields, and his fender lines blended into running boards. His work was integrated and looked made-from-a-piece rather than assembled from disparate elements, which described the process followed by GM's Chassis Engineering department.

Fisher carried photos of Earl's cars back to Sloan, who soon hired Earl as a consultant to design the LaSalle. After finishing his work and reviewing other designs too far along to improve, Earl returned to Don Lee and his celebrity clients. But soon after the LaSalle debut, Sloan contacted Earl again, and on July 27, 1927, Harley moved to Detroit to head General Motors' newly created Art and Colour Section. (Lee was furious. In protest, he gave up his Cadillac franchise to sell Lincolns. That short-lived experiment lasted just two years before Don Lee again was Beverly Hills' Cadillac dealer.)

Earl answered only to Sloan. Art and Colour started with 10 designers and 40 administrative, clerical, and shop personnel to design general-production car bodies, do research, and develop special car designs.

Harley Earl was called manager of the department. He preferred "MistErl," a contraction his designers used for decades to follow. He was an imposing boss, standing 6 feet 4 1/2 inches tall. He had a high voice and stuttered, often beginning his design analyses with "Fe-fe-fellahs. . . ." Those who worked for him never were sure if it was a true impediment or a way to command their attention and allow no interruption.

MistErl's "fellahs" began designing concept and show cars, often painted in a variety of wild colors, which Earl's wardrobe matched. He was known to drive into work in one prototype, dressed in a matching blue suit, and change into a green suit to head out for lunch, only to switch to a black or gray one for his drive home.

One of his most significant concept cars also was Buick's first, a car called the Y-Job, built in 1938. With its blended fenders and concealed headlights, this 20-foot-long two-seater yanked automobile design into the 1940s. Earl put tens of thousands of miles on the car, not only commuting from his home in suburban Grosse Pointe, but also driving it to Watkins Glen, New York, to meet his friend Briggs Cunningham for a race or to Chicago for the opening of an auto show.

Earl hired—and occasionally fired—some of the greatest automobile stylists of a generation. Infatuated with airplanes, he encouraged his designers to experiment with aircraft motifs in their designs. When GM recognized World War II was nearing an end, Harley Earl assigned Frank Hershey's studio to redesign Cadillac's entire product line for 1948. Hershey's young stylist, Bill Mitchell, introduced small tail fins on a fastback coupe, launching a trend that redefined automobile design. The motif carried over into other divisions and appeared on the taillights of Chevrolet's sports car at its introduction in 1953 (and on the tail of Hershey's successful Thunderbird in 1955).

Harley Earl retired in 1958, shortly after approving final design of the 1959 car line, which offered the largest tail fins yet. He introduced two-tone paint, wraparound windshields, clay modeling, the hardtop sedan (which did without the central, or B-, pillar), and tail fins. On April 10, 1969, at the age of 75, he died of a stroke in West Palm Beach, Florida.

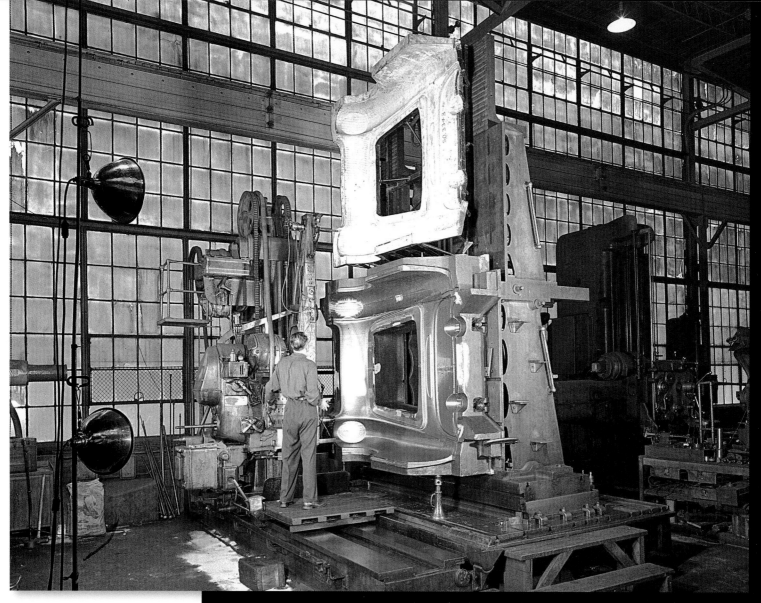

Above: An inspector at Detroit Forging examines the male and female molds for the new Corvette's upper front body panel in late spring 1953. This was the second largest piece on the car. *GM Media Archive*

Right: At Flint Assembly and afterward at St. Louis, the Corvette essentially was a handmade automobile. Technicians glued and bonded body panels together, waited for them to dry and cure, and then sanded them smooth before painting. *GM Media Archive*

1938, and his next one, the 1951 Le Sabre, were assembled on Buick chassis. When GM's board named Curtice executive vice president in 1948 and then president in 1952, Earl's ideas carried greater weight.

New technologies caught Earl's attention. Before the war, he and GM had learned about glass-reinforced plastic (GRP) from U.S. Rubber and Fiberglas from Owens-Corning. His staff had done work and experiments with them. By 1950, these were materials of choice in the boat-building industry. Earl invited chemists and staff from both companies to his studios to introduce his designers and design engineers to new possibilities. They learned that Fiberglas and GRP could reduce prototype development from days to hours.

Above: Zora Arkus-Duntov was the pilot of this low-altitude flight in a pre-production mule at GM's Milford Proving Ground in May 1953. It is safe to bet he logged many more flight-moments as he continued developing the car. *GM Media Archive*

INDUSTRIALIST LUNCHEONS

In Earl's time at GM, the corporation had launched several innovations. Beginning in the 1930s, General Motors invited loyal customers and friends in finance and industry in New York City to preview new products and get an insider's view of design concepts. For a few hours over lunch, these influential men had the ear of equally powerful individuals inside the corporation; each learned the other's interests and concerns.

GM interrupted these industrialist luncheons during the war. Chairman Charles Wilson, who had succeeded Alfred Sloan as corporate president in 1941, reinstated them in 1949. Questions of economic recovery and the impact of the developing war in Korea postponed the luncheons until 1953. GM's marketing staff enlarged the program from a few New York lunches to an 11-city tour renamed Motorama. Chevrolet's new general manager, Tom Keating, had Harlow Curtice's ear, so GM's entry-level division was included for the first time. It gave Chevrolet an opportunity to develop its own concept car.

Earl already had it in mind by 1951. He had started his design staff on a project he code-named Opel to suggest to prying eyes that it was something for the corporation's German division. He planned to surround an existing drivetrain and frame with a stylish two-seat body. He envisioned a price of $1,800, half that of Jaguar's XK120, introduced in 1948 and a favorite on many racetracks around the United States. Through late 1950 and early 1951, he had stylists, body engineers, and clay modelers creating concept after concept without much direction.

The visit from U.S. Rubber and Owens-Corning engineers came with sample products, including a sporty roadster U.S. Rubber's sales director Dr. Earl Ebers had brought along as an example of what was possible. Created in California by boat-builder Bill Tritt, this was a sports car body on a Jeep chassis that he had done for a friend. Called the Boxer, it lit a spark in Earl's imagination.

Earl acquired a Jaguar XK120, more for its packaging concept than its appearance. He installed it in a design studio and asked Bob McLean, a recent engineering and industrial design graduate of the California Institute of Technology, to engineer the car. Duane "Sparky" Bohnstedt drew the assignment to create the body.

Earl and McLean wanted to use Cadillac's or Buick's 188-horsepower V-8. But the upper divisions, including Oldsmobile, with its own new 165-horsepower engine, balked. Earl's power extended only so far, and Olds, Buick, and Cadillac fiercely guarded what they believed was their marketing and technological advantage. This left McLean with Chevrolet's durable but unexciting 115-horsepower inline "Stove Bolt" six.

Earl's message to McLean and Bohnstedt was clear: The XK120 was their target and should be their inspiration. McLean adopted the Jaguar's 102-inch wheelbase, and, aware that contemporary sports car design favored long hoods and short rear decks, he penciled in the passenger compartment just ahead of the rear axle. Earl championed the "longer, lower, wider" look that GM's advertising trumpeted, so McLean and Bohnstedt complied, making their 69.8-inch car more than 8 inches wider (and 1 inch lower) than the Jaguar.

Bohnstedt's body took influence from a small-production Italian car called the Cisitalia more than from Jaguar's XK. Interior stylist Joe Schemansky created the passenger compartment with its symmetrically balanced instrument panel and inset seats. Body stylist Clare MacKichan put finishing touches on the car before its shape was "frozen," prior to management's final review in June 1952.

Earl played showman, first inviting Harlow Curtice to see the car privately. He wanted GM's president on his side in case anyone raised objections. He needn't have worried. After his preview, Curtice joined Chevrolet general manager Thomas Keating and chief engineer Ed Cole. Their response was enthusiastic and immediate. They approved the mockup for Motorama in January 1953. They agreed to advance the project to Chassis Engineering, the next step toward provisional production.

Above: As relentless as the work schedule was at the proving ground, so was the "modeling" schedule to which Chevrolet's ad agency Campbell Ewald subjected the Corvette prototype. Chief photographer Myron Scott who named the car—shot in image-enhancing locations around the United States. *GM Media Archive*

Above, left: Three of the first nine 1953 Corvettes assembled at Flint went to GM's Milford Proving Ground engineering staff. Testing and development continued at an exhausting pace. *GM Media Archive*

Opposite: When the Chicago Auto Show opened its doors on March 14, 1953, visitors got to see not only the Corvette roadster but also a show concept with a removable hardtop roof. The show, 6 weeks after the Motorama debut and some 15 weeks ahead of production start, displayed the car's simple frame in the background. *GM Media Archive*

Alfred Sloan

" Each year, we build the best car we can to satisfy our customer, and then the next year we build another to make him dissatisfied. "

Alfred Pritchard Sloan could see the future. He was not a clairvoyant, but as a perceptive, insightful businessman, he and colleague Donaldson Brown, working together for financier and acting GM President Pierre S. DuPont, were forced to look far ahead as they envisioned and enacted methods to save and enhance a damaged conglomerate.

General Motors was an assemblage of automobile manufacturers that an entrepreneur named William Crapo Durant put together soon after the turn of the twentieth century. But Durant was too much enthusiast and too little disciplinarian. He imagined an organization that owned and controlled every part and product required for auto manufacture. Decades later, this concept earned the name "vertical integration," but Durant's version of it yielded a conglomerate whose too many automakers manufactured too many cars too near the same price, without any central guidance or control. When the U.S. economy collapsed after World War I, money tightened, and Durant learned he had no basic, cheap car to sell. The gaunt and severe Alfred Sloan, born in May 1875 in New Haven, Connecticut, joined GM in 1916 as a vice president following one of Durant's acquisition sprees. Sloan had studied electrical engineering at the Massachusetts Institute of Technology, graduating in 1895. He knew the automobile business inside and out, but when Durant ran amok, he could do little but endure the ride downhill.

DuPont, the giant banking firm that had financed much of Durant's ambition, stepped in to manage its investment in 1920 after the founder walked away from his mess. With Pierre DuPont in place serving as the big fist enforcing hard decisions, Donaldson Brown became GM's financial brain, and Sloan assumed the role of strong backbone. Within a year, the corporation had cars in its lineup from $6,000 Cadillacs to $700 Chevrolets. It was Sloan who put this product array in perspective, characterizing GM's new philosophy: "A car for every purse and purpose."

The turnaround had cost even more money, but DuPont, Sloan, and Brown settled on a policy of patience. "The question," Sloan wrote in his autobiography, *My Years with General Motors*, "is not simply one of maximizing the rate of return for a specific short period of time . . . , the fundamental consideration was an average return over a long period of time."

To help GM's customers, Sloan developed an innovative financing arrangement for buyers who paid interest not to banks but to General Motors. By 1925, GM manufactured one in every five automobiles sold in the United States, and it kept $1 in every $3 of profit the industry earned. By this time, DuPont had returned to his bank in New York, and GM's grateful board elected Sloan as its president. An astute student of his industry, he watched as Auburn Automobile Company introduced fully enclosed bodies for 1924, in dramatic contrast to Henry Ford's open Model Ts. The new Auburns were mechanically identical to 1923 but, as he observed in his biography, featured "...advanced styling and coloring. A sweeping belt line . . . often painted in contrasting colors gave a striking impression." When

Auburn's losses in 1923 turned into profits before 1925, that made another striking impression.

Cadillac still sold bare chassis to wealthy customers who preferred personalized custom vehicles. Sloan learned about the cars Harley Earl was redesigning in Los Angeles, and he dispatched Cadillac general manager Lawrence Fisher to observe firsthand. Soon after Fisher returned, Sloan invited Earl to Detroit to see what he'd do with the new LaSalle. Earl also made suggestions for the mainline Cadillacs, most importantly to expand the division's staid color selection from 3 to more than 500 exterior and interior color options.

Sloan hired Earl to run GM's new Art and Colour Section. The work pace kept Earl busy, a reality that backfired on both men with the 1929 Buick. Some of the Chassis Engineering department management grew jealous of Earl's influence, referring to his studios as "The Beauty Parlor." After Earl finished his concepts for the Buick, he moved on, leaving—and trusting—chassis engineers to finish the car for production. Earl's concept fit the car body down inside the chassis. The engineers "redesigned" it to mount on top of the existing chassis so they did not need to do additional work. Earl's car would have been a design leap forward. Instead, the result was ungainly and top heavy and was quickly nicknamed "The Pregnant Buick" by customers and journalists.

Buick sales plummeted, and Sloan pulled the car from production after one year. Sloan, the backbone and now the fist as well, reacted quickly, tightening his and Earl's authority over manufacturing and production engineers. The Buick showed everyone the sales difference between successful and awful design. Earl hurried a new Buick through design, and this fathered another GM innovation: the annual model change.

"Each year," Sloan wrote in his biography, "we build the best car we can to satisfy our customer, and then the next year we build another to make him dissatisfied." But more than just new versions of previous models came out of Art and Colour. As Earl's impact became clearer, Sloan named him a vice president. This new position allowed Earl not only to update existing models but also to invent new ones. He used his studios, sometimes by invitation only, to advance his pet schemes.

"We all were window shoppers," Sloan wrote, "in the Art and Colour 'sales' rooms. Art and Colour was proposing new designs, presenting new idea sketches, selling progress. As time went by, more and more of these ideas appeared to be feasible."

Sloan retired from GM in 1956, but not before establishing and endowing graduate education programs at his alma mater, MIT, as well as Cornell University, Stanford University, London School of Business, and, along with Charles Kettering, GM's chief experimental engineer, a cancer research and treatment institute in New York City. Sloan died in February 1966 in New York.

It somehow makes perfect sense: One of history's greatest portrait photographers, Yousuf Karsh of Ottawa, Ontario, photographed one of history's greatest automobile executives, Alfred P. Sloan of General Motors, Detroit, Michigan. Karsh took great pains with his lighting, including how he illuminated his subject's hands.

Maurice Olley was GM's chief of research and development. In his career, he had made Rolls-Royce automobiles "handle" and introduced Rolls-Royce-like ride and handling to GM's products. His ideas and skills were in such demand the corporation named him chief engineer, Product Study department. Always interested in performance automobiles, Olley gravitated toward the new sports car. He reasoned that the standard Chevrolet sedan front suspension, revised for 1949 to operate with two parallel wishbones on each side, would work even better for a lower, lighter two-seater.

Chassis stiffness concerned him. He conceived a frame of boxed side-members, and he planned a central crossmember for rigidity. What was atypical in his approach was that his frame rode low enough that the engine and drivetrain ran above the central cross rather than through it, thereby weakening the frame with the driveshaft hole. Olley opted for a Hotchkiss final drive suspended by longitudinal leaf springs at the rear that sloped upward to help induce understeer, that plowing sensation most drivers have experienced when going into a turn. Olley got a new, quicker-reacting Saginaw worm-and-sector steering box.

While Olley prepared its chassis, and Ed Cole and Harry Barr developed its engine, marketing personnel inside Chevrolet and GM's ad agency Campbell Ewald searched for a name for the new car. The project generated enough excitement within the company that they felt sure it would capture the imagination of thousands of viewers at Motorama. Printing time had to be scheduled to be sure enough brochures were available. A process of elimination ruled out hundreds of possible names before Keating, Curtice, and Earl agreed on *Corvette*, which was inspired by the designation of a Royal Navy warship.

Above: Robert Paxton McCulloch began manufacturing automobile superchargers in 1937. He introduced a much-improved version in 1953, and his young engineer Art Oehrli set out to try one on the newly introduced Corvette.

Left: Oehrli was able to borrow 1953 no. 024 from the president of Standard Oil of California. The confined engine compartment forced some clever plumbing solutions to install the new-style VS-57 supercharger.

When the doors opened on Motorama 1953 at New York City's Waldorf-Astoria Hotel, the invitation list extended far beyond influential business leaders. Anyone who had expressed any interest in a GM product throughout 1952 got a pass. Others bought tickets. Roughly 300,000 visitors streamed past elegantly dressed models pointing out the features and fantasies of production and concept cars alike. An orchestra and stage show entertained them. GM personnel moved through the crowd, eavesdropping on so much favorable response to the Corvette that Tom Keating authorized production to start in June 1953. He and Ed Cole knew that using fiberglass for the body would save time and money and would take advantage of the novelty of the show car. Eventually, they agreed, they would shift to a steel body.

For the next five months, Motorama traveled the nation, working its way west to the Pacific Ocean in a 100-vehicle caravan of specially designed and built trucks and buses, stopping in 11 major metropolitan areas where, again and again, they heard excitement and praise for the new Corvette.

Throughout it all, production engineers slaved to make the fiberglass car production-ready. Keating and Cole set a goal of manufacturing 300 in 1953. No sooner had they considered switching to steel bodies for 1954 than realities and costs of producing dies for metal forming reversed their plan. Fortunately, as production engineer Jim Premo told Karl Ludvigsen, "People seemed to be captivated by the idea of the fiberglass plastic body."

Chevrolet division let out bids for manufacturing 12,300 full sets of the body, anticipating demand might dictate 1,000 units per month for 1954. The complications of start-up—with their publicly stated goal of Job One in June 1953—made limiting output to 300 units mandatory. Chevrolet's advertising and sales staffs spun the logistics into a marketing strategy.

Opposite, top: McCulloch added dual gauges that registered pressure out of the supercharger and pressure into the carburetors. McCulloch eventually produced two prototypes from its shops in Venice, California.

Below: In addition to the "Supercharged" logo mounted above the crossed-flag nose badge, McCulloch's only other marketing distinction was converting production steel wheels to wire wheels from the 1953 Buick Skylark convertible. When Chevrolet finished its evaluations, supercharged no. 024 went back to its Standard Oil executive, who reportedly enjoyed it on Los Angeles streets.

Blue Flame Special

Harley Earl's "Opel" was supposed to use either a Cadillac or a Buick V-8. Cadillac's 188-horsepower engine, which had come from two talented individuals—Ed Cole, who had been Cadillac's chief engineer, and Harry Barr, the division's engine specialist—set the standard for V-8 performance at that time and was the engine of choice, but interdivisional rivalries kept V-8s out of Chevrolet's new sports car.

Promotion at GM happens from one division to the next based on the hierarchy of sales numbers, not perceived prestige. For Ed Cole, his success at Cadillac led him to run Chevrolet's engineering operations. He brought Harry Barr with him, so the team that had created the potent Cadillac V-8 was now at Chevrolet, working on designing something similar for GM's best-selling division. But that engine was still a couple of years away from being road-ready, so Earl's sports car would have to make do with Chevrolet's reliable-but-unexciting six.

Chevy's tried-and-true inline six began life in 1941 as a truck motor. In 1950, division engineers had mated it to the Powerglide transmission, and it had become a smooth, even-tempered passenger car powerplant. The total displacement of 235.5 cubic inches came from a bore and stroke of 3.563 inches by 3.938 inches. With aluminum pistons, full-pressure lubrication, and steel-backed connecting rod bearings, all new for 1953, and compression of 7.5:1, the engine developed 115 horsepower at 3,600 rpm. This was fine for sedans and station wagons, but anemic for a sports car.

Cole and Barr reworked the overhead-valve engine. They changed induction from a single carburetor to three single-barrel side-draft Carters with manual chokes. (The side-draft carbs were the only induction possible because a downdraft design would not fit below the car's low hood.) They advanced the timing with a new more aggressive camshaft and mechanical valve lifters with dual springs for each valve, reworked the exhaust, enlarging exhaust valves in the process, and raised the compression ratio to 8:1. This bumped output up significantly, to 150 horsepower at 4,200 rpm. Torque increased from 204 at 2,000 rpm to 223 foot-pounds at 2,400 rpm.

Because Harley Earl targeted Jaguar's XK120, some comparison is valuable. The U.S. version of the British car's 210-cubic-inch dual-overhead camshaft inline six, introduced in 1951, utilized twin side-draft SU carburetors and a compression of 9.0:1 to develop 180 horsepower at 5,300. With its four-speed manual transmission, it was capable of 120 miles per hour. This made it the fastest production car in the world at the time.

One decision haunted Chevrolet engineers as soon as the car appeared: offering a sports car only with the Powerglide automatic. Chevrolet division had no four-speed manual unit and, as historian Karl Ludvigsen pointed out, "The base engine was the Powerglide unit, so it was easiest to build it for use with that transmission." The floor-mounted gearshift, while sportier, also made sense because a column shift linkage would have run through the rear carburetor. With a final drive ratio of 3.55:1, the car was capable of a top speed of 108 miles per hour at 4,800 rpm.

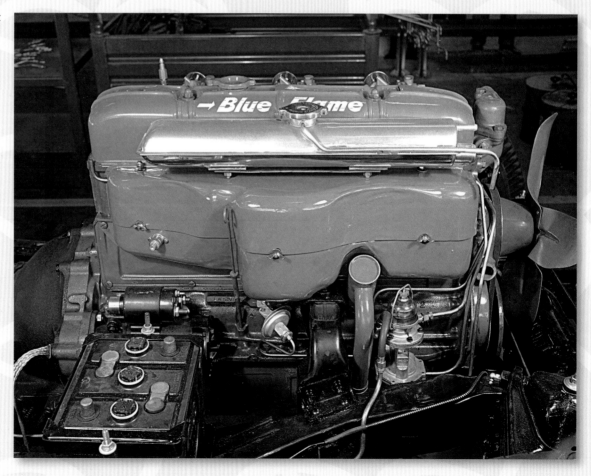

The "Blue Flame Special" inline six was not the engine Harley Earl or Ed Cole wanted for their sports car; however, none of the GM divisions with V-8s in their lineup would share their innovations. *GM Media Archive*

Above: Harley Earl and his design staff scrambled to keep ahead of Corvette interest by showing new concepts at the 1954 Motorama. Chevrolet approved the fastback for production until Ed Cole and others saw dismal 1954 roadster sales results. *GM Media Archive*

Left: In December 1953, Corvette assembly started up in St. Louis, Missouri, with the ambitious goal of producing 1,000 cars a month. As these models inch along the assembly line, they have removable side windows in place. *GM Media Archive*

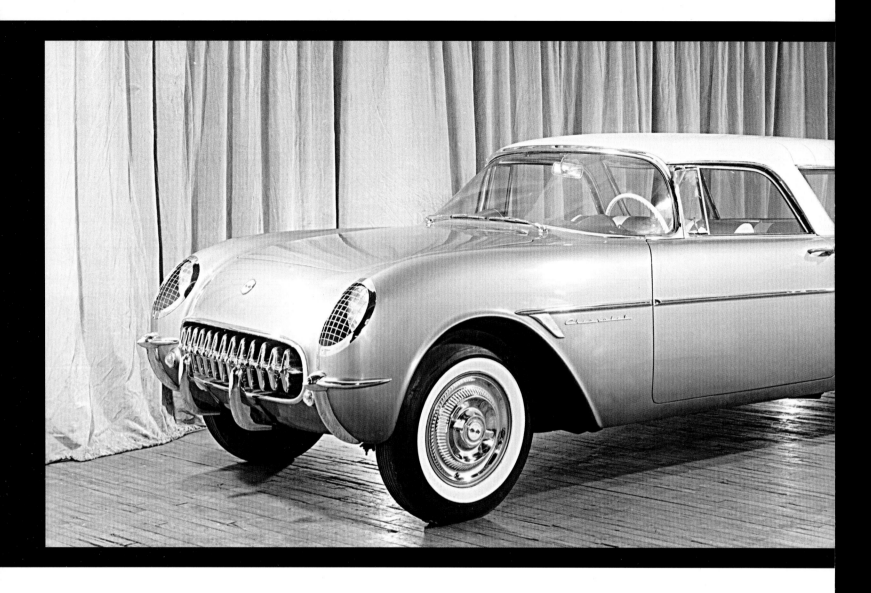

Above: The Nomad Corvette "station wagon" was a huge success at every show. It was such a sensation at New York's 1954 Motorama that Harley Earl phoned his staff from the show to tell them to prepare it for production—but on the full-size Bel Air platform.

Right: Chroming the engine did gain some adherents, including Roger Crispell, one of Earl's interior design studio chiefs. This car, his own, began life as a 1954 Polo White production car; Crispell twice modified it to present new interior design ideas and exterior color schemes to management.

Opposite: Nothing glitters like chrome, especially under the hood of another 1954 Motorama show concept. While it never reached production, it inspired customizers for decades. *GM Media Archive*

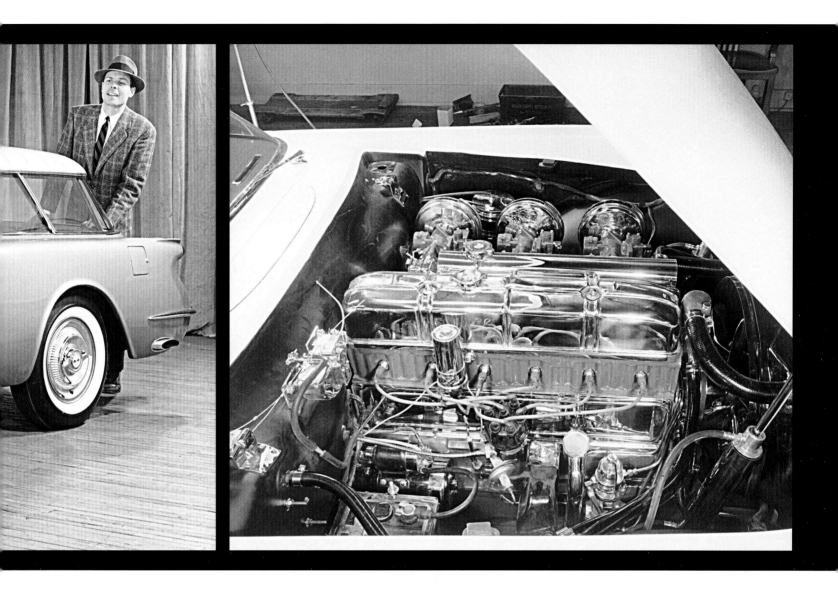

Harley Earl envisioned his sports car selling for around $1,800. This was about half what his benchmark Jaguar XK120 went for. It would have been a bargain. Sadly, costs of improving engine capabilities, creating and testing an all-new frame, and developing technologies to mass produce and rapidly produce a complicated car body in a new material ratcheted production costs up to where Chevrolet introduced the car at $3,490. Complete with Powerglide transmission, whitewall tires, a clock, and an outside review mirror, this positioned the car near enough to the Jaguar to invite comparison.

THE BIRTH OF THE CORVETTE

Production began June 30, and serial numbers 001, 002, and 003 drove off the assembly line on Chevrolet Division Plant 35 near Flint, Michigan, that day. A team of workers hand assembled the 62 major and minor fiberglass pieces, gluing or bonding them together and finishing the bodies by hand. Chevrolet decided to offer the first 300 in Polo White with red interiors. Flint served not only as pilot production, but also as shakedown assembly for the higher-speed lines the division prepared for its St. Louis Assembly plant.

All of Chevrolet's 7,600 dealers throughout North America wanted a Corvette to sell—or at least to draw sedan buyers into their showrooms. General sales manager William Fish held his cards close to his chest. Through discreet words passed through circumspect channels, it became clear that unless you were a performing celebrity, government official, community leader, military hero, corporate captain, sports star, or well-known racer, you had to wait until 1954 to get your Corvette. The largest-volume dealers with the highest-visibility regular patrons got cars. It was an elitist strategy from which Chevrolet and GM hoped for the exclusivity and public envy that characterized Harley Earl's 1920s and 1930s Cadillacs for Hollywood: Place the cars with those who will be photographed in them.

By late September 1953, 50 of the cars had found homes among such owners. At year-end, 183 of the 300 cars had been sold. The others were counted as engineering test vehicles, dealer displays, GM executive perks, and models devoted to national auto show tours.

It was not until September 29 that the division "launched" the car to the media. Engineers and public relations and marketing people moved eight cars to the Milford test track. The program they set up gave each of 50 journalists a chance to drive a car for 7 miles. Tom Keating opened the program by defining the car: "In the Corvette," he said, "we have built a sports car in the American tradition. It is not a racing car in the accepted sense that a European sports car is a race car. It is intended rather to satisfy the American public's conception of beauty, comfort, and convenience, plus performance. Just as the American production sedan has become the criterion of luxury throughout the world, we have produced a superior sports car."

By late March 1954, another picture emerged. Fiberglass manufacturer Bob Morrison remembered in an interview in 1996 that Jim Premo and Ed Cole essentially had moved out of Detroit, ferrying between St. Louis production and Ashtabula manufacture to ramp up assembly to 1,000 units a month. By spring, they knew their target far exceeded public demand.

Briggs Cunningham was among the early customers. He returned his car to his dealer, disappointed by its performance and quality. Had the Corvette come in at $1,800, he could accept leaks in rainstorms and side-curtains in lieu of roll-up windows. Had it cost $3,500 with a 180-horsepower V-8 and a four-speed transmission, he could race it.

Above: One of Crispell's car's most distinctive design-center treatments was its "shark-fin" headlights. GM Styling got feedback from several states that did not allow anything in front of headlights, putting the "fencing mask" grids at risk.

Opposite: Black-and-silver dyed alligator hides covered the seats of Crispell's car. Studio mechanics fitted the prototype three-spoke steering wheel. The center console housed a glove box.

One journalist at Milford that late-September day questioned what Chevrolet had created. In the June 1954 issue of *Motor Trend*, writer Don MacDonald related his struggles to lower and raise the convertible top. GM's concept of the Corvette market, he wrote, is "that no owner will be caught in the rain without a spare Cadillac."

Chevrolet division's strategy of parceling out the car to those it chose may have backfired. Some of them stepped away from their commitments or signed over their option to others who never could have gotten one. Nearly 20,000 anxious potential buyers had left their names with dealers. This left them feeling slighted and insulted. When magazine articles appeared disparaging its performance and its quality, they felt vindicated.

In truth, it wasn't a bad car. Acceleration from 0 to 60 miles per hour took 11 seconds. The XK120 accomplished that in 10. Magazines found the top speed was 106 miles per hour, and even *Motor Trend* later begrudgingly allowed that "Chevrolet has produced a bucket-seat roadster that will hold its own with Europe's best."

The Corvette pushed back against the philosophy Alfred Sloan and Donaldson Brown had advanced decades earlier: Let cars find their market, wait patiently for return on the investment. By mid-1954, voices inside the division and around the board table challenged Sloan, urging GM to cut its losses. Chevrolet manufactured 3,939 Corvettes between June 30, 1953, and December 31, 1954, but it sold 2,863. It began the 1955 model year with a surplus of 1,076 cars not only in Polo White but also Pennant Blue, Sportsman Red, and black. Color made little difference except to brighten the St. Louis plant storage lot.

Then three things happened that made a difference.

In chronological order, a former GM stylist, Frank Hershey, had dinner with a friend who still worked at GM design. Hershey had brought fins to Cadillacs but by 1952 was head of design at Ford. The friend showed him a photo of the Corvette-to-be. Hershey was no sports car enthusiast, but overnight he became one. Harley Earl had fired him for

> " Chevrolet has produced a bucket-seat roadster that will hold its own with Europe's best. "
>
> *Motor Trend*

Above: There was some royal interest in Corvettes, though it took until 1955 for this one to reach Europe. Thirty-five-year-old Baudouin I, King of Belgium, ordered this car for his use in and around Brussels.

Right: The king's tan leather interior came with metric instruments. The speedometer read to 210 kilometers per hour (131.25 miles per hour).

Bottom: Campbell Ewald conceived, designed, photographed, wrote, and published a variety of promotional brochures for the Corvette. Some described the car in general terms; others heralded the arrival of V-8 engine power.

The Birth of Corvette Culture

As Ed Cole and others inside Chevrolet division struggled to understand what this Corvette was that they had created, they looked to their advertising agency Campbell Ewald in Detroit for help in defining the beast. At Campbell Ewald, a succession of clever, articulate, literate, and perceptive writers and observers crafted an evolving image of the car that reflected—and shaped—the culture around it.

Campbell Ewald's first contribution was most significant: the car's name. Agency public-relations photographer Myron Scott already had photographed the car several times for release materials to promote it. The agency had scrolled through a dictionary, coming up with and discarding some 300 names. In a 1991 interview with Amy Lynn Smith for *Corvette Quarterly*, Scott said he had read a story about a new class of fast-pursuit Navy ships called Corvettes. He thought about the name for a couple of days and then sent a memo to Ed Cole that said, basically, "How would you like to take a ride in my Corvette? As you know, the Corvette is the new sports car built by Chevrolet."

Half an hour later, Cole phoned Scott and asked him if he'd like a ride in Cole's new car, "Yeah, a new car called the Corvette," according to the *Corvette Quarterly* interview.

From there, Campbell Ewald's copywriters went to work. Arthur "Barney" Clarke was first. It took Clarke, the Corvette, and the country a while to hit their stride. It wasn't until 1954 when Clarke's prose began to approach poetry that Campbell Ewald placed his series of ads in a medium suitable to the concept: the *New Yorker*. With the tagline "First of the dream cars to come true," Clarke's opening volley led with "Stop dreaming and start driving!" The text of this ad and others that followed delivered facts flavored with image and imagination: "Stay away from this slim temptress unless there's a spark in you that burns bright to the glove-fit of a bucket seat . . . to the competent feel of a big 17 1/4 inch steering wheel . . . to the tingling delight of a car that moves with the cat quick response of a boxer. . . .

"Stay away if your pulse doesn't stir to the silken potency of Corvette's 'Blue-Flame' engine, fueling 150 horses through triple carburetors. . . ." Like the best of any advertising, Clarke was selling a fantasy life to anyone who was reading.

The campaign expanded to *Motor Trend*, to California's *Sunset* magazine, to *The Saturday Evening Post*, *Popular Mechanics*, *Popular Science*, and *Sports Illustrated*. Ads through 1955 suggested the car was "For experts only" and that "You can still buy magic!" But perhaps one of Clarke's finest was a page that appeared in *Esquire* in November 1955. Corvette was fighting for its life against the new Ford Thunderbird, and Barney sought to put the car in perspective. The ad, which ran with the headline "Child of the Magnificent Ghosts," read as follows: "Years ago this land knew cars that were fabricated out of sheer excitement. Magnificent cars that uttered flame and rolling thunder from exhaust pipes as big around as your forearm, and came towering down through the white summer dust of American roads like the Day of Judgment. . . ."

Two months later, the 1956 model appeared with a V-8 engine, roll-up windows, and an optional power top, elements early buyers had criticized as lacking in a true sports car or any car at that price. The roll-up windows civilized the car for road use, but the V-8 engine had quite a different effect. It turned the timid little sports car into a hairy racer. Within months of receiving a proper sporting engine, a Corvette finished first in its class at a major international car race at Sebring in Florida.

The original title for the television show *Route 66* was *The Searchers. Dave Wendt Photography © 2012*

In July, Clarke again struck advertising gold. Photographer Myron Scott captured the Sebring-winning Corvette, filthy after its hours of racing, as crew members refilled its tank and one of its drivers ran toward his replacement. It was an elemental racing moment, and Clarke's headline captured it: "The Real McCoy." The message was clear: The Corvette could hold its own on the boulevard or the track.

At the same time as it earned a reputation as a race winner, the Corvette began to make its presence known in the new medium of television. Starting in October 1956, Chevrolet began promoting *The Dinah Shore Chevy Show*. Though the show seldom specifically showcased the Corvette, the image of the division, inseparable from one of America's most popular entertainers, promoted goodness by association. The show theme song, "See the U.S.A. in your Chevrolet," sung by Shore, often ran over filmed images of Chevrolets on the road. The weekly hour-long variety show ran through 1961.

It wasn't long before television producers began to recognize the star power of the Chevy's two-seater, however. Seeing the U.S.A. in a Chevrolet became the theme of another television series that debuted in October 1960. *Route 66*, created by Herbert Leonard and mostly written by Stirling Silliphant, rarely stuck to the highway that led from Chicago to Los Angeles. Instead, like the Corvette its two stars used to get them from one adventure to the next, the show name became a symbol of a population a bit disaffected, a bit confused, in search of its identity and its purpose in life. When Chevrolet heard a pitch for sponsorship, it quickly recognized the role its sports car could play. Chevrolet management made a good decision; often Silliphant and the show's other writers treated the Corvette as a character equal to stars Martin Milner and George Maharis.

Following the lead of GM's Motorama motorcades, Herbert Leonard's production company lived out of trucks and trailers and motels, like gypsies, ever in search of the next interesting location and story idea. From 1960 through 1963, the large mobile crew worked as many as 40 weeks a year producing hour-long dramas that riveted viewers to their televisions on Friday nights. For young viewers, the idea of escaping with a friend rang true and spoke volumes. For the older audiences, the scripts, often variations of classic myths from centuries of literature, pulled them into the lives of two strangers, on the road, seeing the U.S.A. in their Corvette.

running an outside business manufacturing ashtrays—outside jobs of any kind were prohibited at GM in those days—and Hershey assembled a small team of designers, acquired an XK120, and worked around the clock. About the time GM opened its doors on Motorama 1953 in New York City, Henry Ford II approved the team's concept for production as the 1955 Thunderbird.

Second, Ed Cole, frustrated by Cadillac's and Buick's attitudes, assigned Harry Barr to produce a V-8 for Chevrolet division. Such an engine already was planned before Cole and Barr arrived at the Bowtie division. One of the first running prototypes went into the Motorama show car, recycled as a proving ground test vehicle; results led engineers, product planners, and management alike to recommend the 195-horsepower 265-cubic-inch V-8—with either the Powerglide two-speed or a manual three-speed transmission—as an option for 1955 production.

Third, and most significant over the long term, was the arrival of a character straight from Russian literature named Zora Arkus-Duntov. Duntov saw the car at the Waldorf-Astoria Motorama show. He wrote to GM, introduced himself, presented his credentials, and, impetuously—but typical of Duntov—offered his ideas to improve the car.

ZORA

Duntov, a Russian born in Belgium, studied engineering in Germany. Following his ambitious letter, Ed Cole hired him into Chevrolet engineering in May 1953. He reached GM too late to affect pre-production but in time to influence what came later.

Barely a month after joining Chevrolet, Duntov took a "vacation" to drive a Cadillac-powered Allard at Le Mans in June. It did not finish, and the lessons registered on Duntov. In a December memo, he proposed that Chevrolet develop,

Above: As Harley Earl's design staff experimented with ideas for the 1956 model year, they developed the coves and removed the taillight fins. They experimented with routing the exhaust pipe through the rear quarter, as they had done with the Nomad show car, or out through a vertical trim piece. *GM Media Archive*

Opposite: Was this an early casting test for *Route 66* with actor Martin Milner in the passenger's seat? Series production 1956 convertibles introduced side coves in contrasting colors and provided standard roll-up windows.

market, and sell its own performance parts so Corvette enthusiasts who might race the car wouldn't "meet with Allard trouble—that is, breaking, sooner or later, mostly sooner, everything between flywheel and road wheels. Since we cannot prevent people from racing Corvettes, maybe it is better to help them do a good job at it."

Duntov's efforts at understanding the car were frustrating. The rear-spring inclination that Maurice Olley gave the car to induce understeer to comfort unfamiliar drivers, worked against the front suspension taken from sedans. As Zora wrote in his test report, "We had a car in which the two ends were fighting with each other." He installed a larger anti-roll bar at the front and limited spring travel in the rear. Soon he had the Corvette doing controllable, predictable drifts.

Duntov took the next assignment from Olley. The car's aerodynamics caused exhaust to stain the rear of the car and the gases to flow into the passenger compartment. The "Ventipane," a wide air vent just ahead of the windshield that opened from inside the passenger compartment, caused this. When it was open, it reversed airflow from front to back. Duntov experimented with new locations for the exhaust tips, taking them inboard from the rear fenders. He extended their length and reset them about a foot in from the outside edge of the car, eliminating the fumes and staining problems.

Duntov quickly became the go-to guy for Corvette engineering challenges. Engineering development of the V-8 continued for 1955 while stylists tried to breathe new life into their ailing product. For the 1954 Motorama, Clare MacKichan and his staff concocted three new ideas, all offering roll-up side windows. One offered a fiberglass hardtop. Another, dubbed "Corvair" and designed by Joe Schemansky, was a sleek-looking fastback coupe that

Opposite, top: In Harley Earl's mind, the Corvette was a Chevrolet full-line vehicle, with the Nomad wagon and Corvair fastback in 1955 and this five-passenger, two-door Corvette Impala hardtop that debuted at the 1956 Motorama. *GM Media Archive*

Opposite, bottom: Arctic Blue was a new color for 1956. All Corvettes in 1956 used the 265-cubic-inch V-8 that developed 210 horsepower in the base model and up to 240 horsepower when equipped with a high-lift camshaft and two four-barrel Carter carburetors.

Below: Some of the 1956 models relied on grandparents for power. Chevrolet sold these pedal cars through its dealer network. *GM Media Archive*

Fiberglas

Given that nearly all other production automobiles in the United States were (and are) made of steel, Chevrolet's decision to produce Corvette bodies in Fiberglas was (and remains) something of a novelty. It had cost Harley Earl's styling studio roughly $60,000 (about $500,000 today) to create the Motorama show car, a somewhat smaller figure than the more than $1 million show-car costs of 2010. Fiberglas was one of the reasons the expenditure was so low.

Fiberglas body panels usually are created either by hand-laying the glass fiber sheets, spraying chopped and shredded glass fibers, or pressure molding the sheets. This latter method can involve metal-to-metal dies or even vacuum bags that press the molds by withdrawing air (and extra resin) from the bags. For greatest consistency—and manufacturing ease and economy—pressure molding was the choice of Chevrolet's Corvette production engineers.

Bob Morrison in Ashtabula, Ohio, won the contract to make the Corvette bodies. To build these, he estimated that he would need 15 large presses that each exerted between 250 and 500 tons of pressure onto the pliable glass-and-resin compound, squeezed between two "matched metal" molds. The largest single piece of the first-generation car was the one-piece underbody that ran from the firewall all the way to the rear bumper. The press for this piece alone was 7 by 12 feet. The piece itself measured 6 by 10 feet and 2 feet deep.

Each body consisted of 30 major parts and another 32 minor pieces. The recipe for the Corvette called for 136 pounds of Fiberglas, 153 pounds of polyester resin (to bond the fibers), and 51 pounds of inert filler. While this totaled 340 pounds, the completed body, with door hinges, rear deck lid hardware, tail and headlights, grille, and other elements, came in at 411 pounds.

In an interview in 1996, Bob Morrison recalled the biggest manufacturing challenge for his staff came when removing the huge underbody piece from the molds. At the point called the kick-up, where the floorpan rose to clear the rear-wheel arches, the hot composite material was too weak and often broke as Morrison's workers struggled to lift it from the mold. Watching his employees fail to remove one expensive molded piece after another, he got an idea. He grabbed a pile of shop towels and buckets of cold water. As soon as the matched-metal molds opened, he threw wet towels on the kick up. This cooled them rapidly, firming up the material enough for his crews to handle the big piece. He never lost another underbody after that.

The 18-month contract ordering the production of 12,300 full sets of Corvette bodies was worth $4 million dollars (a little more than $32 million today) to Morrison and his partner, Jim Lunn. As the process began, Lunn "vacuum-bagged" parts into existence until the matched-metal dies reached his and Morrison's plant. At one point, they had five molds making the underbodies, and they had employees working six days a week around the clock. According to historian Karl Ludvigsen, each of these largest molds was worth $14,000 (roughly $112,000 in 2011). Had Chevrolet decided to produce the Corvette in steel, the first car would have appeared as a 1955 model. It would have taken two additional years—and $4.5 million more dollars (more than $36 million today)—to get the steel panel molds produced. Morrison said that Chevrolet's recipe for the Corvette remained basically unchanged—though slightly modified—through the 1990s.

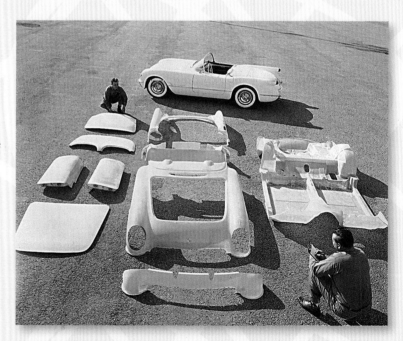

Fiberglas offered car designers many benefits such as lighter weight and lower manufacturing costs (the pressure molds cost a fraction of what matched-metal dies took to produce). In addition, it's likely the two men in this photo positioned each piece for the photographer without needing a forklift truck. GM Media Archive

Above: The shapes and forms of the 1956 and 1957 Corvette remain the purest and simplest in many enthusiasts' eyes. The unadorned sides of this 1957 convertible, missing the cove crossed-flag logo, suggest it was a pre-production model for photos. *GM Media Archive*

Right: By 1957, the Corvette had earned the respect and patronage of true sports car enthusiasts like those running in the Lake Michigan Mille Miglia. The SCCA sanctioned the rally, which ran a convoluted 1,000-mile lap around Lake Michigan and Lake Superior. *GM Media Archive*

4260.2   12-4-57

PG No. 2-7906 Chevrolet Corvette V8 1958 Sports 2-Passenger
Front and Rear

had production approval until poor sales threatened the existence of any Corvette at all. The third was a Corvette "station wagon" called the Nomad, designed by stylist Joe Renner. From the 1954 Motorama floor, Harley Earl called MacKichan and told him public response was so good that he and Renner had to prepare the Nomad for production, but on the full-size car body.

MEDIA DARLING

Chevrolet ran its first ad for the new car just as production began. In the *Detroit News*, readers were invited to see "America's Sensational Sports Car" at the Michigan Motor Show from June 2 through 7. A series of ads launched in early 1954 promoted the car's image. It appeared several times in the *New Yorker*, calling it the "first of the dream cars to come true."

The design studio created face-lifts for the 1955 model, accentuating its new V-8 power. A proposed egg-crate grille better reflected the sibling relationship with the full-size Bel Air. If 1953 sales sobered Chevrolet management, however, 1954's figures terrified them. They canceled the face-lift. Rumors floated that the entire car might suffer the same fate.

Product planners added new colors—Pennant Blue, Sportsman Red, and black—to spark up the appeal of the car. By creatively rewriting order forms so the Powerglide automatic transmission was a mandatory option, Chevrolet appeared

Opposite, top: Often brochure and advertising art—as for these 1958 convertible and hardtop models—was artwork. Staff illustrators and outside contractors for Campbell Ewald produced the paintings or airbrush works.

Opposite, bottom: Staffers at Milford Proving Ground documented each new production model when it reached them, as with this 1958 hardtop. This way, the engineers had a point of reference for any modifications that happened intentionally or otherwise.

Below: Assemblers at St. Louis had their hands full with the new 1958 models. They had many new body panels, a new instrument panel, and new interior materials.

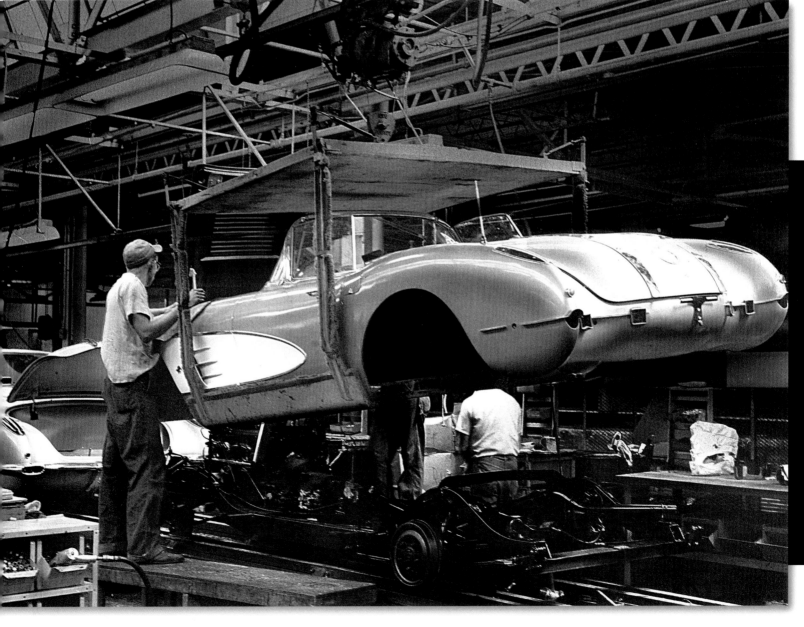

"If Corvette dies, it is admission of failure. Failure of aggressive thinking in the eyes of the organization, failure to develop a salable product in the eyes of the outside world."

The Soviet government in Russia celebrated the launch of its Moscow ExpoCenter in late July 1959 by inviting the United States to show its products. As this six-week exhibition started, then Vice President Richard Nixon met Soviet Premier Nikita Khrushchev and argued culture and philosophy in an American kitchen display. *GM Media Archive*

to drop the price from $3,498 to $2,774. Assembly at St. Louis, Missouri, offered economies that made up some of the price drop. On its best day, Flint turned out 50 cars a month. St. Louis could produce 1,000 or more each month. Yet because of the slow reception of 1953 models, the division revised assembly projections down from 12,000 to 10,000 for 1954. Chevrolet slowed manufacturing and cut employees. By year-end, although St. Louis had assembled 3,640 cars, Chevrolet sold only 2,780.

Years later, Ed Cole confessed to historian Karl Ludvigsen Chevrolet's uncertainty of the nature of the car. "We had no real feeling for the market," he said. "Was the Corvette for the boulevard driver or the sports car tiger?"

For the 1955 model year, Cole gave both the boulevardier and the tiger more teeth with the new V-8. Still, the car remained a vehicle in search of an identity. Ford Motor Company introduced its 1955 Thunderbird at the Detroit Auto Show in February 1954. It struck a clearer note with buyers. Its handsome looks, standard V-8 engine, electric window lifts, and other creature comforts helped push more than 16,000 of them out of Ford dealers through the model year. Chevrolet cut production at St. Louis back to Flint levels and manufactured just 700 cars, 693 of them with the new V-8.

Understandably, the car got a public vote of no confidence from GM chairman Harlow Curtice, who told the *Detroit News*, "America is not in favor of sports cars. . . ." This prompted a quick counterattack two days later from Duntov to Cole and Maurice Olley. "If Corvette dies," he wrote, "it is admission of failure. Failure of aggressive thinking in the eyes of the organization, failure to develop a salable product in the eyes of the outside world."

Again, European sports cars affected the Corvette concept as designers styled a new look for 1956 in hopes of new sales energy. Recessed headlights framed behind the "fencing mask" went away, as did the bullet taillights. The chrome-tooth grille remained, but now headlights rose vertically in the fenders, inspired by the Mercedes-Benz 300SL roadster appearing early in 1954. To provide visual interest to the body side, designers sculpted bullet-shaped coves that started behind the front wheelwell and ended in the doors. Colors expanded to include Polo White as well as Cascade Green, Aztec Copper, Arctic Blue, Venetian Red, and Onyx Black.

Zora Duntov gained a greater degree of input, and he increased high-speed stability, enhanced steering wheel response, and improved rear-axle traction through turns for 1956. Engineers Harry Barr and Russell Sanders redesigned

One of Bill Mitchell's first concept cars, the 1959 XP 700—a car he dubbed the Phantom—set the stage for a generation of more wild ideas created for him by his designers. While the front end of the Phantom never saw production, its backside showed up on production 1961 Corvette models. *GM Media Archive*

St. Louis assembled 10,261 Corvettes for model year 1960, and this was the first one off the line. Nearly a third of those cars were finished in Ermine White, and St. Louis delivered 9,104 of them with whitewall tires. *David Newhardt © 2012*

Above: Zora Arkus-Duntov climbs into his 1955 convertible after a day of making his Harvest Gold convertible dirty. Zora and his wife, Elfi, enjoyed powerboating and owned a home in suburban Grosse Pointe Woods near Lake St. Clair, where they kept their boat.
GM Media Archive

Right: In the late 1950s, Cadillac planned to resurrect its LaSalle line under the code name "Q project." For this sportier, better handling version of the big sedans, engineers conceived this rear transaxle system, a configuration that Zora Arkus-Duntov immediately envied for the Corvette.
GM Media Archive

Zora Arkus-Duntov

Zachary Arkuss was born in 1910, the son of Russian-Jewish parents working in Belgium at the time. The family returned to St. Petersburg when Zora, their diminutive nickname for Zachary, was young, the first of many family moves. As a seven-year old, Zora witnessed the February 1917 Bolshevik revolution. Zora's mother, Rachel, joined the movement, according to Duntov biographer Jerry Burton. Eventually his parents divorced. Rachel remarried a man named Josef Duntov, and in the early 1920s, they relocated to Germany. Enthralled with cars, racing, and high performance, he became a friend of Alfred Neubauer, head of Mercedes-Benz racing.

Zora Arkus-Duntov graduated in 1934 from Berlin's Institute of Charlottenberg with a degree in mechanical engineering. While in Berlin, he met young Elfi Wolff, a ballet dancer whom he dated in his Bugatti Type 30. Keith Bradsher's *New York Times* obituary of Duntov reported that he left Nazi Germany for France, where he joined the French air force and flew as a tail gunner at the start of World War II. In 1939, he married Elfi, who was dancing at Paris' Follies Bergère. When Paris fell, they escaped to Portugal. In late 1940, they immigrated to the United States, landing in New York City.

Arkus-Duntov and his brother, Yura, ran Ardun Mechanical, a successful munitions company during the war. After the war, they turned their engineering and mechanical talents to developing overhead-valve conversions for flathead V-8 Ford engines. While the Ardun heads performed well and were of very high quality, they were expensive and few sold. The stress of this business fractured Duntov's marriage to Elfi, and they separated for several years.

Hoping to establish a racing career in the United States, he entered the Indy 500 in 1946 and 1947, but he failed to qualify both times. Leaving Yura to run Ardun, Duntov returned to England. Carmaker Sydney Allard was looking for an engineer with knowledge of America V-8 engines that Allard could install in his cars for more competitive racing. In 1952, Duntov drove a Cadillac-powered Allard J2R model in the 24 Hours of Le Mans, but he failed to finish.

He returned to New York in late 1952, reunited with Elfi, and in January 1953, saw the Chevrolet prototype Corvette at Motorama. He wrote an ambitious letter asking for a job, outlining his ideas to make the Corvette an even better car. General Motors hired him to work with Maurice Olley in Chevrolet Research and Development as an assistant staff engineer. He started work on May 1, 1953, but left five weeks later. He had committed to co-drive an Allard at Le Mans. The engine failed after 65 laps, and he returned to Chevrolet.

He quickly established a reputation as a brash and outspoken but innovative engineer. His experience a decade earlier developing and attempting to sell Ardun heads in a competitive hot-rod industry gave him insight into marketing performance to enthusiasts. Despite Harley Earl's styling, Chevrolet division offered lackluster products with an inline six-cylinder, the only engine available. Ford's equally handsome offerings came with V-8s, and sales accelerated Ford into first place, generating stories in newspapers and enthusiast magazines.

In mid-December 1953, Duntov wrote a memo destined to wake up the Chevrolet division. He argued that Chevrolet should manufacture and sell high-performance parts itself, rather than leave outsiders to direct the market and reap the profits. His experience with Allards, first with Ford and Mercury V-8s and later with Cadillac and Chrysler power, was that these hybrids often mismatched power to chassis. In his memo, he pointed out how Allard's reputation suffered. He argued that if racing enthusiasts installed non-Chevrolet parts, the Corvette's reputation might bear the burden even if the incompatible pieces failed.

When his efforts to get Chevrolet into the performance game succeeded, he moved forward. Through friends in Paris, he gained an invitation to drive a Porsche at Le Mans in 1954. He won his class, earning an invitation to meet with Porsche's engineers working to improve the handling of their rear-engine 356. Having worked for Olley a year by this time, he shared ideas and techniques, leaving an indelible mark on the Porsche. He drove again in 1955 to another class victory.

By then he had begun to put his own imprint on the Corvette. The mark of Zora became a wide brushstroke as years went on, as one innovation or idea after another improved performance, handling, and sales. He earned another nickname, "Father of the Corvette," which was not really accurate, as Harley Earl had filled that role. Duntov certainly was its protector and champion, however.

He retired in 1975, having seen generations of "his" cars win the hearts of increasing numbers of enthusiasts and trophies for vast numbers of racers. He and Elfi remained in their comfortable home in Grosse Pointe Woods near Lake Ste. Claire on which they continued to enjoy boating. In the years after retirement, he collaborated with outsiders to turbocharge the Corvette V-8, and he took up flying again, planning in his last years to install a powerful motor on a small stunt plane. According to longtime friend and Corvette museum founder Dan Gale, Duntov intended to claim the world speed record for a small aircraft without a jet engine.

He died in April 1996, at age 86. Elfi died in 2008. She spent her last years ensuring the place Zora Arkus-Duntov's legacy held in Corvette history.

cylinder heads, fitted die-cast aluminum rocker-arm covers and a new cast-iron exhaust manifold. These changes and other subtleties raised power to 210 horsepower at 5,200 rpm. Installing a second Carter four-barrel carburetor and mounting both on a new aluminum intake manifold increased horsepower to 225, also at 5,200 rpm. When the car, delayed by so many changes, finally appeared at Motorama in January 1956, it came with an impressive resume. Just days earlier, Duntov clocked an official 150.583 miles per hour at Daytona Beach. One of his secrets had been his "Duntov cam," which pushed engine horsepower up to 240 at 5,800 rpm. Chevrolet offered it as RPO 449, a $188.30 option available only with the dual four-barrel RPO 445 V-8 (for $172.00). It was a package meant for racers, though Chevrolet managed to sell 1,570 (out of a total of 3,080) of these engines coupled to the Powerglide transmission. The T-Bird influence was rubbing off. Still, those numbers meant that another 1,510 of the RPO 445 buyers chose the manual. The Corvette effect was settling in. The base Corvette with a 210-horsepower V-8 and three-speed manual gearbox sold for $3,120. Venetian Red was the most popular color that year, while Cascade Green cars were hardest to find. Total production for 1956 reached 3,467 automobiles. It wasn't great, but great was coming. In the meanwhile, Corvette survived several serious death threats.

THE YEAR EVERYTHING CHANGED

Among engine historians and Corvette enthusiasts, 1957 is the year everything changed. First, Harry Barr succeeded Ed Cole as Chevrolet chief engineer following Cole's promotion to division manager. Barr's engineers bored out the 265-cubic-inch V-8 another 1/8 inch. This yielded total displacement of 283 cubic inches, the first of the legendary

designations. In standard trim, the new engine provided 220 horsepower and ranged up to 270 with dual four-barrel carburetors. The engineers had another innovation: fuel injection. With Rochester's new mechanical system, Chevrolet offered 250- and 283-horsepower options that achieved a long-held goal to develop 1 horsepower per cubic inch of displacement.

The base price crept up $56.32, to $3,176.32. Nearly as many cars sold in Onyx Black (2,189) as the next two colors combined, Venetian Red at 1,320 and Polo White at 1,273. The least popular color was Inca Silver, with only 65 produced.

Model year 1958 may go down in automotive design history as the pinnacle of chrome excess in GM styling. Not even Chevrolet's sports car was exempt. First, it stretched in length, from 168.0 inches overall to 177.2. It expanded in width from 70.5 to 72.8 inches. New dual headlights got chrome bezels to surround them. The toothy grille shrunk slightly, but designers trimmed new air intakes for front brakes in chrome. The front hood grew mock louvers that resembled a washboard. On the rear deck lid, carried over from 1956 and 1957, two new chrome spears divided the curved surface. Styling redid the interior as well, fitting the car with a new dashboard providing a grab bar for the passenger and a central instrument pod with a large 160-mile-per-hour speedometer encircling a centrally located tachometer. Bright metal kick-panels on the doors kept the chrome motif alive.

All this decoration had not come cheap. The 1957 base Corvette with its 220-horsepower engine and three-speed manual transmission had sold for $3,176.32. The 1958 price jumped to $3,591, similarly equipped. The top-performing carbureted engine, with two Carter four-barrels, delivered 270 horsepower at 6,000 rpm, while the Rochester fuel-injection versions provided 290 at 6,200. Despite Chevrolet increasing the price more than 10 percent, however, the car struck a clearer note with the buying public. In 1957, Chevrolet manufactured 6,339 Corvettes; for 1958, production increased to 9,168. In a marketplace characterized by sparkle, Corvette found its place, and the division discovered

Opposite: It had to be more fun than the expressions on these boys' faces suggest. Perhaps they just resented the photographer asking them to stop their 1961 Corvettes in the Kiddie Corral so he could take a picture. *GM Media Archive*

Below: One of the world's most important automobile shows takes place every second year in Frankfurt, Germany, and in 1961, drew a record crowd of 950,000 visitors. The Corvette took GM's center stage for the biennial show. *GM Media Archive*

Above: Chevrolet's advertising promoted the Corvette as the sports car among equals. Campbell Ewald sent photographers, cars, and models to important racing venues such as Wisconsin's Road America; a red convertible, a good-looking couple, and a great background were a photographer's dream come true. *GM Media Archive*

Right: As calendar year 1960 became model year 1961, St. Louis assembly staff raced the last of the 1960 cars out the door. The 1961s offered new rear bodywork and a new grille, which was missing its chrome teeth.
GM Media Archive

The V-8

While Ed Cole and Harry Barr had brought Cadillac's V-8 into existence, by the time they arrived at Chevrolet, Cole's predecessor, E. H. Kelley, already had begun developing one for General Motors' most important division. Kelley's version displaced 231 cubic inches. Cole, Barr, and engineer Russell Sanders enlarged the engine to 265 cubic inches, with a 3.75x3.0-inch bore and stroke. Significantly, Barr and Sanders designed the engine with plenty of room between cylinder centers: 4.4 inches. This allowed room for growth. Then Sanders and Barr updated the combustion chamber design and replaced the old-style heavier case rocker arms with new lighter stamped ones, allowing higher engine speeds. The engine was a natural fit for the Corvette.

The new V-8 brought two other significant improvements to the cars it inhabited. First, it weighed 41 pounds less than the "Stove-Bolt" six. And it was shorter and lower, so it improved front-end balance and overall handling.

Because of the far-sighted view of its designers, this powerplant grew again and again. By enlarging bore from 3.75 to 3.875, overall displacement grew to 283 cubic inches, starting with 1957 models. It did require one quick redesign to ensure cylinder walls didn't grow too thin.

For 1956, three separate Carter carburetor packages varied output. Starting with the base 210 horsepower featuring a single two-barrel carburetor, a buyer next stepped up to Regular Production Option (RPO) 469, which developed 225 horsepower using two four-barrel carburetors. The most potent engine was RPO 449, which hinted at the direction Chevrolet management meant to take the engine. Ordering instructions warned buyers that this option package was "for racing purposes only." While Chevrolet didn't reveal official output, it was widely known to be 240 horsepower, thanks to its two large Carter four-barrels and "Special High-Lift Camshaft." Chevrolet fitted new dual-point distributors to both 225- and 240-horsepower engines.

For the 1957 model year, the Carter-carbureted engines maintained their displacement, but other improvements increased output to 220 and 245 horsepower.

Above: Chevrolet's new 265-cubic-inch V-8 engine debuted in 1955 series production Corvettes and passenger cars. The engine developed 195 horsepower; Chevrolet engineers fitted a chrome distributor and ignition coil protective cover (visible on top, behind the carburetor and air cleaner). *GM Media Archive*

Left: With two four-barrel Carter carburetors, Chevrolet's new 283-cubic-inch engine developed either 220 or 270 horsepower for Corvette models in 1958. The "twin-carb V-8" was a popular option, selling slightly more than 3,500 out of 9,168 cars produced. *GM Media Archive*

black ink for the first time on its Corvette ledgers. According to Corvette historian and consummate researcher Michael Antonick, Snowcrest White outsold all other colors at 2,477 examples. Once again, Inca Silver trailed the eight-color field with only 193 manufactured.

EXIT HARLEY EARL

Harley Earl retired as vice president of Styling in 1958, but not before reviewing and approving corporation-wide design changes for 1959. It has been suggested that one of the earliest roles his successor played was tempering Earl's exuberance. That certainly was the case with the 1959 Corvette. Bill Mitchell removed the washboard and rear chrome spears.

Under the bodywork, engineers revised the rear suspension, adding trailing radius rods—the so-called parallelogram suspension—from mounting points on top of the axle back to rear edges of the frame. This controlled the rear axle's tendency to twist from the torque and horsepower the engine developed. Engine outputs repeated 1958 figures. The base car sold for $3,875, and the division manufactured 9,670. Chevrolet painted a third of its production Snowcrest White, the final tally in at 3,354. Most difficult for a modern collector to find is Classic Cream, with just 223 assembled. It was a one-year color.

Few changes differentiated 1960 model-year cars from those produced in 1959. Engineers and product planners agreed that fuel-injected engines should be sold only with manual transmissions, but engine output did not change for

Below: Once Mitchell got started, there was no stopping his creative imagination— or his ego. If the XP-700 Phantom had teased auto-show attendees with the look of future Corvettes, his XP-755 was the future. *GM Media Archive*

Below: Mitchell and Larry Shinoda added a third taillight, gave the rear windows a fancy split-glass treatment, and sent this XP-755 out on the show tour to test the public sentiment. The Mako Shark, as Mitchell called it, was near enough to the production car that management trusted the enthusiastic reactions. *GM Media Archive*

the third model year in a row. The instrument panel received more-legible letters and numbers, answering a complaint from customers and journalists. To improve handling, Duntov enlarged the front anti-roll bar again and added one on the rear. Production set a benchmark, reaching 10,261 units. Base price dropped $3, to $3,872. Ermine White led the customer choices, while Cascade Green, back on the chart after a two-year absence, counted just 140 examples.

Plans emerged in early 1958 to introduce a new Corvette for 1961. While Chevrolet division was successful, the Corvette became profitable only late in 1958. GM management shifted the project back. Other improvements, already scheduled, were easier to introduce. Headlight bezels went to body color and a new grille retired the chrome teeth. A newly designed back elevated the rear deck and introduced twin pairs of small round taillights to the Corvette design language dictionary. The rounded surfaces of Harley Earl's influence at the front merged into creases his successor Bill Mitchell favored at the rear.

The base engine for 1961 remained the 230-horsepower Carter-carbureted V-8. Improvements to fuel-injection metering and larger intake ports in the engine's new aluminum cylinder heads, as well as an increase in compression from 10.5:1 to 11:1, boosted top output to 315 horsepower. Chevrolet planned to introduce this package for 1960, but aluminum casting inconsistencies caused the delay till 1961. Another significant aluminum improvement reached production as well: Chevrolet introduced aluminum core radiators that offered 10 percent greater cooling capacity at half the weight of the previous units.

Fuel Injection

Carburetion once was viewed as a precise technology. Inside the carburetor, gasoline pumped through venturis then vaporized and misted into an airflow. The vacuum that the engine created with each cycle sucked the mixture through an intake manifold that somewhat equally distributed it among the several combustion chambers.

Fuel injection shoved that technology back to the horse-and-carriage era.

As fuel-injection historian Robert Genat defined it, there are three basic types of injection systems. One of those is "a direct timed-injection system [in which] the fuel is directly injected into the combustion chamber via a nozzle within the chamber at a specific instant prior to combustion. On a timed port-injection system, the nozzle is mounted outside the combustion chamber and is designed to spray fuel only when the intake valve is open. The final type [which GM chose] is continuous-flow port injection." Genat described this as a system in which "the fuel nozzle is located outside the combustion chamber and fuel flows even when the intake valve is closed. This design is less costly to build than one that requires a timing device for the release of the fuel."

Ed Cole, Harry Barr, Zora Arkus-Duntov, and others generally credit John Dolza as the GM engineer who made the Rochester system work reliably on the Corvette. According to Genat, Dolza studied fuel-injection systems on aircraft engines. To make any system deliver fuel, it is essential to understand and calculate the density of air flowing through, how to meter fuel, and how to coordinate all that with engine speed. In order to even out fuel-air mixture flow to multi-cylinder powerplants, engineers typically design engines so intake valves are adjacent to each other. But engine fuel-flow demands change with power demands, so any system has to be a compromise between best- and worst-case needs.

With the Rochester system GM selected and Dolza developed, this narrowed the range drastically from worst to best and delivered a much more useful air-fuel mix equally to each cylinder. As work continued, performance increased and horsepower output rose. For 1958, 1959, and 1960, peak output exceeded the 1:1 ideal as Corvettes developed 290 horsepower. These kinds of outputs resulted from another innovation: the Cold Air Box.

Engineers already knew cold air was denser than hot air. For 1957, the rarest option—and therefore the most collectible today—was a car with RPO 579D. The "D" specified "air box." This brought air from outside the car directly to the fuel-injection fresh-air intake. It also directed excess cool air to the hard-working front brakes.

For 1961, the final year Chevrolet offered the 283-cubic-inch V-8 in the Corvette, Dolza and his colleagues coaxed 315 horsepower out of the overachieving small-block. If anyone doubted Chevrolet had capable engineers, this package silenced them. And then came 1962.

Right out of the box, Chevrolet's new 327-cubic-inch V-8 developed 300 horsepower on carburetors (almost while coasting). With fuel injection, the new "small-block fuelie," known on order sheets as RPO 582, established a new benchmark: 360 horsepower.

The next year, with an otherwise entirely new car, the engine changed designations. As the L84, the 327/360 launched a new legend. And set in motion an entire new world of performance. With fuel injection. And without.

Rochester fuel injection arrived in 1957 (along with a four-speed transmission). Displacement increased to 283 cubic inches, and peak output matched the displacement: 283 horsepower. Fuel injection was a $726.30 option that only 43 buyers selected. *GM Media Archive*

Base price for the 230-horsepower three-speed inched up to $3,934. The most popular option, at $31.55, was whitewall tires. The dual-quad-equipped 270-horsepower 283 V-8 was nearly 28 times as popular as the 275-horsepower fuel-injected engine, at 2,827 manufactured versus 118. Price played some role in that decision. The carbureted engine was a $182.95 option, while the "fuelie" went for $484.20, for either the 275- or 315-horsepower power plants. Chevy manufactured 1,452 of the 315s. It was the final year for dual four-barrel carburetors.

Again, according to Antonick, Ermine White claimed most car bodies at 3,178, followed by Roman Red at 1,794. At the opposite end of the color chart, Sateen Silver again claimed rarity with just 747 produced.

Few outside General Motors imagined what Chevrolet had in store for Corvette buyers for 1963, so 1962 sales surged, climbing to 14,531 cars manufactured. The all-new base engine provided 250 horsepower at 4,400 rpm, introducing the next legend in Chevrolet small-block history, the 327. To achieve this displacement, Harry Barr's engineers bored out the 283 from 3.875 to 4.0 inches and lengthened stroke from 3.0 to 3.25 inches. The most potent fuel-injected variation delivered 360 horsepower at 6,000 rpm, and Chevrolet assembled 1,918 cars with this engine.

Base price came at $4,038, and for the first time in Corvette history, the heater no longer was an option but came included in the price of the car. Almost from the start, it had been the most-purchased option, but perhaps for accounting and product-planning purposes, it cost extra (at $102.25 for the previous three years) until model year 1962. The St. Louis plant assembled 14,531 of the 1962s. Throughout the year, assemblers were reconfiguring the plant and retraining themselves for the second-generation Corvette, coming soon to dealers everywhere.

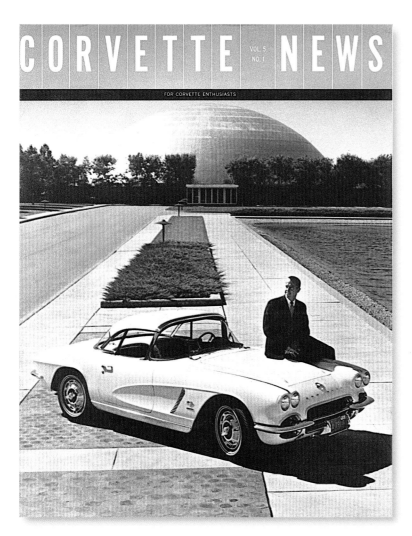

Left: NASA's Mercury astronaut Alan Shepard was a Corvette enthusiast from the start, buying his first, a 1953 convertible, in 1954 from his father-in-law. A 1957 followed, and then *Corvette News* editor Joe Pike convinced Ed Cole that Shepard needed a state-of-the-art 1962 'Vette in 1962. *GM Media Archive*

Above: For its final year, the C1 lost the chrome trim outlining its style-statement side coves. Engine displacement increased from 283 to 327 cubic inches, spawning a new generation of "must-have" V-8s for the Corvette. *GM Media Archive*

2 FROM DOMINATION TO DISCO

THE SECOND AND THIRD GENERATION

The assignment Bill Mitchell delivered to his designers in November 1958—create a new Corvette—excited Zora Duntov as well. GM had a concept under development for a sedan with a transaxle-type rear transmission-and-differential combination using a fully independent rear suspension. Duntov believed the same piece should find a home in any new Corvette, perhaps even one with a rear engine. This secret project bore the designation "Q" and was considered for introduction on a new Cadillac model, with versions for other divisions to follow. Advanced engineering developed the transaxle with both manual and automatic transmissions, and they mounted rear brakes "inboard," alongside the differential. While Bob McLean's research studio won the assignment for the Corvette's styling, Duntov provided the chassis layout this time. He shortened the wheelbase from the existing 101.85 inches to 94. To lower the car and to provide more chassis rigidity, he conceived a Porsche-type platform frame of steel. Rumors circulated that with production targets in excess of 10,000 units per year, Chevrolet was switching to a steel body for the Corvette.

By early December, McLean's clay modelers had completed a full-size mockup of the Q Corvette. But its many engineering innovations, which by this time had grown to include an all-aluminum engine with a dry-sump oil lubrication system to lower the engine in the chassis, became economic liabilities to a company squinting into the future. GM financial planners recommended belt tightening, and the board canceled far-reaching programs such as the Q. By New Years, Chevrolet placed its Q concepts on hold. As historian Karl Ludvigsen summarized it, Duntov recognized that the 1960 Corvette "was going to be the best car he could make out of his 1959 model."

Opposite: Chevrolet Design staff wraps its gift to auto enthusiasts with a bow in the Design Center lobby during the 1962 Christmas holidays. The body style, originally created in 1958, went into production as a 1963 model. *GM Media Archive*

Above: The entire bodywork of the 1963 Sting Ray was startling and dramatic. Its divided rear window provoked considerable quarrels between design boss Bill Mitchell and chief engineer Zora Duntov. *David Newhardt © 2012*

Above: Chevrolet offered the 1963 Corvette in coupe and convertible forms. The design and engineering were so appealing that production surged 50 percent over 1962 output. *David Newhardt © 2012*

Right: The 1963 model's interior dipped between outer frame rails on an all-new chassis. Independent rear suspension greatly improved ride and handling. *David Newhardt © 2012*

Duntov did not give up. Looking at other configurations for the Q transaxle, he began in early 1958 to develop his own version of a mid- or even rear-engined Corvette. He ran a proposal past Ed Cole, who encouraged him to move forward, at least experimentally. Armed with new fiberglass production-cost appraisals, Duntov stepped forward and backward at the same time, returning to a steel frame and abandoning the steel body as he began experimenting with engine placement behind the driver. But packaging logistics and stylists' creativity began to thwart his efforts. While Duntov believed a midengine vehicle could be shorter even than the Q Corvette concept, the need to provide for driver and passenger comfort and legroom and the design department's devotion to the long-nose/short-tail sports car form made for some tense moments between Duntov and Mitchell. Their relationship was destined to deteriorate further as the next-generation Corvette took on more sharply defined forms.

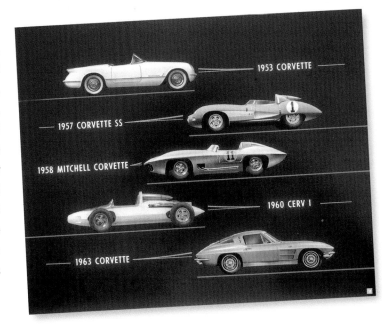

SECOND GENERATION A GO

During the fall of 1959, Mitchell got word that Chevrolet division had written funds for a new Corvette into the budget. The ill-fated Q coupe and roadster came from designs that Peter Brock and Chuck Pohlmann had done in Bob McLean's research design studios. Mitchell retired Brock's coupe when the project was postponed. However, in late 1958, he had set Larry Shinoda to work adapting Pohlmann's open car to the Corvette SS mule chassis to create a race car for himself. Mitchell's Caribbean deep-sea–fishing holidays inspired him to name his new racer the Sting Ray. Shinoda and Corvette SS designers Tony Lapine and Bob Cumberford sometimes worked as pit crew for Mitchell and kept the car running for designated driver Dr. Dick Thompson. It raced through 1959 and 1960. As Mitchell explained it to interviewer Dave Crippen in 1984, when it came time to develop the second-generation Corvette, "I took the lines right off that car." He took its name as well.

The plan for a production Sting Ray moved forward, and Duntov made the best of what he felt was a compromised situation. He petitioned Chevrolet chief engineer Harry Barr to support his ideas for better visibility front and rear. Duntov

Left: Chevrolet carried over the base 1962 engine and transmission for 1963. However, they offered three optional powerplants ranging from 300- and 340-horsepower carbureted variants to this 360-horsepower, top-of-the-line fuel-injected version. *David Newhardt © 2012*

believed the wheel bulges on Mitchell's Sting Ray racer and on later Shark show cars blocked forward vision, and a coupe greatly limited what the driver could see to rear.

Zora forged ahead, developing a new ladder frame strengthened by five thick crossmembers. He sacrificed the Q's 94-inch wheelbase and settled on 98, still nearly 4 inches shorter than the 1962 production car. Positioning the passenger compartment inside the frame rails and, as Bob McLean had done for the 1953, putting the driver and rider as far to the rear as possible lowered the center of gravity (from 19.8 inches above the ground to 16.5 inches) and shifted weight balance toward the rear axle. Saving money by using Chevrolet sedan front suspension members again (but in different positions) gave him funds to develop a three-link independent rear suspension, a concept he first explored in his open-wheel research vehicle CERV. With Mitchell's new body configuration, Duntov had no room for longitudinal leaf springs or even for traditional coils on either side of the rear axles. A year earlier, his friends at Porsche had introduced a transverse leaf spring mounted rigidly to the differential but whose ends were free to rise and fall with the half shafts. This was technology he had seen on countless production and racing cars in Germany while he was in school. For Duntov, this solution, which transferred wheel loading from the tire on the outside of the curve to the one inside, not only fit the space and improved ride and handling but also eliminated the first generation's solid-axle hopping during hard acceleration.

Duntov was content with the year-old 327-cubic-inch engine, so Chevrolet made only one change when advancing it into the production Sting Ray: What they had designated RPO 582, the 360-horsepower fuel-injected V-8, became the L84 for 1963. With the engineering improvements and the configuration of the new body, weight distribution settled at 53 percent on the front tires of the 1963 coupe with 47 percent on the rear tires. Nonetheless, Zora Duntov had one more battle to lose. Already unhappy at the idea of an enclosed coupe, he told biographer Jerry Burton he was "aghast" when he saw the rear treatment Mitchell had in mind for the new car. A fastback was one thing. One with a tapering

Below: Some concepts for what became the 1963 Corvette explored a variety of rooflines and rear-end treatments. This clay model allowed Bill Mitchell and others to imagine the car in closed and open versions. *GM Media Archive*

Above: Design Center engineers and fabricators created this fastback mockup on a 1961 Corvette convertible. There is no indication whether this was a road-going mule or a wind tunnel test unit. *GM Media Archive*

Left: Engineers favored several methods to determine airflow during wind tunnel tests. One system used strands of thread taped to the body. For this test, ink dots set on the bodywork run with the air currents. *GM Media Archive*

Above: By the 1930s, Bugatti, a French automaker, was renowned for great engineering and sensational design, including this 1936 Type 57SC Atlantic. This rear styling inspired Bill Mitchell's center spine and split window on the 1963 Sting Ray. *Randy Leffingwell © 2012*

Right: Another influence for Bill Mitchell and his Corvette designers came from the 1956 Oldsmobile "Golden Rocket" show car. Fabricated in fiberglass, the car debuted during the 1956 Motorama show season and appeared at the Paris Auto Salon. *GM Media Archive*

Split Windows

From what mind did the controversial but stylish split rear window originate? Early car designers needed to split the rear window for the same reason that windshields were two pieces: until the 1940s, glass was not strong enough to open up a broad expense of roof without shattering because of poor roads and car body flex.

One of the most famous split-window designs in automotive history was Jean Bugatti's striking Type 57 Aerolithe, introduced at the Paris Auto Salon in October 1935. Splitting this rear window was a styling decision dictated by another manufacturing reality. Bugatti manufactured the Aerolithe body out of Elektron, a feather-weight magnesium alloy that was challenging to weld or to hammer into shape. Jean turned an engineering challenge in to a design statement, developing a spine of the folded metal panels that his fabricators riveted together. The 1935 car inspired a small production run in Duralumin, an aluminum alloy, called the Atlantic, starting in 1936. Bugatti fabricated six underslung chassis, designated the 57S, and Jean assembled three cars initially, each customer choosing to maintain the stylish spine and semi-boattail rear end. Over subsequent decades, another three cars came into being.

But even Bugatti's Aerolithe had precedents. At the 1933 Berlin Motor Show, the German custom bodymaker Erdmann and Rossi showed a streamlined Mercedes 170 coupe with a spine dividing the rear window and running down the rear of the car to a boattail.

In the United States, Cadillac startled Century of Progress Exposition visitors with its 1933 V-16 Aero-Dynamic Coupe. This long-nose, two-door fastback finished with a gently curved back end set off by a large rear glass split down the center. Based on visitor reaction, Cadillac put these coupes in production with both V-12 and V-16 engines starting in 1934. In this same year, Chrysler Corporation introduced its radical airflow in coupe and sedan configuration with split rear windows. The car was far advanced for its time stylistically and in its engineering. Even more radical, the Czechoslovakian Tatra T77, introduced in 1934 using a rear-mounted air-cooled V-8, had no rear window but a prominent spine that became a rudder-like wing as it reached the rear of the car.

Soon after Bugatti's Atlantic coupe, Talbot-Lago introduced its 1937 T150-C-SS models. For the Paris show car prototype, body designers Figoni and Falaschi created a subtle notchback roof style nearly identical to their pure fastback; it used twin rear windows (that mimicked the shape of the car's front grille) separated by a subtle crease. Talbot-Lago produced at least four cars with this split rear window.

After World War II, the split rear window motif reappeared. While some designers considered the treatment old-fashioned, Nuccio Bertone, the Italian designer in Turin, was among the first to resurrect the feature. It first appeared on his Fiat-engined Abarth show car for 1952. Then Alfa-Romeo approached his design company Stile Bertone to explore the possibilities of car design with special attention to aerodynamics and drag. Bertone had done research and design studies for aircraft wings and had developed profiles that managed airflow. His chief designer, Franco Scaglione, created the bodies on Alfa 1900 platforms. The first of the legendary series of Berlinette Aerodinamica Tecnica coupes, known among enthusiasts by their acronym "BAT," appeared at the Turin Motor Show in 1953. BAT 5, as the car was known, had a prominent spine that ran down the rear window to become a shark-like fin on the rear deck. In 1954, Alfa and Bertone showed BAT 7, and the series concluded with BAT 9 for the 1955 motor show circuit. (The missing numbers were drawings only.) Each of the cars introduced large wings and a split rear-window treatment with a central wind-splitting spine.

In 1955, Mario Felice Boano, who had grown up designing cars for Ghia in Turin, founded his own firm and soon produced a custom-bodied Alfa-Romeo 6C3000 coupe for Argentina's president Juan Perón. The striking fastback featured a prominent central spine along the roof, splitting the huge rear window. Its low beltline emphasized upper and lower body forms and functions.

GM did its first split window in 1956 with the Oldsmobile Golden Rocket concept car. In typical Harley Earl style, the Motorama show car appeared in gold paint with rudimentary fins and rocket nose cone–like projections at the front. Doors opened traditionally, but panels above each rose gull-wing style, and the seat came up and swiveled to meet the driver or passenger.

Harley Earl and Bill Mitchell returned from the Turin Motor Show in early November 1957, and Mitchell announced to his staff that he wanted to do a new Corvette for 1960. He had pictures of a new Pininfarina-designed land-speed-record car from Abarth that had been on display at Turin. It featured rounded bulges that accommodated wheels in the low fenders and a prominent horizontal body beltline. He initiated a contest among the studios. A recent hire out of California's Art Center College of Design named Peter Brock won the competition. After studying Brock's concepts, Mitchell asked for a roadster as well. Another young talent in McLean's studio, Chuck Pohlmann, a friend of Brock's, drew the open-car assignment. For weeks, they worked on their designs. Mitchell concluded his best shot for production was to show the open car first, so the roadster moved out of research and into more public development.

In an interview in 1996, Peter Brock clarified another mystery: "The coupe was originally done with a large rear window, a single piece of glass," Brock said. "That split rear window was actually put on later. Mitchell imposed that hard line down the roof and rear window because he loved the Bugatti type 57SC Atlantic. He wanted the flavor of that car on the Sting Ray."

Right: Four prototype Sting Ray coupes raced at the Riverside International Raceway at Riverside, California, in October 1962. As the race went on, Chevrolet parked a new coupe and convertible above the track for publicity photos. *GM Media Archive*

Below: Chevrolet supported a few of its private racers who entered the first Grand Prix of Puerto Rico at *Auto Pista de Caguas* in San Juan. A public relations team brought a coupe and this convertible and photographed them all over San Juan. *GM Media Archive*

tail, with a rear window divided by an unnecessary spine, was another all together. As their arguments disintegrated into profane name-calling, Duntov heard the stakes go up. Mitchell, who had learned from Harley Earl to push a speed-dial phone number whenever anyone disagreed with him, threatened to yank Duntov's independent rear suspension from underneath the new car. That was power Mitchell possessed. Duntov got a sense of how little he held.

Still, he could not let go. He went to Ed Cole with his concerns. But Cole understood what Duntov did not: Mitchell's designers exerted greater impact on the balance sheet bottom line than did Duntov's engineers.

Mitchell got his split window, and although he let it go away for 1964, he was not done with Duntov. He barred the engineer from entry to the design department, and he forbade his staff from rendering any help to Duntov projects. These arguments came to a head as Zora was developing a set of world-beater racing cars based on the new Sting Ray: the Grand Sport. This proved a costly miscalculation when the car's aerodynamics created an unsolvable problem with front-end lift.

FOUR SEATS?

Those concerns barely affected regular customers who flocked to the new cars in record numbers. By model-year-end, Chevrolet had assembled 10,919 of the convertibles and 10,594 coupes for a record total output of 21,513 cars (up nearly 50 percent from the previous year's 14,531 convertibles). Chevrolet delivered the base car with the 250-horsepower 327-cubic-inch V-8 and three-speed manual transmission. While the most popular option for the Corvette remained the $31.22 whitewall tires, second most widely selected was the $188.30 four-speed manual gearbox. In an effort to convince buyers the Corvette was a true Grand Touring automobile, Chevrolet offered option C60: air conditioning. Just 278 buyers specified the $421.80 luxury. Among the least-purchased options were those that made the car a potent competitor: N03, the 36-gallon fuel tank for coupes only (only 63 produced, until midyear,) and Z06, the "special performance equipment" package that cost a pricy $1,818.45. Production figures suggest that Chevrolet manufactured 198 coupes and a single convertible with that option.

Below: To hedge his risks against the popular four-seat Thunderbird, Ed Cole commissioned a prototype four-seat Sting Ray. Its proportions nearly worked, but rear seat access was difficult.
GM Media Archive

Above: Technicians spray fiberglass composite material onto the 1963 Sting Ray floorpan mold. This early version incorporated footwells for potential rear seats. *GM Media Archive*

Right: In addition to stylish external exhaust pipes, the special 1963 coupe that Bill Mitchell built for Harley Earl provided an assortment of instruments for the passenger's amusement. The two large dials were an accelerometer on the left and a 24-hour clock. *David Newhardt © 2012*

Above: Harley Earl had retired, but he was not forgotten. Bill Mitchell's design staff developed a special 1963 hardtop coupe for his former boss.
David Newhardt © 2012

By 1963, Ford's Thunderbird had been a four-seat coupe for five years. Sales figures had remained impressive, far exceeding what it had done as a two-seater. This prompted Ed Cole to suggest Chevrolet hedge its bets and develop a four-seat Sting Ray as well. The Design staff stretched the wheelbase 10 inches to accommodate rear seats and create some legroom. Duntov worried the four-seater would blur the image of Corvette as the sports car he had worked so hard to sharpen. But the project died when, as Larry Shinoda explained to Jerry Burton, "GM Chairman Jack Gordon got stuck in the back seat of the prototype at Design Staff. He stormed off, and that was the end of the four-passenger Corvette."

For 1964, the most notable change was that Bill Mitchell's split-window treatment disappeared. While he quietly had acknowledged Duntov's point about visibility, a different consideration dictated the design change. Production engineers had widened the central pillar to give it strength and rigidity during the assembly process, and it gained more mass than Mitchell wanted. Designers also removed the mock vents in the front deck lid, though they retained the insets. Base engine and transmission packages remained unchanged with 250 horsepower from the 327-cubic-inch engine, delivered to the road through the three-speed manual transmission. Whitewall tires just barely outsold the four-speed manual gearbox, each at significantly more than the 19,000 produced. Annual assembly totals tilted toward convertibles for 1964 with St. Louis manufacturing 13,925 of the open cars against 8,304 of the coupes. Prices held steady at $4,037 for the convertible and $4,252 for the coupe, exact repeats of 1963 figures. Besides the one-piece rear window, the other significant improvements were under the hood. Engineers coaxed another 25 horsepower out of the 327-cubic-inch engine by installing a new long-duration high-lift camshaft and a Holley four-barrel carburetor. Output reached 365 at 6,200 rpm. The same camshaft increased fuel-injected output by 15 to 375 horsepower, also at 6,200 rpm.

(CONTINUED ON PAGE 81)

" *GM Chairman Jack Gordon got stuck in the back seat of the prototype at Design Staff. He stormed off and that was the end of the four-passenger Corvette.* "

75

XPs, the Q, and Ocean Aggressors

Military aircraft and the acronyms and code names that the armed forces used for them fascinated Harley Earl. It's only natural that Earl would express the language of military aircraft, both literally and figuratively in the form of design language, in automotive design.

Following on the heels of a 1956 limited-production SR model, which was meant to legalize the Corvette as a "production Sebring Racer"—hence the SR–Earl assigned his staff designers and engineers to create a Corvette-based race car for his son, Jerry. He designated this second race special the SR-2, presumably meaning "Sebring Racer 2." The SR appeared little different from production Corvettes, but under the hood, racer John Fitch and a collection of Chevrolet engineers, including three-time Indianapolis 500 winner Mauri Rose, transformed the stock convertible into a potent competitor for Sebring and other venues such as Daytona, Florida, and Road America, Wisconsin.

Soon after completing SR-2, they commenced work on another Earl creation meant to shame Chevrolet management into supporting racing. This was labeled the XP-64 among styling staffers. Earl's long friendship with Air Force General Curtis LeMay introduced him to several designations he adopted for Styling such as "Experimental Pursuit"

(XP) aircraft. Zora Duntov did the engineering, and body stylists Bob Cumberford and Tony Lapine created the shape of the car, which was inspired by Jaguar's new D-Type sports racer and based on the tube-frame of Mercedes-Benz's racing 300SL models. By 1957, the car was named the Corvette SS. It was destined to race at Sebring where problems related to insufficient development brought an early retirement.

All of General Motors retired from racing in June 1957 when the corporation signed on to the American Automobile Manufacturers Association's recommendation that no U.S. carmaker participate in or promote "any race or speed contest, test or competitive event involving or suggesting speed." This had an effect similar to that of the constitutional amendment prohibiting production and consumption of alcohol. Racers still got special parts and even support checks; they just had to go to the building's back doors.

Harley Earl named Bill Mitchell vice president of Styling in December 1958, upon Earl's retirement. Mitchell soon learned that plans to introduce a new Corvette for 1960 were on hold due to a dim economic outlook. As if to prove the hypocrisy of the AMA ban, Mitchell acquired the 1957 SS Corvette development mule and re-bodied it with the roadster

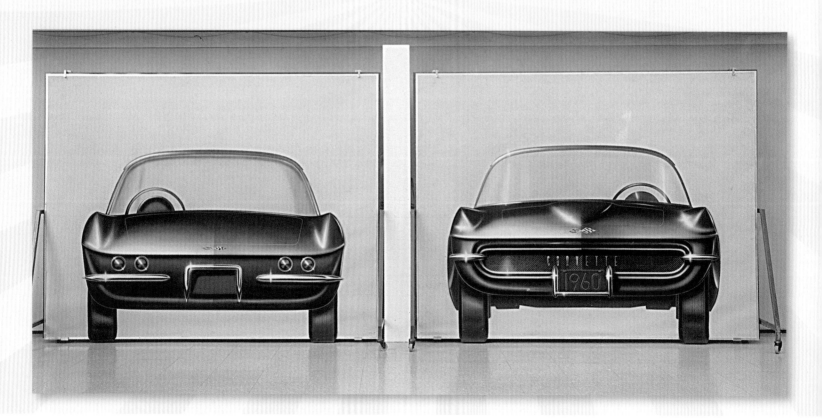

Opposite: The Peter Brock/Chuck Pohlmann concepts reached full-size renderings by October 10, 1958, as a potential Q Corvette. Bill Mitchell intended these as 1960 introductions if the mockup license plate is any indication.
GM Media Archive

Left: By February 1960, Neil Madler's photo showed that the Q Corvette had undergone subtle evolution. The spine and split rear window were in place.
GM Media Archive

Below: No sooner had the world seen the 1963 Sting Ray than Mitchell got his designers considering wild possibilities for the next generation. Styling photographer Dean Zeeb shot this mid-engine XP-807 with a 427-cid motor on June 5, 1963.
GM Media Archive

concept he had approved for 1960 production. Internally, the car was known as the XP-87.

Mitchell had vacationed in the Caribbean and took a deep-sea fishing trip, where he watched a variety of fish and other sea creatures passing beneath the boat. The stingray particularly fascinated him with its undulating movements. These reminded him of the surfaces of cars his designers had developed. He christened his race car the Sting Ray, although there was no Chevrolet or GM identification on it. Still, because Mitchell was the entrant, journalists and race fans assumed this was a preview of the next Corvette.

After its debut race in April 1959, GM Chairman John Gordon called Mitchell on the carpet and told him to quit racing. When Mitchell effectively argued that racing sold cars and that he had grown deeply interested in car design because of racing, Gordon relented, telling Mitchell to get the car off GM grounds and off GM books. Mitchell paid for the next two racing seasons out of his own pocket. His Sting Ray racing efforts culminated with driver Dr. Dick Thompson winning the SCCA C Modified class championship in 1960. By this time, Mitchell knew a new Corvette was due for 1962, and he resurrected the designs from which his Sting Ray originated.

Throughout this time, Mitchell followed Earl's pattern of assembling special cars for himself and others within the corporation. A "Special

SR-2" had gone to GM president Harlow Curtice. He created for himself the XP-700 Phantom, a stylized hint at things to come. For this car, Mitchell picked up several concepts for the rear ends of the proposed 1962 car designed by stylists Peter Brock and Chuck Pohlmann. The front end featured quad headlights and an elongated oval nose with flanking openings for brakes and other functions. Because the rear end too faithfully represented what was coming soon, Mitchell assistant Larry Shinoda revised it with a steeper drop.

As development continued on the car destined for 1963 introduction, styling and engineering efforts took place under the code name XP-720. To keep interest alive in existing Corvette production, Mitchell released a steady stream of concepts for the auto shows. Next on his roster was the 1961 XP-755 "Shark." This car, as a roadster with a Harley Earl–era double-bubble glass top, was close in lines and forms to the new production car. Mitchell again tapped Larry Shinoda to create this iteration of the Pohlmann/Brock cars.

The Shark, rechristened the Mako Shark, remained on the show tour circuit until 1965, when it was updated as the Mako Shark II, code-named the XP-830. Little did viewers know that this car previewed shapes to come in the third-generation Corvette models beginning in 1968.

Above: Milford Proving Grounds engineering staff subjected 1964 prototypes to hundreds of miles on the "rough road." This test broke or shook loose components and electrical connections. *GM Media Archive*

Top: In 1962, the first snowfall of winter leave a couple of inches on the cars in Zora and Elfie Duntov's driveway. At the time, Zora had one "company car" and regularly drove home in a prototype to evaluate engineering changes during his commute. *GM Media Archive*

CORVETTE '61 BY CHEVROLET

(CONTINUED FROM PAGE 75)

As had been the case in recent years, red, specifically Riverside Red, remained the most popular color choice, followed by Ermine White.

If the first two years of the Sting Ray had delivered really good cars to Chevrolet customers, model year 1965 brought greatness. Following extensive testing and development, Corvette engineering mounted 11.75-inch-diameter disc brakes on all four wheels. These were highly capable four-piston, two-piece caliper units with ventilated rotors. Previously, performance enthusiasts opted for sintered metallic brake linings on the finned drum brakes. But these needed to be hot to work best.

Above: Chevrolet changed the 1964 coupe and convertible in several large and small ways. The coupe lost its split window and both cars gave up the faux-grille work on the front hood. *GM Media Archive*

BIG-BLOCK POWER

To test the new brakes, Chevrolet offered the first variation of its "big-block" V-8 as option code L78 beginning in mid-March 1965. This put a 396-cubic-inch engine under the hood. With a bore and stroke of 4.09 by 3.76 inches and a four-barrel carburetor, this package produced 425 horsepower at 6,400 rpm. It fit in the car under a modified front deck lid with a prominent bulge to enclose the large air cleaner. In a coupe weighing 3,135 pounds, the big-block accelerated the car from 0 to 60 miles per hour in 5.7 seconds and through the quarter mile in 14.1 at 103 miles per hour. If a Corvette buyer sought maximum performance, there was no question this was the choice: while the fuel-injected L84 375-horsepower 327 was a $538 option, Chevrolet charged barely half as much ($292.70) for the 396. The big-block signaled the disappearance of fuel injection from Corvette engines for more than a decade.

A new blue arrived on the Corvette color charts, and it went straight to the top of buyer choices. Nassau Blue represented 6,022 of the 23,564 cars manufactured for 1965. They broke down as 15,378 convertibles and 8,186 coupes, open sports cars taking the preference nearly two-to-one. The second most popular color was Glen Green with 3,782 cars produced.

Above: *Corvette Summer*, produced in 1978, gave high school shop student Kenny Dantley, played by Mark Hamill, a chance to build his dream Corvette. He did so well his car was stolen. He chased it and the bad guys to Las Vegas to retrieve it. The producers gave it right-hand steering so Dantley would be close to the curb when he drove past young girls on the sidewalks of Los Angeles. *Randy Leffingwell © 2012*

Right: In the 1975 film *Death Race 2000*, David Carradine played a racer named Frankenstein who charged across the United States with others in a coast-to-coast race. Cars, such as this one for Frankenstein, were fitted with lethal teeth and fangs because the rules of the contest awarded drivers extra points for every pedestrian they killed. *Ed Baumgarten ©2012, courtesy Mid America Motorworks*

Corvettes of Death and Corvettes of Summer

Even before Martin Milner and George Maharis, starring as Tod Stiles and Buz Murdoch on the television series *Route 66*, pulled into their first fictional stop in Garth, Alabama, the Hollywood and entertainment industry celebrities, sports stars, and community leaders around the country had noticed and embraced the Corvettes. It may have taken V-8 engines and four-speed manual transmissions, but steadily the car caught the eye and opened the pocketbook of the very audience Harley Earl and Ed Cole had sought in 1953.

CBS and Screen Gems had renewed *Route 66* through 1961 and 1962, and as the new car approached, Chevrolet again signed on as major series sponsor. There was no better "vehicle" on television to promote their vehicle. While a Tasco Turquoise convertible was used in the series' inaugural year, cinematographer Jack Marta had trouble. The light blue reflected more light on the black-and-white film and sometimes faces went too dark. For the next three years, Tod and Buz drove Fawn Beige cars. Some viewers wondered how two barely employed young men got a new car each year, and why, with the show's name, episodes took place thousands of miles from U.S. Highway 66.

Perhaps the Fawn Beige settled better with viewers, or more enthusiasts tuned in during the series' third year. There are no figures available to reflect the impact of Friday night's show on Saturday shoppers, but production numbers rose by nearly a third from 1961 to 1962.

Two buyers in 1962 had nothing to do with the show but already had achieved their own stardom. Jan Berry and Dean Torrence, both Los Angeles natives, began recording music in the late 1950s while they were going to college. With many successful songs under their belts, the two bought new Corvettes in 1962. They met and worked with Brian Wilson, co-founder of the Beach Boys. Berry and Wilson co-wrote nearly all their music from that point on. Their songs reflected the twin Southern California cultures of surfing and fast cars. As they released "Surf City," "Drag City," and "Little Old Lady from Pasadena" in 1963, they updated their year-old convertibles with new Sting Rays, inspiring the 1964 hit "Dead Man's Curve." That song, based on a fictional race through Beverly Hills between a Jaguar XK-E and a Sting Ray, became eerily prophetic when, in 1966, Berry crashed his Sting Ray into a parked car barely a block from the curve in the song. He survived, but it was more than a year before he could make music again.

Brian Wilson had been writing music for a band he was in with his brothers Carl and Dennis, as well as Mike Love and Al Jardine. After their first recorded song, "Surfin,'" was released in 1961, the record producer renamed the band The Beach Boys. Over the next year, Wilson immortalized Chevrolet's big-block V-8 in a song called "409," and then with Capitol Records with "Little Deuce Coupe" and the Corvette-themed "Shutdown," a song about a drag race between a Super-Stock Dodge and a fuel-injected Sting Ray.

Another racing classic, this time on the silver screen, not black vinyl, made good use of a 1964 silver coupe. The 1965 hit *Red Line 7000*, directed by Howard Hawks and starring, among others, James Caan, told the story of loves and lives lost on and around the stock-car circuit in 1965. Shot on several oval tracks across America, including the Daytona 500, and incorporating many well-known drivers of the period, Hawks also pulled in film clips from other events.

Then in 1968, director Gordon Flemyng gathered a virtual who's who of Hollywood and TV actors for a film titled *The Split*. It set up the premise of dividing loot following a half-million dollar theft during a football game at the Los Angeles Coliseum. A red 1965 coupe was one of the getaway cars when it came time to split with the proceeds.

In the early 1970s, Corvettes began picking up cameo roles in foreign films. In 1973, Federico Curiel used a white 1955 convertible in several scenes in a violent spy thriller *Misión Suicida*. In it, Soviet spies kidnap a war criminal and then kidnap a Corvette-driving cosmetic surgeon to change his face.

The same year, Alfredo Crevenna directed one of a series of films about a masked wrestler, Santo, who was asked to help save a friend's hacienda from intruders. In the film *Santo y el Aguila Real* (Santo and the Royal Eagle), a 1953 Corvette appears in a number of scenes.

In the 1975 production *Death Race 2000*, Paul Bartel directed a Roger Corman science fiction film in which a group of wildly modified cars race across country, picking off pedestrians for points. David Carradine, often wearing a mask, played Mr. Frankenstein and piloted a spined, buck-toothed green Corvette convertible through events such as Euthanasia Day at a local hospital in this R-rated cult classic.

In 1978, the Corvette starred in a movie co-written by independent producer Hal Barwood and director Matthew Robbins, starring Mark Hamill and Annie Potts. It was a coming-of-age film that met the road-trip cinema concept with auto theft and a few good chases thrown in. A wildly customized 1973 Sport Coupe, converted to right-hand-drive so its young star could chat up the ladies as he drove it slowly through traffic, was stolen in the film by bad guys and in reality from the studio storage lot by feuding film trade unions. Light-hearted summer entertainment, the distribution company changed the film's name from *Stingray* to *Corvette Summer* when they learned a far poorer production was being rushed to completion, having stolen their title.

The other 1978 film, the one titled *Stingray*, involved drug dealers, a red Stingray, and cases of mistaken identity when two hapless rubes, Al and Elmo, buy a 1964 convertible, complete with roll bar, in which stolen drugs are stashed. The movie's promotional "tag" lines says it all: "Get wrecked! Get chased! Get smashed! Get it on! The big red hot one is in town!"

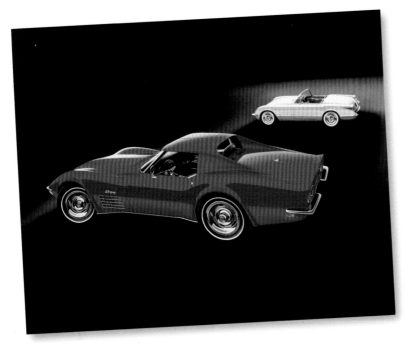

An internal rule at GM had limited the largest displacement engines to the full-size models through 1965, hoping to appear responsible to lawmakers, insurance companies, and its customers. Product planners, monitoring surging interests in performance, showed sales projections to chairman Frederick Donner, who abandoned the restriction for 1966. The Corvette and other Chevrolet products added 427-cubic-inch engines to their options list. Piston stroke remained unchanged at 3.76 inches, but bore grew to 4.25. Chevrolet offered two versions. The L36 developed 390 horsepower at 5,200 rpm. This engine used hydraulic valve lifters. The higher performance version for 1966 was the L72 with solid lifters, high-flow cylinder heads, and a high-lift long-duration cam. Producing 425 horsepower at 5,600 rpm, this engine accelerated the Sting Ray from 0 to 60 miles per hour in 4.8 seconds.

Performance potential sold cars. In 1966, Chevrolet manufactured 17,762 convertibles and 9,958 coupes. Base prices for models with the 300-horsepower 327 engine with three-speed manual transmission dropped $22 to $4,084. The coupe enjoyed a similar price reduction, by $26 to $4,295. Virtually every one of the 27,720 cars went off the St. Louis line with the $199.10 AM-FM radio. The next most popular option was the Positraction limited slip differential. The two poorest sellers were the newly introduced A85 shoulder harnesses, with only 37 delivered at $26.35, and the M22 racing four-speed gearbox. Just 15 of these left the assembly line at $237 each. Nassau Blue remained the most popular color with 6,100 cars produced, and Milano Maroon (3,799) edged out Rally Red (3,366) for second place.

Magazine journalists had heard rumors in 1965 that a new Corvette was coming for the 1967 model year. Once again, Chevrolet kept its enthusiasts on the edge of their seats. When economic and production considerations slipped introduction back a year and the final Sting Ray appeared as a 1967 model, few people were disappointed. Chevrolet

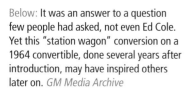

Below: It was an answer to a question few people had asked, not even Ed Cole. Yet this "station wagon" conversion on a 1964 convertible, done several years after introduction, may have inspired others later on. *GM Media Archive*

Above: The front hood of the 1965 model went flat, losing the depressions on the 1963 and 1964 models. The three diagonal louvers behind the front wheels were functional. *David Newhardt © 2012*

Left: Model year 1965 saw the last fuel-injected Corvette engines for 17 years. This L84 327-cubic-inch V-8, developing 375 horsepower, cost $538, making it an expensive engine option. *David Newhardt © 2012*

manufactured 22,940 of the coupes and convertibles. These cars finished the evolution from most-adorned to least with this final edition. Production of coupes (at 8,504) consistently trailed convertibles (at 14,436). Base prices, still with the 300-horsepower V-8 and three-speed manual, rose to $4,240.75 for the open cars and $4,388.75 for the coupes. Air conditioning had come down $9.20 from introduction in 1963, to $412.90, and up considerably in popularity, with 2,235 coupes and 1,553 convertibles manufactured with the climate system for a total of 3,788 of all Corvette production.

RACING ENGINES

Again, the big news was greater performance potential. Five optional engines ratcheted output up from the L79 350-horsepower 327 to the L71, a 427-cid V-8 that Chevrolet rated at 435 horsepower at 5,800 rpm. In between, buyers could select the 390-horsepower L36, an L68 version that developed 400 horsepower at 5,400 rpm, or a curious and costly racing-derived L88 that the division declared was capable of 430 horsepower.

The L88 was one of the most powerful engines Chevrolet ever sold to the public. To discourage unknowing buyers, product planners priced it at $947.90, more than double the figure for the 435-horsepower engine at $437.10. It was one of Zora Duntov's latest creations, and while Chevrolet had to make it available to regular customers to qualify it for racing, engineers hoped its price might deter anyone who didn't know exactly what he or she was getting. Rumors described output in excess of 480 horsepower, 530 horsepower, even 560, all at nearly 6,000 rpm. It was the single priciest option for 1967, though it was not the least produced. That distinction fell to the L89 aluminum cylinder head option for the 435-horsepower L71 (16 sets produced), and the 36-gallon racing fuel tank for the coupe (just two cars were manufactured with this option).

Above: This prototype 1965 coupe with clean body sides was photographed in March 1963 in Design Center storage. Mitchell's designers considered introducing Zora Duntov's Grand Sport front hood to production. *GM Media Archive*

Left: Chevrolet hoped to entice youngsters into becoming future Corvette owners. This scale-model 1965 coupe offered one child-power performance. *GM Media Archive*

For much of the time that Chevrolet produced the Sting Ray, designers and engineers worked on the next-generation Corvette. As Karl Ludvigsen wrote in his book *Corvette: America's Star-Spangled Sports Car*, for this new car, Mitchell "wanted a narrow, slim, 'selfish' center section and coupe body; a prominently tapered tail; an all-of-a-piece blending of the upper and lower portions of the body through the center; avoiding the look of a roof added to a body; and a sense of prominent wheels which, with their protective fenders, were distinctly separate from the main central body section, yet were grafted organically to it." This was, Ludvigsen concluded, "the launching pad for the missile known as Mako Shark II."

Before it was the Mako Shark II, designer Larry Shinoda had created the car as XP-830. It was one of many show cars and concepts that Bill Mitchell had his staff working on to tantalize division heads, excite auto show audiences, and to study and presage what the next models might look like.

Through this same period, engineers were doing the same kind of noodling. Zora Duntov had taken what he learned from the open-wheel CERV and developed a mid-engine all-wheel-drive sports racer he named CERV II.

Although officially forbidden to race, Chevrolet had a good reason for looking the other way while Duntov pursued his supposedly prohibited on-track research. Ford Motor Company had blatantly cast aside the AAMA racing ban early in 1962. By 1964, the world had seen Ford's GT40, a machine meant to beat Enzo Ferrari and every other sports racing carmaker. CERV II looked like Zora Duntov's ideal competitor to Ford's GT. Zora ceased being circumspect in testing the car, and this led many magazines and enthusiasts to wonder if the third-generation Corvette would follow this configuration.

Opposite: For model year 1966, Chevrolet offered two engine displacements for the Corvette. The 327 sat under the standard hood; the new 427, developing either 390 or 425 horsepower, required a power bulge to accommodate its air cleaner. *GM Media Archive*

Below: Bill Mitchell's XP-802 was one of the generative models toward his XP-830 Mako Shark. This February 1963 clay model carried forward the pointed nose and modified exhaust treatments introduced with the 1961 XP-755 Shark and later show cars. *GM Media Archive*

The V-8 Gets Bigger

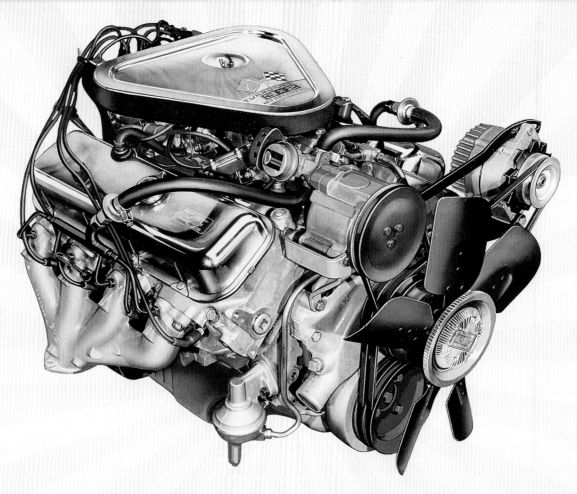

Above: The L71 for 1969 gave Corvette owners breathtaking performance. The 427-cubic-inch-displacement V-8 used a 4.25-inch bore and 3.76-inch stroke to develop 435 horsepower at 5,800 rpm. It was a $427.10 option. *GM Media Archive*

Opposite: By early April 1964, Chevrolet engineering had 427-cubic-inch engines in test mules. This installation was new enough that engineers had not yet connected spark plug and coil wires to the distributor. *GM Media Archive*

By 1963, when the Sting Ray appeared, Chevrolet's 265-cubic-inch V-8, which developed 195 horsepower when Chevrolet introduced it in 1955, had grown to 327 cubic inches (with a bore and stroke of 4.00x3.25 inches). The mechanically fuel-injected L84 version output reached 360 horsepower. The finest hour for the original small-block came in 1970 when, as a carbureted 350-cubic-inch LT1 with solid valve lifters, the engine produced 370 horsepower. But that also was the zenith of the muscle-car era, and 370 was nowhere near enough.

Every innovation that Harry Barr and Ed Cole devised with their V-8 in 1955 had made the new engine compact in dimensions. Thin-wall iron-casting techniques and a valvetrain and rocker-arm development that did away with the rocker-arm shaft saved many pounds over previous designs.

In performance circles, small and lightweight is good. But bigger is still better, so Chevrolet responded in 1965 with its first "big-block," the L78, displacing 396 cubic inches and developing 425 horsepower. The shaftless valve-rocker arm system carried over onto this new engine, enabling design

engineers to mount the valves in the heads in positions and at angles where they worked most efficiently for intake and exhaust flow. This left valve stems and rocker arms pointing in odd directions and earned the mysterious new engine the nickname "porcupine head." By physical size and interior displacement, this new engine was "the big-block." In its earliest appearances at racing events, the big-block was referred to around the pits as Chevrolet's "mystery motor." It didn't take long before the smaller engine became known as the "mouse motor" and the larger displacement engine became the "rat motor."

The 1965 L84 fuel-injected 327 developed 375 horsepower, sufficient to accelerate the Sting Ray from 0 to 60 miles per hour in 6.3 seconds and through the quarter-mile in 14.4 and 99 miles per hour. The new L78 396 with 425 horsepower got the car to 60 miles per hour in 5.7 seconds and on through the quarter in 14.1 at 103. Both cars used a 3.70:1 final drive.

The next year, the 427-cubic-inch L72 produced 425 horsepower but, thanks to the use of a 4.11:1 rear axle, 0-to-60 times dropped to 5.6

seconds and the quarter-mile passed in just 13.4 seconds at 105 miles per hour. Then came the next iterations: L88 and ZL1.

These engines used aluminum to lighten their weight. The L88, introduced in 1967, displaced 427 cubic inches and with its aluminum cylinder heads weighed only 60 pounds more than the 327-cubic-inch L79. However, the L88 developed 435 horsepower compared to the small-block's 350. The L88 added $947.90 to the purchase price. Because Chevrolet engineering designed it primarily as a race engine, publicity and price lists understated its power and set its cost high. Nearly comparable performance was available in a more tractable engine, the 427-cubic-inch L71, with claimed horsepower of 435. Option lists priced it at $437.10, and optional aluminum cylinder heads (RPO L89) for this engine were another 368.65. While just 16 buyers added the aluminum heads, a total of 3,754 customers went for the L71. The age of big-block performance had arrived.

Above: This was Chevrolet's most potent performance engine yet—the L72. It provided 425 horsepower and was a popular option, with 5,258 manufactured in 1966. *David Newhardt © 2012*

Right: As great as the L72 was, something more powerful was coming. This engineering prototype—with Zora Duntov at the wheel—housed a prototype 1967 L88 engine inside a 1966 body mounted on a 1965 chassis. *GM Media Archive*

Opposite: The bulging hood provided bragging rights. The 427-cubic-inch L72 engine added $312.85 to the window sticker of these $4,084 convertibles for 1966. *David Newhardt © 2012*

Below: GM engineering created this 1967 Goodwood Green coupe for Chevrolet Division chief Ed Cole. Underneath the hood, they installed the famous "Tri-Power" triple Holley carbureted 435-horsepower L71 engine. *David Newhardt © 2012*

Right: To discourage regular customers from ordering the competition-oriented L88 engine, Chevrolet developed this L71 and rated it at 435 horsepower, supposedly 5 horsepower more than the L88. For 1967, Chevrolet charged $437.10 for this option but wanted $947.90 for the L88. *GM Media Archive*

Frank Winchell's R&D team had created XP-819, a lightweight (2,650 pounds) coupe with its 327-cid engine mounted behind the rear differential. This configuration put 70 percent of the car's weight on the rear axle and provided handling characteristics that defeated the best test drivers.

A third idea used basic Corvair running gear and body variations. It received little engineering support because Winchell and Duntov each had their own candidates.

REALITY TRUMPS FANTASY

Reality pulled the next Corvette far away from either of their fantasies. Corvettes always had come together from parts manufactured for other Chevrolet models, and no pieces existed to assemble the dreams that Duntov or Winchell put forward. By the time this became clear, however, designers and engineers were closing on a deadline.

Mitchell named Larry Shinoda's concept XP-830 the Mako Shark II. He renamed Shinoda's earlier 1961 XP-755 Shark show car the Mako Shark I. This appeared to create a linear progression from Sting Ray to Shark. Chevrolet introduced the Mako Shark II at the New York International Auto Show in April 1965. For the Paris Auto Salon the following October, engineers on the design staff installed a Mark IV 427-cid V-8, and Mitchell showed both cars on General Motors' stand. The two Sharks, which together had cost Design around $3 million to create and engineer, toured Europe and North America, trolling for favorable public opinion and reviews.

By November 1965, Mitchell's production studio under Henry Haga's direction had created full-size clay models that turned the Mako Shark II into something St. Louis could mass-produce. But no sooner had production engineers gotten the models into a wind tunnel than the sleek shapes tried to take off. A ducktail lip at the rear helped hold that end down, but that brought the nose up; the new shark nose proved more flight-prone than the Sting Ray had been. Duntov affixed a strip of chin spoiler well below the small air intakes. It helped some.

Below: **Design chief Bill Mitchell created this 1967 Tri-Power L71 convertible for his wife, Marian. The body-length wide red stripe frames the full red interior.**
David Newhardt © 2012

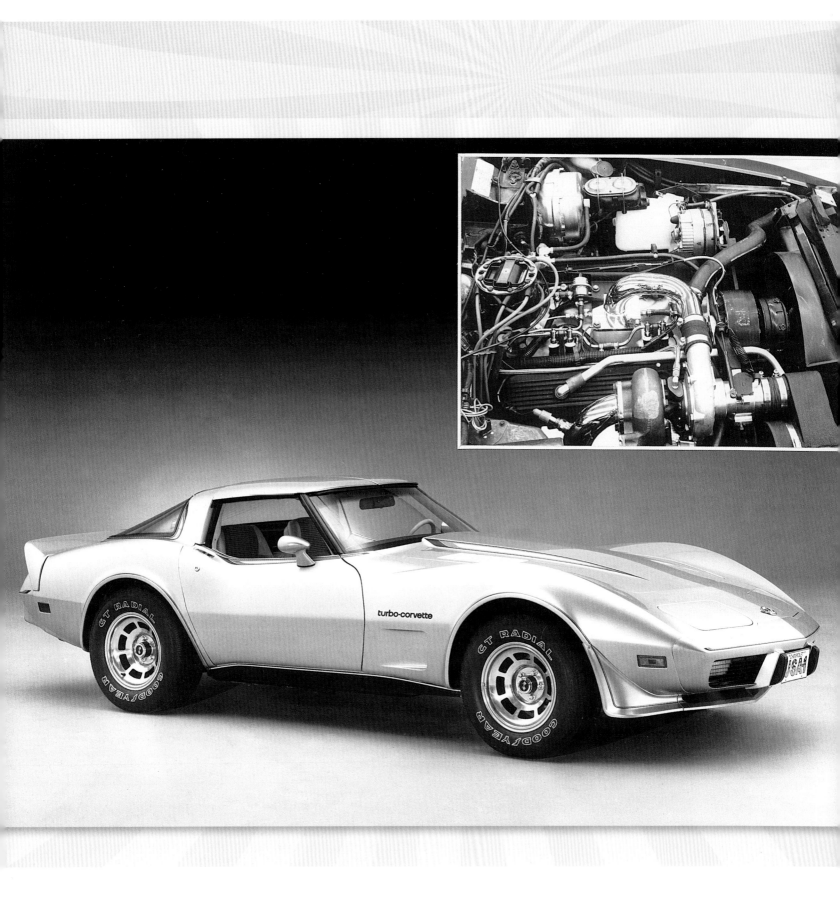

Legislating Performance

Responding to voter interest and pressure for federal action on vehicle safety, in 1966, Congress initiated public hearings, and, among other immediate effects, it passed laws making seat belt installation mandatory and created the U.S. Department of Transportation (DOT) in October 1966. This became effective in April 1967. It was an umbrella organization for a variety of agencies monitoring, directing, and regulating aviation, railroad, highways and maritime transportation and industry in the United States. The Highway Safety Act of 1970 established the National Highway Traffic Safety Administration (NHTSA), which was charged with setting and enforcing vehicle safety standards.

A succession of environmental concerns led to a variety of U.S. congressional acts, beginning with the Air Pollution Control Act of 1955. The Clean Air Act followed in 1963, and automobiles fell under special scrutiny starting in 1965 with the Motor Vehicle Air Pollution Control Act. This legislation established initial limits on exhaust emissions to go in effect for 1968 based on percentages of emissions measured in 1963. This, plus subsequent acts, amendments, and extensions, led to the formation of the U.S. Environmental Protection Agency (EPA) in December 1970 by President Richard Nixon.

For automotive engineers, these limits forced the development of apparatuses and technology that seemed at first to signal the end of high-performance vehicles. Air pumps, exhaust gas recirculators, catalytic converters, and other equipment challenged engineers to reduce over time the toxins that internal-combustion engines produced.

Beginning in 1972, the EPA required auto manufacturers to provide fuel economy information using driving "cycles" that simulated rush-hour Los Angeles at that time. Figures for city and highway mileage appeared on the "Monroney" price window sticker. (The sticker is named for Oklahoma Senator Mike Monroney, who sponsored the Automobile Information Disclosure Act of 1958 requiring that specific information appear uniformly on each automobile.)

As engineering staffs worked to meet ever-stricter safety and exhaust emissions standards, the 10-member Organization of Arabian Petroleum Exporting Countries (OAPEC) initiated an oil embargo against the United States in protest of American support of Israel during the Yom Kippur War. The embargo began in October 1973 and ended in March 1974. Crude oil prices quadrupled from $3 per barrel to $12, taking gasoline prices from an average of 38 cents per gallon to 55 cents in four months. Politicians called for national gas rationing. President Nixon requested service stations stop selling gasoline on weekends; most complied, but this led to long lines at stations on weekdays. Politicians and car buyers demanded more fuel-efficient vehicles.

For automotive engineers, this combination of challenges was irresistible if not by their nature as problem solvers, then by law and popular demand: clean the air; make cars safer; make them go farther on a gallon of much more expensive gasoline. Clean air and safety equipment added weight to cars, increasing the burden on engines.

Opposite: As Environmental Protection Agency (EPA) and California Air Resources Board (CARB) regulations reached their tightest standards, Chevrolet prepared a turbocharged 350 V-8 to provide the performance that the emissions devices hampered. The 1980 Turbo Corvette never went into production as a Chevrolet product. *GM Media Archive*

Left: While Chevrolet never put its Turbo into production, Zora Duntov, in his retirement, collaborated with an outside group to market the Duntov Convertible. It was not legal in California. *GM Media Archive*

MADLER 7·14·64   57766

Above: As design concepts advanced from stylized sketches on paper, designers created full-size renderings of their ideas using black tape. GM Styling had its own photographer, Neil Madler (and later a photo staff), who documented thousands of creations. Madler explained that negatives were identified and numbered in case an image got out to competitors or the public. *GM Media Archive*

Opposite, top: Neil Madler, the styling staff chief photographer, began using color to document design projects when GM's European studios complained about differentiating chrome from black-and-white images of the cars. This model went into the Design Center auditorium for management review on September 28, 1965. After a number of tweaks to its nose and rear end, it entered production as the 1968 Corvette. *GM Media Archive*

Opposite, bottom, left: The "Bat 'Vette" was perhaps one of the more unusual "custom" 1967 coupes to come out of GM Design. Chuck Jordan, sitting on the car, created it for the *Batman* television series starring Adam West. *GM Media Archive*

Opposite, bottom, right: The final test and design validation for the new 1968 coupe came in the wind tunnel. Ink trails indicated what the car's shape did in airflow. *GM Media Archive*

Haga's production studio staff had carried over Larry Shinoda's extreme front fender bulges. Again, Duntov found himself battling Mitchell. This time, he was the one with allies: Chevrolet had a new general manager, Pete Estes, who came from Pontiac. Like Ed Cole, Estes had been Pontiac's chief engineer before he managed the division, and he also worried about driver visibility. The models went back to the sculptors.

Meanwhile, engineers and designers worked around the clock on Chevrolet's new Camaro, GM's answer to Ford's Mustang and Pontiac's GTO. This was to be Chevrolet's foot soldier in the muscle-car wars looming on the near horizon. The Camaro had to come out in 1967. The Corvette didn't need to appear then. It slipped back to 1968.

This was not a bad thing. It provided Shinoda and Haga's designers time to experiment with an idea for a removable roof panel that had been on drawing boards since the 1950s. Engineering experiments showed that the new body and its barely revised frame were not stiff enough to support the car with so much upper bodywork but no roof. Haga's team adopted a concept from Gordon Buehrig, an outside industrial designer who had developed a central spine over the driver and passenger that incorporated removable panels. Buehrig called it the T-roof.

With the revised schedule, the cars, named simply "Corvette," began coming off the production line. Duntov, frustrated that the new car was all design on an unimproved chassis, authored an angry memo to Chevrolet chief engineer Alex Mair. Chevrolet management viewed this as one objection too many. GM disbanded Corvette engineering and assigned Duntov public relations duties, including attendance at the advanced press introductions. When those were completed, Duntov joined a pool of roving engineers, jacks-of-all-trades meant to solve problems of all kinds. Others less fortunate or prominent found they had passenger car responsibilities. This meant, however, that the Corvette's teething problems went ignored.

The reviews went to press just as series production began filling showrooms. *Car & Driver* magazine's editor Steve Smith was damning. He had scheduled their review for the December 1967 issue. Instead, he wrote, "We won't. The car was unfit for a road test. No amount of envious gawking by the spectators could make up for the disappointment we felt at the car's shocking lack of quality control. With less than 2,000 miles on it, the Corvette was falling apart."

Chevrolet division manager Pete Estes restored Corvette Engineering and named Duntov its chief engineer. The group worked magic. In the December 1968 issue, *Car & Driver* readers named the 1968 Corvette "Best All-Around Car in the World." The runner-up was Lamborghini's mid-engine Miura, a car Duntov had suggested as a target.

SUCCESSFUL SHARK

Not only was it the magazine's best car, it also was Corvette's bestseller. Chevrolet assembled a record 28,556 of the new models with convertibles, eclipsing coupes nearly two-to-one, 18,630 versus 9,936. Pete Estes added a third shift at St. Louis assembly to meet demand. Of course, he also had held the price close to previous editions, barely increasing the coupe from $4,388.75 to $4,663.00 and the convertible from $4,240.75 to $4,320.00. The base package still provided buyers the 300-horsepower 327-cubic-inch V-8 with three-speed manual. The most popular engine option was the L79 version of the 327 with 350 horsepower. Posi-traction went on all but about 1,500 of the cars; however, only 80 buyers checked the options boxes for the L88 engine, the 430-horsepower 427, along with the M22 close-ratio four-speed manual gearbox. Together, those two rarities added $1,211.20 to the price of the car. For those who chose to let Chevrolet shift gears for them, engineers introduced the durable M40 three-speed Turbo Hydra-Matic to replace the long-lived two-speed Powerglide. St. Louis manufactured 5,063 of the new cars with the new automatic, a $226.45 option. Most popular color: British Green, but only by a few dozen over Le Mans Blue (4,779 versus 4,722).

Product planners returned a name to the car for 1969, this time spelling "Stingray" as one word. Duntov's engineers made small but meaningful changes, such as reducing the steering wheel diameter from 16 to 15 inches to improve ingress/egress and seating comfort. Inside the engine, they redesigned the crankshaft, lengthening the piston stroke from 3.25 inches to 3.48. This increased overall displacement to establish yet another Chevrolet engine milestone: 350 cubic inches displacement. Base horsepower, set at 300 in the 327, remained the same with the new engine, but where Chevrolet offered five optional power plants for the 1968 Corvette, it provided seven engine options for the 1969 Stingray. One cost nearly as much as the coupe itself.

Right, top: **The 1968 Corvette carried over much from the 1967 chassis beneath its sleek body. Convertibles outsold coupes nearly two-to-one, and Chevrolet produced just 80 Corvettes in either body style with this L88 engine option.** David Newhardt © 2012

Right, bottom: **Bill Mitchell's designers were students of other car styling features. The 1968 coupe's "sugar scoop" rear window inset had appeared on earlier Porsche and Ferrari racers.** David Newhardt © 2012

Above: The L88 added $1,032.15 to the price of the base convertible's $4,438 bottom line. Chevrolet assembled 116 cars with L88 engines in 1969, the largest output of all three years. *Randy Leffingwell © 2012*

Above: Chevrolet engineering created cutaway 1969 convertibles for display at state fairs and major exhibitions around the United States. Corvette production reached 38,762 cars for 1969, counting both open cars and coupes. *GM Media Archive*

Top: Chevrolet continued manufacturing the 427-cubic-inch L88 engine through the 1969 model year. The last one installed in a convertible ended up in this car, sold new to a customer in San Diego, California. *Randy Leffingwell © 2012*

Bill Mitchell

Bill Mitchell was a GM man through and through. While he had drawn cars in his youth and painted illustrations through school and his first job, he never designed an automobile until he joined GM Art and Colour. Then, for the next 42 years, he learned from his mentor Harley Earl, became his hand-picked successor, and finally ran the department.

Mitchell was born in Cleveland, Ohio, on July 2, 1912. His father owned a Buick dealership, and by the time Bill was in his teens, Dad was bringing home Stutz and Mercer trade-ins. Bill had a natural talent for art, and he constantly drew cars, but his father worried that this was no way to make a living. He sent his son to Carnegie Institute of Technology. One of

the instructors noticed Mitchell's true talent and encouraged him to transfer to the Art Students League in New York City. By this time, Mitchell's parents were divorced, and his mother was living in New York. He visited her in summers and took classes and workshops.

He found a job as an office boy at Barron Collier Advertising, which at the time specialized in ads on street cars across America. Mitchell moved into the art department where Collier's sons, Barron Jr., Sam, and Miles, noticed the drawings he did in his spare time. He became a weekend regular at Collier's estate in Tarrytown, New York, and began competing in events sponsored by the American Racing Car Association (ARCA), which

Right: Bill Mitchell took his promotional obligations to new heights, coordinating his suit, shirt, hat, and socks to match the color schemes of show cars he exhibited. He posed alongside a 1961 Corvair concept car. *GM Media Archive*

Opposite, top left: Bill Mitchell followed in Harley Earl's footsteps not only as design chief but also in producing show cars for his own use. This XP-700 appeared in late 1958, even before Earl had retired. *GM Media Archive*

Opposite, bottom left: Based on a stock 1958 convertible, Mitchell created the XP-700 to test his concepts for future Corvette styling. The rear end was enough like the production 1961–1962 version that in 1959, before a long show series, designers had to modify it away from the coming car's appearance. *GM Media Archive*

Opposite, far right: During Bill Mitchell's career, he worked as a stylist in the Cadillac Division. One of his concept sketches early in the 1950s proposed a two-seat Cadillac sports car. *GM Media Archive*

the Colliers had co-founded. Mitchell became the official illustrator for ARCA, and his drawings, watercolors, and sketches hung in the clubhouse and appeared in their newsletter. One weekend, a Detroit insurance agent friend of both Barron Collier and Harley Earl asked Mitchell if he ever had thought of designing cars. He offered to get Mitchell's portfolio to Earl, who liked what he saw. Mitchell started at GM on December 15, 1935.

Earl divided design assignments into studios for individual makes the following summer. Surprised by Mitchell's work, Earl gave the 24-year-old the responsibility of creating an all-new entry-level model for Cadillac, the 60 Special for 1938. "That was in the summer. There was no air conditioning," Mitchell told Dave Crippen in an interview in 1984. "I remember the cars were all modeled in a row in a room where, if the temperature dropped, the clay would crack and the front end would fall off."

The war interrupted Mitchell's design career; he served in the Navy from 1942 till mid-1945 but then returned to GM Styling. Mitchell stayed, learning not only design but office politics, the skill of selling a concept car to a division manager, and the management technique of direct-dialing Chairman Alfred Sloan or President Harlow Curtice. In 1954, Harley Earl infuriated the board—but not Sloan or Curtice—by appointing his own successor. As Earl prepared for retirement in December 1958, Mitchell encouraged the design staff to "go all out on fins and chrome," believing it would be the last gasp of this design excess. When Virgil Exner's entire Chrysler lineup proved even wilder for 1959, Mitchell knew he had guessed correctly and, under his direction, he shifted styles toward what he characterized as a blend of Ferrari and Rolls-Royce, introducing sharper edges—"wind splitters," he called them. As he explained to Crippen, "It

took me years to learn how to use sweeps. Now you can design a car with a T square and a triangle."

Mitchell was an enthusiast. He raced cars on tracks—sometimes against direct corporate orders—and around the roads surrounding GM and its test tracks. He rode motorcycles hard and fast and enjoyed parties and socializing the same way. He was coarse and crude in a time when that style, like the appearance of automobiles, was changing. In countless conversations and interviews in the years after Earl retired, he praised his mentor for the systems and styles Earl had created.

When Mitchell took over GM Styling, he had a staff of 90. Within a few years, he changed the name to Design and assembled an empire with nearly 1,500 modelers, designers, engineers, craftsmen, technicians, and managers. He played board officers against division managers, always to his advantage. There were stories that Harley Earl dressed to match his show cars, and there are photos that prove Mitchell did. The images show Mitchell dressed in, for example, a cherry-red three-piece suit, hat, and shoes, to complement the interior of a prototype, or a jacket, shirt, tie, and hat in the same yellow as a show-car exterior. While he abandoned some Earl practices, he magnified others. Management, afraid of a third generation of manipulative and outspoken design leaders, denied him the chance to groom and select his successor. Despite phenomenal successes with his 1963 Sting Ray and Buick Riviera, as well as the 1970 Camaro, the directors had endured enough. When Mitchell retired in 1977, after 19 years as vice president of design, bringing to a close 50 years of powerful personalities in charge of the appearance of GM's cars, the pendulum swung far the opposite direction. Bill Mitchell died on September 12, 1988.

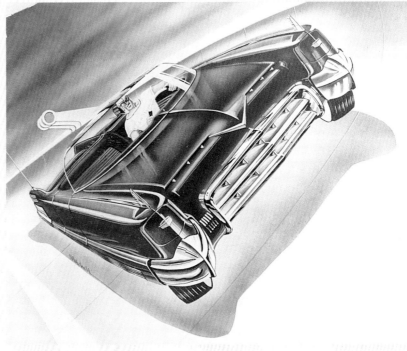

Everything Chevrolet had done right in 1968 reflected in the 1969 production numbers (albeit counted within an extended model year). Coupes, up from a respectable 9,936 in 1968, shot up to a staggering 22,129. For the first time coupes exceeded convertible production, which slipped from 18,630 in 1968 to 16,633 for 1969. The total: 38,762. This performance came despite a two-month autoworker's strike that delayed delivery and created a backlog of orders for 1969 models. If anything validated Mitchell's impact on sales (and Shinoda's design flair), it was those numbers.

Engineering helped. Not only did the optional L46 return (now 350 cubic inches developing 350 horsepower—12,846 produced) as well as the L36 (427/390 with 10,531 of them out the St. Louis factory door), but also the 400-horsepower L68 (2,072 manufactured), the L71 (427/435 with optional aluminum cylinder heads—2,077 in all, 390 of which had the lighter weight heads), and the already legendary L88 (427/430 racing engine, now at $1,032.15, which did not deter 116 customers from buying it) returned to the lineup. Duntov's engine designers weren't finished, however. They created an all-aluminum-block 427-cubic-inch ZL1. It created no more horsepower than the L88, but it weighed 100 pounds less. For racers, reducing weight means improved performance, and that translates to winning races. Without much effort, the engine took the Stingray through the quarter-mile in 12.1 seconds at 116 miles per hour.

SMALL BLOCK, BIG POWER

For Duntov, even the aluminum ZL1 set too much weight on the front end. Late in the 1969 model year, Chevrolet announced the engine Zora wanted, the 350-cubic-inch LT1. Frederick Donner had retired. The board relocated Ed Cole to one of the top-floor corner offices suitable for his new title as president of General Motors. He had earned the trust of chairman James Roche, who was not an engineer but understood sales numbers. Cole's ideas since the 1950s had brought the corporation ever-increasing profits. With Cole and Roche, performance no longer was banned. Thus, even an engine such as the LT1 with lighter weight, but without the outrageous potential of the ZL1, found a place on the option list.

Chevrolet achieved its impressive 1969 production numbers cleverly. Pete Estes moved on to a corporate vice-presidency. He followed Ed Cole's proven footsteps, ascending to GM president on November 1, 1967, soon after the L88 appeared. In Estes' trail, John Z. DeLorean had followed, promoted to Chevrolet division after his success turning the Tempest, an uninspiring midsize coupe, into America's most sought-after muscle car, the GTO. His contribution to 1969 Chevrolet sales was resetting the calendar to introduce 1970 models in February of that year. But, compared with previous years, even that short season (eight months) netted impressive numbers: 10,668 coupes and 6,648 convertibles assembled for 1970.

Above: The G81 "optional rear axle ratio," known in years past as "Posi-Traction Rear Axle, all Ratios," was a most useful option to Michigan skiers. The "Sun N Snow" ski shop in Cadillac, Michigan, has served winter sports enthusiasts since the 1960s. *GM Media Archive*

Above: There were few changes to the appearance of the 1971 Corvette from the 1970 models. This brochure mockup illustrates the optional "Custom Interior Trim" and air conditioning. *GM Media Archive*

Top: Model year 1970 production started in early January that year, leading to low sales and manufacturing totals that did not reflect the popularity of the car. Design made subtle changes to the body, including widening wheel flares to better trap road debris. *GM Media Archive*

Designations inside Chevrolet sparked rumors and joined some of the great mysteries auto enthusiasts debated decades later: that someone somewhere designated the LT1-equipped 1970 Stingray ZR1 will forever lead loyalists to believe it stands for Zora's Racer version 1.0. (And because there was a bigger-bore sibling in 1971 by which time Duntov had made his peace with heavy big-block front engines—dubbed ZR2—only reinforces the strength of the lore: Zora Racer version 2.0.) For 1970, St. Louis delivered 1,287 of the LT1 engines at $447.60. Only 25 of the ZR1 packages went out the door; these included the LT1, close-ratio four-speed manual M22 gearbox, and an assortment of suspension and brakes options, at $968.95. (It was capable of 14.2-second quarter miles at 102 miles per hour, despite the assessment that its configuration was more oriented toward road racing than drag strip runs.) Meanwhile, the base coupe and convertibles came with the 300-horsepower 350-cubic-inch engine and a manual four-speed for the first time.

Federal government exhaust emissions laws that first began to be implemented in 1966 had a noticeable effect on performance by 1971. Anticipating the horsepower-strangling effects the engineers knew these new devices were going to have on engine output, they increased displacement of the 427 to 454 cubic inches for the 1970 model year, with bore and stroke of 4.25 by 4.0 inches. They intended to match the performance of the 1968 and 1969 models. Engine compression fell to accommodate lower-octane unleaded fuels. Across the Chevrolet lineup, performance options contracted. The 454 LS6 (at a very expensive $1,221.00) developed 425 horsepower; the $295 LS5 454 produced 365. The LT1 remained in the lineup but with only 330 horsepower. Chevrolet manufactured just eight ZR1 LT1 packages and 12 ZR2 LS6 models. Each of these left St. Louis assembly without a heater or radio to emphasize their racing purpose.

Production for a full 12-month 1971 model year crept back up to a total of 21,801 cars comprising 14,680 coupes and 7,121 convertibles. The AM-FM radio, followed by power steering, led the popular options. War Bonnet Yellow was the most frequently ordered exterior color, with Brands Hatch Green close behind.

By 1972, the base 350-cubic-inch V-8 delivered 200 horsepower, while the optional LS5 offered only 270 (and this was not available to California buyers). The LT1 produced 255. The most popular options were power steering and AM-FM radio. Ontario Orange took the color lead, followed by Elkhart Green. One option since 1968, the UA6 alarm system, became standard equipment in 1972. Despite diminished performance potential, Corvette production numbers rose again for 1972 to a new record of 27,004 cars, split between 20,496 coupes and 6,508 convertibles.

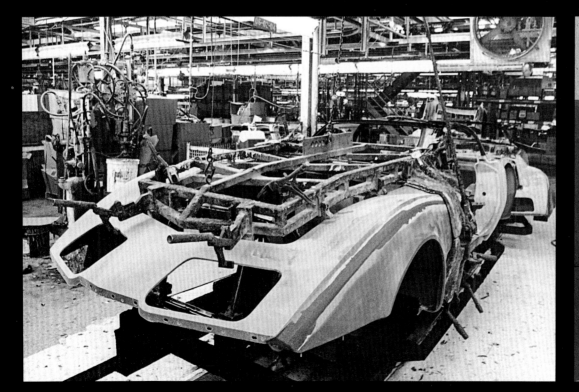

Astros, More XPs, and Ocean Predators

Larry Shinoda collaborated on a several projects with Frank Winchell's research and development group during 1966 and 1967. One became a running rear-engine prototype, the XP-819, sometimes called Astro I. Its lines were a subtle variation on the front-engine third-generation cars. Mounting its V-8 engine behind the rear wheels led to a car that had what could be charitably described as challenged handling.

A short time later, Shinoda and Winchell updated the concept with the XP-880, the 1968 Astro II, in which Winchell mounted the engine behind the driver but ahead of the rear wheels in true midengine fashion. Handling improved, but the car still was ahead of contemporary tire and wheel technology. GM encouraged Winchell to continue on this project, fearing Ford Motor Company had planned to introduce road-going versions of its GT40.

The other extreme from Astro II was 1968's alternate show car, the front-engined Astro-Vette. Additional body cladding extended the front and rear of the car and spats entirely hid the rear wheels. It was strictly a "dream" car.

The Mako Shark II, project XP-830, which introduced customers and enthusiasts to the looks of third-generation Corvettes for 1968, reappeared as the 1969 Manta Ray. Styling changes were evolutionary, not revolutionary. Revolution came with the 1970 XP-882, a very up-to-date examination of the midengine design theme, this one with a V-8 mounted transversely behind the driver and passenger. The body revisited the boat-tail tapered-end of the passenger compartment that Chevrolet introduced with the 1963 Stingray coupe and the 1965 Mako Shark II. It first appeared to the public at the New York Auto Show in April 1970.

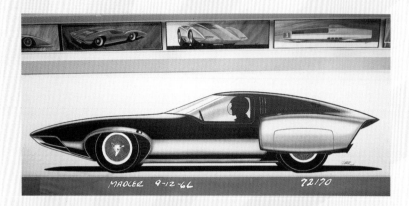

Right, top: Phil Clark started his career with GM design, then moved to Ford in 1962 and was best known for creating the Mustang running horse logo. He apparently freelanced this concept back to GM through his longtime friend Larry Shinoda. *GM Media Archive*

Right, middle: This XP 882 concept was the first, in 1969–1970, of three mid engine design-and-engineering prototypes to explore the concept of a mid engine Corvette. It used a transverse-mounted 400-cubic-inch V-8 with an automatic transmission. *GM Media Archive*

Right, bottom: General Motors invested heavily in testing and developing the Wankel rotary engine for use across the full line of its products. Clare MacKichan, who had created the shape of the 1953, had overall charge of the GM design staff that created the prototype in 1971 and 1972. *GM Media Archive*

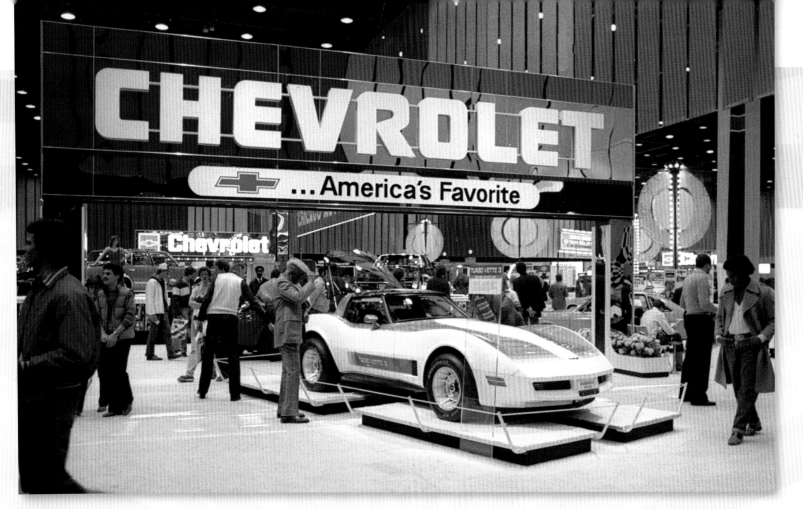

Next on the scene was the XP-895 for 1972. This show car filled a commission to GM Design from Reynolds Aluminum. Reynolds hoped to convince GM to use aluminum for bodies. This unibody integral frame-and-body construction weighed 500 pounds less than comparably equipped Corvettes at the time. The design introduced forms that appeared on later Camaro and Firebird models. It also used a transverse 400-cubic-inch V-8.

A year later, as if to settle any dispute over body material, GM Design showed the XP-898. This show car, with hints of shapes to come in the next generation, was fabricated using a fiberglass "sandwich" that incorporated a foam filler. The material offered design engineers the capability of varied thickness to increase strength in impact areas and reduce weight on less critical surfaces. GM did not put the process into production.

GM engineering became captivated by Wankel rotary engines, and the 1972 compact XP-987GT was first to explore that territory with its two-rotor powerplant mounted amidships. Engineers used a Porsche 914 platform, which enabled them to produce the show car on a short enough deadline to propose it to GM's board, according to Karl Ludvigsen. The board reviewed it in late summer 1972 but passed on the idea. It remained under cover for a while. Its first public appearance came at Germany's influential Frankfurt Motor Show in September 1973. It was named "Corvette 2-Rotor."

Zora Duntov recycled the 1970 XP-882 show car, reworked its platform, and with Gib Hufstadter's help, installed two twin-rotor Wankels in a car. Inspired by what Duntov was trying, Design stepped up and Jerry Palmer developed a sleek new body with bi-folding gullwing-type doors and severely angular front and rear-end treatments. It debuted at the Paris Auto Salon in October 1973 as the Aerovette and was displayed facing the 2-Rotor on GM's stand. Palmer's Aerovette led him to many of the design elements he incorporated in the fourth-generation cars introduced in 1984, over which he supervised design.

SAFETY BUMPERS

For 1973, Design and Engineering collaborated on a new front bumper that met federal 5-mile-per-hour crash standards. Chevrolet chose a composite urethane material stretched over a honeycomb framework. This added 3 inches to the length of the car, and assemblers painted the new collision-absorption system to match the car body. New side-impact protection beams ran through both car doors. The base 350-cubic-inch engine delivered 190 horsepower in response to ever more effective emissions controls and fuel economy demands. The LT1 disappeared, replaced by a 250-horsepower 350-cubic-inch L84. The 454 LS4 variation produced 275 horsepower. None of this discouraged buyers. Chevrolet set another production record, rolling 30,464 of the coupes and convertibles (25,521 and 4,943, respectively) out the St. Louis factory doors. Power steering (27,872) and power brakes (24,168) topped the options list. Steel-belted GR70-15 radial tires first appeared for 1973, a $32 option that 19,903 buyers selected.

Rear body-colored urethane bumpers arrived on 1974 models. Production rose again, to 32,028 coupes and 5,474 convertibles, totaling 37,502 cars. The base engine output increased slightly to 195 horsepower, the L82 held its 250 horsepower, but the LS4 slipped once more to 270. It was the last year Chevrolet offered large displacement V-8s in the Corvette for many decades. Power steering, power brakes, and air conditioning led the options favorites. As the Corvette sacrificed performance options, it became more a personal luxury car, a true grand tourer in the American sense. However, even touring in the American sense slowed considerably in 1974 with the introduction of the mandatory 55-mile-per-hour speed limit in response to gasoline shortages and price hikes that began in 1973.

Model year 1975 marked three significant changes at Corvette. Having reached mandatory retirement age of 65, Zora Duntov stepped down as chief engineer, to be replaced by Dave McLellan. Duntov had seen the car from convertible prototype to capable racer. The convertible body style also retired at the end of 1975. Under steady assault from consumer

Opposite, top: **Prior to the 1973 model year, Corvette owners could remove the rear window for better ventilation. Zora Duntov maintained it caused buffeting, so Chevrolet fixed it solidly.** *GM Media Archive*

Opposite, bottom: **This catalog illustration emphasized the body-color "soft" rear bumpers with the insets for the license plate and taillights. This was a one-year-only two-piece rear bumper.** *GM Media Archive*

Left, top: **The long collaboration between Baldwin Motors, a Chevrolet dealer on New York's Long Island, and "tuner" Joel Rosen of Motion Performance rarely yielded subtlety. His 1974 "Motion Spyder" offered customers a return to 1970 performance.** *David Newhardt © 2012*

Left, bottom: **Testing at Milford for cars like this 1975 coupe was a year-round and an around-the-clock effort. As emissions standards became the law of the land, carmakers not only had to provide EPA fuel use estimates but also perform 100,000-mile long-term tests.** *GM Media Archive*

safety activists who belabored rollover injury risks, Chevrolet watched convertible sales slip from a high of two-to-one against coupes to one of every eight Corvettes produced in 1975. The division manufactured only 4,629 convertibles compared with 33,836 coupes (with the T-roof) for a total of 38,465 units.

The third change occurred under the front hood. While the base engine output dropped again to 165 horsepower, the only displacement available for 1975 was Chevrolet's 350-cubic-inch V-8. The one performance option, the L82, offered 205 horsepower for $336. Just 2,372 buyers were interested. Power steering and brakes, air conditioning, and tilting/telescoping steering wheels led the options lists. The Corvette was ever more comfortable. Only 144 cars left St. Louis assembly with the "off-road suspension and brake package" for racers. Classic White outsold silver nearly two-to-one; together, they were the two most popular exterior color choices, according to historian Mike Antonick.

It seemed no one missed the convertible in 1976. Corvette manufactured 46,588 T-roof coupes at a $7,604.85 base price with the 180-horsepower 350-cubic-inch V-8 and four-speed manual transmission. Corvette's most expensive option was air conditioning at $523, yet seven times as many buyers selected that over the optional $481 L82 V-8 with 210 horsepower. Again, white and silver led color choices.

Production inched up again through 1977, to 49,213 coupes, all with standard leather seats or optional cloth-insert leather. Base price reached $8,647.65. The most popular option was the tilt/telescoping steering column ($165) and the least was a new trailer-towing package (just 289 takers at $83). Cruise control appeared for the first time on option lists, and 29,161 buyers ordered it (available with the Turbo Hydra-Matic only). A new center console housed heat and air-conditioning controls and provided room for Delco's new AM-FM radio with eight-track tape player. For a third year, Classic White won the popularity contest, but black edged out Corvette Light Blue for second choice.

Chevrolet celebrated Corvette's 25th birthday in 1978 with a redesigned coupe with a fastback glass rear window. The division manufactured 40,274 of the cars. Last-minute hardware cost analyses eliminated a planned lifting-hatchback feature. Nonetheless, the new design gave owners substantially greater luggage capacity as well as a cargo cover to hide it from view. A commemorative Silver Anniversary Edition provided buyers two-tone silver treatment. At $399 for the option, 15,283 ordered this package.

PACE CAR

Early in the model year, Chevrolet announced that Indianapolis Motor Speedway had selected the Corvette as pace car for the 500-mile race, the car's first such designation. Many buyers presumed the Silver Anniversary paint scheme had been chosen as well, but Indianapolis officials opted for a black-over-silver combination. Besieged with orders, Chevrolet promised to produce one for each of its 6,502 dealers. Many of them substantially marked up the $13,653.23 price, some to nearly double the figure. As a result, some dealers had unsold pace-car replicas on their lots months later.

Model year 1979 set a benchmark for Corvette production, reaching 53,807 cars assembled. Chief engineer Dave McLellan had navigated through the tangles of emission and safety regulations in his first few years as boss. Both base and optional 350-cubic-inch V-8s went up slightly in power because of new less-restrictive mufflers; the base L48 increased further by adopting the optional L82's improved air-intake. Output for the base engine rose from 185 to 195 horsepower while the L82 went up to 225. Base price topped $10,000 for the first time, at $10,220.23. The single most popular option was the $45 sport mirrors package. The adjustable steering column was next, followed by air conditioning. Perhaps as an indication of a healthy economy or else inspired by the appearance of the pace car in 1978, black was the most popular color for 1979. St. Louis turned out 10,465 of those, followed by 8,629 Classic White and 7,331 silver cars.

Below: The new 1978 model year fastback body gave owners considerably more storage space, although economic factors killed a proposed opening-hatchback rear glass. Wind tunnel testers liked the way the tufts fluttered on these prototypes. *GM Media Archive*

V-8 Engines for the Next Generation

While most of these all-aluminum ZL1 engines ended up in Camaros destined for drag racing, Zora Duntov managed to secure a few for Corvettes. Two ended up in 1969 production models (as a $4,718.35 option) and a handful did service in engineering prototypes at Milford.
GM Media Archive

If engine weight was the problem, aluminum was the solution, and the ZL1, introduced in 1969, provided the ultimate answer. This all-aluminum block weighed 100 pounds less than the L88, which was 85 pounds less than the cast-iron 327. Yet it produced the same horsepower as the L88. (Chevrolet engineering rated these engines conservatively so as not to set off alarm bells with insurance agents and law enforcement agencies.) The ZL1 set buyers back $4,718.35. While most ZL1 engines went into Camaros for drag racing, two buyers ordered the aluminum blocks for their Corvettes. Another group of ZL1-equipped cars remained with engineering.

As Environmental Protection Agency (EPA) regulations began to choke engine output, Chevrolet bored out the 427 to 454 cubic inches. For 1970, Chevrolet offered a 390-horsepower LS5 with 10.25:1 compression for the Corvette. Its more powerful cousin, the LS7, produced 465 horsepower (at 12.25:1 compression), but Chevrolet parceled these out only to known racers. Not only was the EPA gaining strength, but automobile safety organizations had found their voice as well.

In an effort to appear environmentally conscious, GM reduced compression of all its engines for 1971 so the powerplants would operate on lower octane unleaded fuels. Compression plummeted to 8.5 and 9.0:1. This reduced the output of the LT1 to a still respectable 330 horsepower

and of the 454 LS6 to 425. It was the start of a long slide that saw the LS4 big-block 454-cubic-inch engine erode to 270 horsepower in 1974. At that point, the 350-cubic-inch displacement base engine only produced 195 horsepower. The big-block engines disappeared at the end of 1974.

From that point on, the outlook for performance-oriented drivers dimmed. Environmental requirements and safety needs further diminished engine horsepower output and added weight to the cars. It took a long, measured, careful march from the lowest point—the 165-horsepower base 350 V-8 in 1975 to recapture driving excitement. Bragging rights were more than a decade away. From 1975 through 1980, Chevrolet kept an optional 350-cubic-inch engine, the L82, on its Corvette order forms. But engineers gained a clearer understanding of what new laws meant and how engines might work. The L82 output inched up from 205 in 1975 to 230 in 1980.

Then even that disappeared. In 1980, California held the strictest limits in the United States. Those requirements forced Chevrolet engineers to develop a 305-cubic-inch V-8 that produced just 180 horsepower, 15 less than Corvette's first V-8 in 1955. This situation lasted one year only, for California alone. Regulations standardized for all 50 states starting in 1981. But horsepower stayed down.

By 1980, with few people honoring the national 55-mile-per-hour speed limit, automakers fit speedometers that read a maximum 85 miles per hour. These began to appear in late-1979 model-year cars. A slight facelift provided integral spoilers to the urethane nose and tail of the car. These functioned to reduce the coefficient of drag (Cd) from 0.503 to 0.443 over a similarly equipped 1979 model. In all, Chevrolet manufactured 40,614 of the cars with a base price of $13,140.24. The two most popular options were rear-seat speakers (36,650 equipped) and the rear-window defogger (36,589 were installed). Least popular was the decision to order the car without a radio at all (just 201 cars went out with no sound system), and next was the trailer package (at only 796 mounted). White edged out black for color supremacy at 7,780 versus 7,250.

It was a tough year to be a car buyer in California. New state regulations meant that automobiles manufactured for the other 49 states still emitted too much. As a result, McLellan's engineers fitted California-bound Corvettes with the Chevrolet passenger car 305-cubic-inch V-8 that delivered 180 horsepower. This proved unmotivating to California buyers, who only consumed 3,221 of the cars in 1980. But California's challenge lasted a single year, and for 1981, all 50 states had a single 350-cubic-inch 190-horsepower V-8 for the cars. That deterred few buyers, who kept production up at 40,606 units, despite a base price that rose to $16,258.52. St. Louis and the new plant at Bowling Green, Kentucky, combined produced 36,893 cars. Most popular option: the rear window defogger, a $119 feature. Next, 36,485 sets of aluminum wheels were produced, at $428 for four.

Production switchover from Missouri to Kentucky was a gradual and overlapping process. The first car came out of Bowling Green on June 1, 1981; the last car drove off the St. Louis line two months later on August 1. One principal

Opposite, top: When Chevrolet first discussed providing the Corvette to Indianapolis Motor Speedway (IMS) management as the 1978 Indy 500 pace car, everyone agreed the 25th Anniversary model would serve well. IMS reconsidered and changed it to this black-over-silver scheme. *Randy Leffingwell © 2012*

Opposite, bottom: New high-back seats appeared in 1979 models, along with front and rear spoilers carried over from 1978 Indianapolis 500 pace car replicas. *GM Media Archive*

Left, top: Model year 1979 was Corvette's best ever: St. Louis manufactured an all-time record of 53,807 coupes. It also was the first year the base coupe cost more than $10,000, at $10,220,23. *GM Media Archive*

Left, bottom: The high-backed seat introduced in 1979 carried through 1980 and provided better lateral support. Engineers moved the fold-point higher up the seat back to improve access to rear storage. *GM Media Archive*

reason for the move was to improve Corvette paint quality. Two-tone paint schemes were possible, topped with clear-coat enamel from Bowling Green's state-of-the-art paint shop.

The last of the third-generation Corvettes emerged from Bowling Green, ending a 14-year run that set several milestones in place. With the C3, Corvette crossed 250,000-, 500,000-, and 750,000-unit production thresholds. Prices multiplied from $4,663 for the base coupe in 1968 to $18,290.07 in 1982, and higher, considering the Corvette Collector Edition, painted in silver-beige with matching interior and functioning glass hatchback. That went for $22,537.69, nearly five times the base price at the beginning of the run. In all, Chevrolet produced 542,861 of the C3 models, counting the 18,648 base coupes and 6,579 commemoratives in 1982. The engine for both models was the 200-horsepower 350-cubic-inch V-8 with "Cross-Fire" injection, coupled to the new four-speed-plus-overdrive automatic transmission. Chevrolet offered neither optional engines nor manual transmissions for 1982.

Enthusiast magazines had leaked stories and spy photos for more than a year that showed in increasing detail what the next-generation Corvette looked like. As an all-new car, the complicated processes to design, engineer, and produce it and to make it comply with a litany of new emissions and safety standards that went into effect for 1984 models led Chevrolet general manager Bob Stempel, a former Chevrolet chief engineer, to skip the 30th anniversary 1983 model year all together. It was a hard decision, one that everyone noticed, commented on, and lamented.

Until the next-generation Corvette arrived. Then everyone noticed, commented, and celebrated.

Right: Manufacture began at the new Bowling Green, Kentucky, plant on June 1, 1981, and ceased at the St. Louis, Missouri, factory on July 31, two months later. The overlap allowed seamless assembly and gave workers in Kentucky time to get up to speed. *Randy Leffingwell © 2012*

Opposite, top, left: Though not quite so modest a paint shop as these facilities, one key motive for transferring Corvette assembly from St. Louis over to Bowling Green during 1981 production was to improve paint quality. *Randy Leffingwell © 2012*

Opposite, top, right: The 1982 Corvette developed 200 horsepower, whether it was on Chevrolet Engineering's chassis dynamometer or on the road. A new "cross-fire-injection" system metered fuel flow and was responsible for the 10-horsepower gain over 1981 models. *GM Media Archive*

Opposite, bottom: For 1982, the final year of a body structure first introduced in 1968 and a chassis brought out in 1963, Chevrolet developed the Collector Edition. The functional rear hatchback was unique to this series. *GM Media Archive*

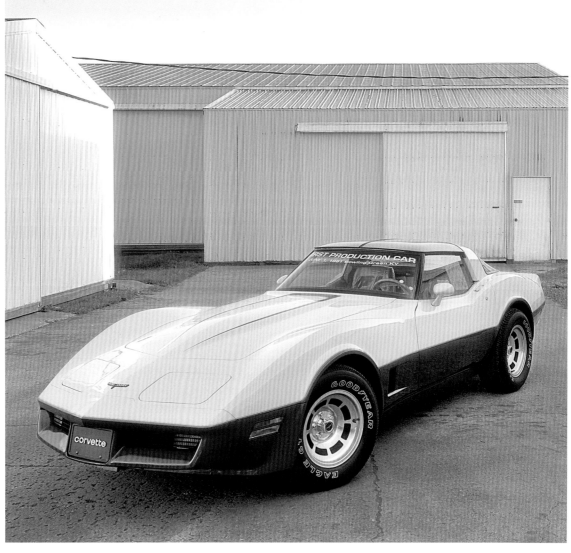

3 RECLAIMING THE THRONE

THE FOURTH, FIFTH, AND SIXTH GENERATIONS

"All of our engineering energy had been focused on surviving the onslaught of regulations,"

Enthusiasts and journalists hounded Chevrolet, wanting to know why the third-generation Corvette went on so long. C1 lasted nine years. C2 remained in production for five. C3, much longer. Dave McLellan, chief engineer for Corvette from the day Zora Duntov retired, explained that it was not from lack of desire or initiative. "All of our engineering energy had been focused on surviving the onslaught of regulations," he wrote in his insightful history, *Corvette from the Inside*. "Emission and safety regulations were coming at us from several states. Until the onslaught subsided, and we had developed adequate technical responses to them, we were in no position to start a new car."

The Corvette had lost performance options. It had gained weight. With mandatory safety and emissions fixtures, it crossed the scales at 3,600 pounds. Emissions standards in 1975 had strangled engine output to no more than 205 horsepower. This, the customers reminded anyone at Chevrolet who would listen, was a Corvette, not a Thunderbird.

Zora Duntov waged a screaming battle against a howling windstorm. As sales built in the early 1970s, Zora, ever the Don Quixote tilting against windmills, continued to advocate midengine configurations. McLellan understood what was at stake, however. A midengine Corvette was the answer to a question only Duntov and a few designers were asking.

So was a V-6. The front office, worried about EPA and DOT mandates, fretted about gasoline prices and sweated fallout from environmental and safety groups. It told Bill Mitchell's successor Irv Rybicki to have his Chevy studio re-size, restyle, and reinvent the popular Aerovette show car to accommodate a smaller turbocharged V-6. Rybicki provided options. It proved to be another idea that few people other than board members cared to see. Handsome design studies appeared. No one cared.

Above left: This was an unsigned, undated flight of fancy. First, Bill Mitchell and then Irv Rybicki gave their designers free rein to stretch their imagination for the fourth-generation Corvette. *GM Media Archive*

Right, top: A collection of federal environmental and safety regulations went into effect for 1984. Although Chevrolet assembled several dozen 1983 models for testing and media introductions, General Manager Bob Stempel decided to hold the model year introduction to January 1984. *GM Media Archive*

Right, bottom: For media introductions that took place in December 1992, Chevrolet engineering, design, and public relations developed models, drawings, and placards to explain everything new about the "1983 Corvette." Journalists tested the car around Riverside International Raceway outside Los Angeles. *GM Media Archive*

McLellan was a pragmatic realist where Duntov had been a belligerent idealist. McLellan believed Corvette had not gone far enough in answering the questions customers were asking. Potential existed to take the front-engine-rear-drive-long-nose-short-tail V-8 much farther than anyone had done yet.

Modern technology helped. It gave the Corvette a stiff unibody that combined the birdcage-and-frame assemblies of the 1960s and 1970s with high-strength steel and a new GRP formula that allowed engineers to eliminate transverse ladder-frame cross tubes. They could lower the seat even further and drop the roofline. The unibody dissipated engine torque over a much longer "frame," allowing engineers to use softer engine mounts. These isolated noise, vibration, harshness, the dreaded NVH acronym that every board member knew enough to criticize but few understood.

NEW CHASSIS

McLellan's staff devised a central spine that housed the driveshaft, exhaust, fuel lines, and the wiring harness for electrical needs at the rear of the car. The spine also provided mounting points for the five-link SLA short- and long-arm independent rear suspension.

With no time to do anything else, McLellan carried over the 1982 Cross-Fire injection small-block. He coupled this, at first, with the four-speed automatic Turbo Hydra-Matic. Later in the 1984 model year, the Doug Nash–derived 4+3 automatic came on line. This system provided "overdrive" in second, third, and fourth gears. The 4+3 transmission, programmed to maximize performance and fuel economy, often got its purposes confused. While it delivered the 25-mile-per-gallon EPA fuel economy ratings GM needed to avoid gas guzzler taxes on the Corvette, few enthusiasts embraced this innovative gearbox. McLellan made sure buyers had a four-speed manual gearbox available at no extra cost.

Designer Jerry Palmer understood equally clearly what the car meant to its longtime customers and enthusiasts. Although he created midengine masterpieces for Duntov, the XP-895 Reynolds Aluminum design study and the Aerovette among them, he drew from his Aerovette as he developed a front-engine vehicle. But he adapted the blunt rear-end

Opposite, top: Designers developed dozens of schemes for what the fourth-generation Corvette was to look like. Engineers and design staff still wrestled with the question of front versus mid-engine placement. *GM Media Archive*

Opposite, bottom: An alternate interior proposal still followed the aircraft cockpit theme with digital readouts but used round instruments rather than squares. Designers believed the bold graphics made information accessible more quickly. *GM Media Archive*

Below: One of the fourth-generation Corvette's most controversial features was its highly graphic digital instrument panel. Interior studio manager Bill Scott sought to replicate the business-like environment of a contemporary jet fighter. *GM Media Archive*

The Death and Rebirth of V-8 Performance

EXHAUST GAS RECIRCULATORS.

POSITIVE CRANKCASE VENTILATION VALVES.

AIR PUMPS.

CATALYTIC CONVERTERS.

CARBON DIOXIDE EMISSIONS.

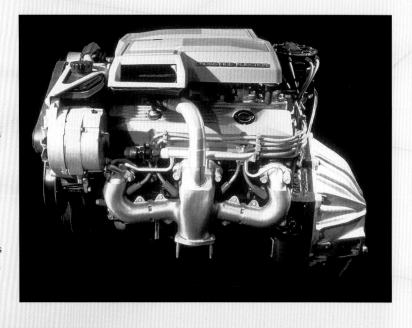

This was quite the opposite mandatory-equipment list from what big-bore, high-octane, tire-burning horsepower-makers needed. These were the devices and considerations that strangled performance from the early 1970s through the late 1980s. In 1972 the optional 350-cubic-inch displacement LT1 V-8 offered customers 255 horsepower. It wasn't until 1990 that Chevrolet had even 250 horsepower again as standard equipment for a Corvette. Of course, that year represented another first-in-a-long-time: The optional engine returned to price lists. This was the LT5 as part of the ZR1 package. This "beast," as engine historian Anthony Young characterized in his book *The Heart of the Beast*, came from a joint development with Lotus Engineering. It developed 375 horsepower at 6,000 rpm. The LT5 increased to 405 horsepower at 5,800 rpm for 1993 through 1995. A bore and stroke of 3.90-by-3.66 inches yielded total displacement of 349 cubic inches.

Right, top: The fourth-generation Corvette carried over the 1982 third-generation L83 engine. With 350 cubic inches of displacement, and incorporating twin throttle-body fuel injection, it developed 205 horsepower and 290 foot-pounds of torque. *GM Media Archive*

Right, bottom: Chevrolet engineering sliced into an early 1989 pre-production LT5 engine for the ZR1 to show off its overhead cams and other features. Co-designed with Lotus Engineering in England, the LT5 was manufactured for Chevrolet by Mercury Marine. *GM Media Archive*

Opposite: The exploded drawing scarcely does justice to the complexity and ingenuity of the LT5. The all-aluminum engine, with 3.9-inch bore and 3.66-inch stroke, displaced 349 cubic inches and developed 375 horsepower at its introduction. *GM Media Archive*

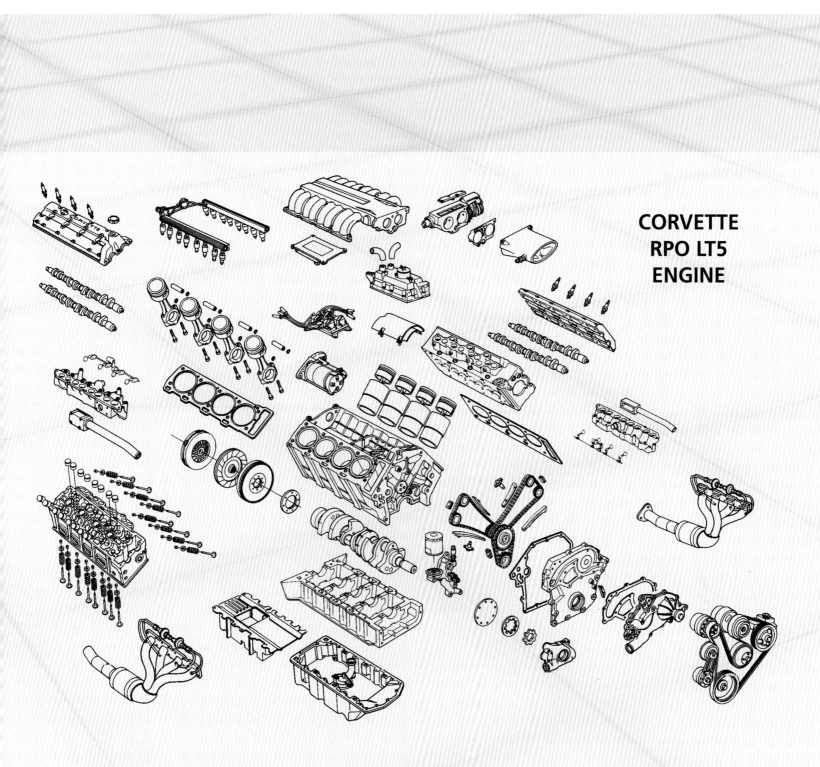

CORVETTE RPO LT5 ENGINE

Chevrolet's engine-assembly plants had no capacity for producing anything in such small batches as the LT5, so Chevrolet contracted with Mercury Marine in Stillwater, Oklahoma. The hand-assembled, dual-overhead cam, four-valves-per-cylinder engines met all the emissions standards and were fuel-efficient enough to avoid the Gas Guzzler tax in place at the time.

When the fifth-generation Corvette debuted as a 1997 model year introduction, it arrived with an LS1 346-cubic-inch 345-horsepower V-8. For 2001, both the base coupe and convertible and the new Z06 model got a new 346-cubic-inch casting that, with other improvements, allowed Dave Hill and his team to pull 385 horsepower out of the engine for the resurrected Z06. This jumped in 2002 to 405 horsepower in a far more tractable package than the 1990's ZR1 had been.

The C6 arrived in model year 2005. Chevrolet's goal from the start was to deliver Z06 horsepower in the base car. They created a new 364-cubic-inch engine that made the step up to 400 horsepower relatively easy. For 2006, the Z06 designation returned with a new 427-cubic-inch engine that developed 505 horsepower. Over the next two model years, engineers worked on two big ideas: The first boosted base horsepower out of the 364 to 430 horsepower. The second effort perfected the fine art of twin supercharging and that work yielded the 638-horsepower ZR1. This kind of published performance matched the unspoken estimates of output from the all-aluminum ZL1 engines of 1969. Because the new 427 was an aluminum block with alloy heads, it left open to the imagination what would come next.

dictated by Dr. Wunibald Kamm's aerodynamic studies. Kamm had proven that as moving air clung to extended tapering surfaces, long tapered tails created more aerodynamic drag than those chopped short and clean. Long hoods and short rear decks required no translation from Dr. Kamm's German research papers as Palmer reinterpreted Corvette's long-lived design language.

Palmer worked with interior studio manager Bill Scott to create a suitable environment for a Corvette pilot and co-pilot. The two men got a chance to sit in a Grumman F-14A Tomcat jet fighter; they came away inspired by its efficiency and purposefulness. Liquid crystal display (LCD) technology was available and the designers loved the clarity it offered in displaying complex but interrelated bits of information at a glance right in front of the driver's eyes.

Development continued at a fast pace to introduce the car as a 30th anniversary edition. Then GM chairman Lloyd Reuss insisted that the new Corvette provide a Porsche Targa-like fully removable roof section. He did not want the T-roof system carried over from the C3. McLellan's staff had to re-engineer the car completely. Complicating matters further, new federal emissions and safety regulations were scheduled to take effect for 1984. The new C4 would be a one-year car before it was illegal. Chevrolet general manager Bob Stempel made the difficult decision to slip introduction back to model year 1984.

As supplies of 1982 C3 models dwindled, Chevrolet invited journalists to Riverside International Raceway east of Los Angeles to meet the C4 in December 1982. (With full 1984 specifications, Chevrolet assembled and serial-numbered

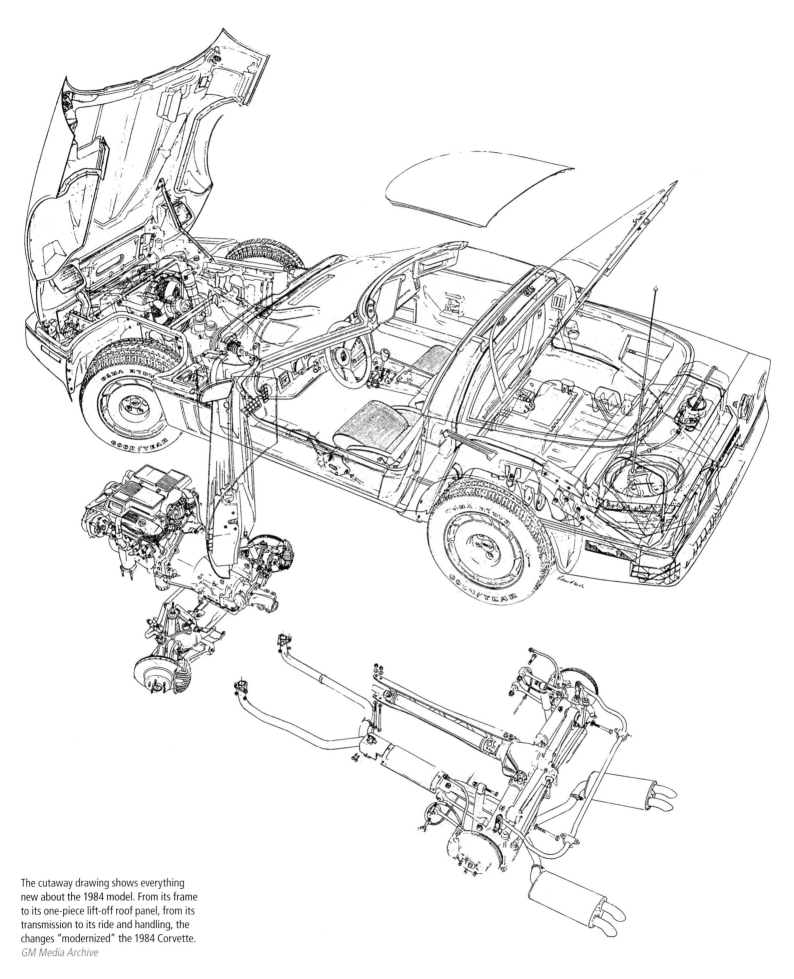

The cutaway drawing shows everything
new about the 1984 model. From its frame
to its one-piece lift-off roof panel, from its
transmission to its ride and handling, the
changes "modernized" the 1984 Corvette.
GM Media Archive

these cars as 1983 production.) Between the smooth road surfaces of the racetrack and the follow-up phase running around the mountain roads behind Santa Barbara, the cars earned rave reviews. (Few journalists, however, were wild about the LCD instrumentation.) Test cars equipped with the optional Z51 Performance Handling Suspension answered all the criticisms that C3s had lost the sports-car ride and feel. Deliveries began in California in January 1983, and Chevrolet had the car available nationally in March.

LONG YEAR, BIG SALES

The 17-month-long model year led to a near-record output of 51,547 cars at a base price of $21,800. For this figure, buyers got a 205-horsepower 350-cubic-inch V-8 with the four-speed automatic transmission, AM-FM stereo sound system, cloth seats, and removable roof panel. Nearly twice as many cars in Bright Red (12,942) went out the Bowling Green factory doors as black (7,906) or white (6,416). Only 6,443 buyers opted for the no-extra-cost four-speed manual. Most popular options included the new Goodyear Gatorback unidirectional P255/50VR16 tires and wheels developed for the new car (51,547, at $561.20), though the fact that 100 percent of production Corvettes were equipped with these tires for the 1984 model year really pushes the concept of "option." Next up in the popularity list was cruise control (49,830 at $185), followed by power door locks (49,545 at $165), power driver seat (48,702 at $210), and rear window and side mirror defoggers (47,680 at $160). Only 104 wanted no radio at all, while 178 chose their sound system with the optional citizens band two-way radio. The Bose sound system designed specially for the car, a first for passenger cars, was Corvette's most expensive option at $895, and Bowling Green installed 43,607 of them. That audio package received enthusiastic praise from everyone. By midyear, dealers learned it was a deal breaker: no Bose, no sale.

Before midyear, buyers in the frost-belts of the country had concluded that the optional Z51 Performance Handling Package gave them too stiff a ride for their rough roads. Complaints to dealers fed back to McLellan and his engineers, who quickly began to revise what the Z51 did, stepping back some from its initial potential. Meanwhile, they encouraged dealers to probe their buyers' intentions carefully before recommending the ride and handling option.

Opposite, top: Cincinnati Milacron robots clamp and weld hundreds of points on the C4 platform. After a superhuman 1984 production of 51,547 coupes during the long manufacturing year, production seemed slow during a normal 1985 with 39,729 coupes from Bowling Green Assembly. *GM Media Archive*

Opposite, bottom: Retired Air Force Brigadier General Chuck Yeager, the first man to fly faster than the speed of sound, was a longtime Corvette enthusiast. He had to slow his regular pace somewhat when he served as 1986 Indy 500 Pace Car driver. *GM Media Archive*

Below: The convertible returned to the Corvette lineup for the first time since 1975. While the official Indy 500 pace car was painted yellow, Chevrolet designated that all convertibles were pace-car replicas and Bowling Green assembly delivered each one with a set of decals. *David Newhardt © 2012*

The Corvette Indy and CERV III

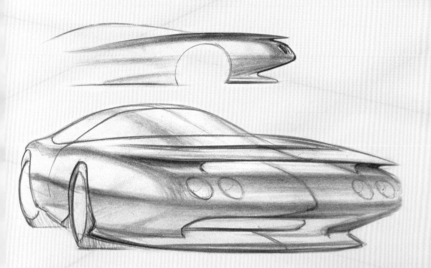

> *The engine guys, McLellan, who had never used their engine as in integral part of the chassis structure, couldn't believe that we were serious.*

General Motors' third "Corporate Engineering Research Vehicle," the CERV III, began life as an engineering-and-design concept car that Chevrolet first showed at the North American International Automobile Show at Detroit in January 1986. At that time, Chevrolet called it the Corvette Indy. It was an all-wheel-drive platform that grew out of the relationship Dave McLellan had established with Lotus Engineering.

As McLellan explained in his book *Corvette from the Inside*, the Indy "was to be an ultra-sophisticated mid-engine active-suspension technology show car. In this car, the engine, transaxle, graphite composite central structural backbone, and suspension points were all an integral structural unit. The body was carried on this frame assembly on isolation mounts." Stylist Jerry Palmer created the striking bodywork.

McLellan and his staff had considered using the engine and transmission as stressed chassis elements, much like contemporary race-car technology. "But the engine guys," McLellan went on, "who had never used their engine as an integral part of the chassis structure, couldn't believe that we were serious." In the prototypes and the show car, the carbon-fiber structure, resembling two "Y" pieces butted end to end, supported the front transmission at one Y and a transverse-mounted 2,650cc (161.7-cubic-inch) V-8 at the other. This was the Chevy "Indy" engine running in several cars in the Championship Auto Racing Teams (CART) Indy car series.

Above: When the Indy debuted at the Detroit International Auto Show In 1986, it did not run. Engineering subsequently created two additional running models, using a variation of the 2.65-liter Indy engine developing something near 600 horsepower. *GM Media Archive*

Right: Inspired by the marriage of Chevrolet and Ilmor Engineering and their offspring, the Ilmor-Chevrolet Indianapolis racing engine, Design V.P. Chuck Jordan asked his staff to create a show car that used and promoted the engine and its new racing venue. Archive *GM Media Archive*

Bottom: J. Carter's June 6, 1985, interior proposal for the Corvette Indy looked like something more appropriate for a space pod than an earthbound vehicle. This concept reflected the styling tone of the entire car. *GM Media Archive*

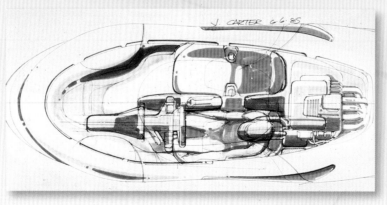

Above: When the Corvette Indy next appeared with all-wheel-drive and all-wheel steering, it was reconfigured as the CERV III. This powerplant, a twin-turbocharged 5.7-liter V-8, developed 650 horsepower. *GM Media Archive*

Top: Whether the "C" in CERV stood for Corporate or Chevrolet or Corvette, the rest of the acronym was clear: Experimental Research Vehicle. From left, 1993 CERV IV(a) (the first C5 prototype); 1964 CERV II (all-wheel-drive midengine); 1959 CERV I (rear engine); 1990 CERV III (midengine); and 1993 CERV IV(b) (second C5 development mule). *Ed Baumgarten © 2012, courtesy Mid America Motorworks*

To this engine, Lotus added four-wheel drive, four-wheel steering, and active suspension. In such a system, microprocessors read pavement inputs and hydraulic controls instantly adjusted ride and handling to accommodate a full range from pothole modulation to racetrack agility.

Engineers continued to develop the active suspension system after the Detroit show debut. Engineering believed the potential would apply to the ZR1 that was on the horizon. However, the necessary pumps and plumbing made the system too heavy for a car on which engineers counted every additional ounce as a compromise in performance.

Following the late 1989 press introduction of the ZR1, Chevrolet reintroduced the Indy as the CERV III, still with full-time four-wheel drive. Engineering fitted it with a twin-turbocharged version of the LT5 that developed 650 horsepower and launched the car from 0 to 60 miles per hour in 3.9 seconds.

The legacy of the Corvette INDY and CERV III was that the car essentially ended the midengine sports car discussion within Chevrolet and Corvette engineering and design. McLellan wrote that the engine team rejected the concept of using engine and transmission as stressed members "as way too big a stretch." McLellan concluded that if he were unable to get some of his extended team to consider so radical a solution as the Corvette Indy, they would have even greater difficulty selling the idea to management and Corvette customers. However, many of the breakthrough technologies that grew out of the Indy and CERV III did appear on late-generation Corvettes.

For 1985, Chevrolet also retreated slightly with the LCD instrument panel. Not only journalists but also buyers missed the analogue dials, so engineers reworked graphics, enlarging the numerals and toning down the colors. These were well-timed improvements; they coincided with the introduction of Corvette's new tuned-port Bosch electronic fuel injection. This system precisely metered the fuel entering each cylinder rather than averaging flow across each bank of cylinders as the previous injection did. It increased horsepower from 205 in 1984 to 230 for 1985, and raised torque from 290 to 330 foot-pounds. It also provided the engine with nearly 11 percent better fuel economy. The top speed of the Corvette went from 142 miles per hour to 150, achieving a long-held target for McLellan and his engineering staff.

Base price rose to $24,403, equipped as it was in 1984. Production topped at 39,729 units, of which 35,998 had the Bose sound system installed. Bright Red remained the largest color choice, followed again by black, then white. The least popular color was Light Blue Metallic, according to Corvette historian Mike Antonick.

After a 10-year absence, convertibles returned to Corvette's product line for 1986. Chevrolet launched the open car with a highly visible presence as the Indy 500 pace car (in yellow) and then labeled every 1986 convertible as a pace car replica regardless of color. Chevrolet delivered the cars with decal packages for later installation. Base price for the convertible was $32,032, and Chevrolet assembled 7,315. Coupes cost $27,027 and the factory produced 27,794 units. Out of a total run of 35,109 vehicles, only power door locks, power driver seat, and cruise control appeared on more cars than the Bose sound system. Still priced at $895, Corvette assemblers installed 32,478 of them.

Aluminum cylinder heads arrived midyear, providing the standard engine with a 5 horsepower gain due to more efficient intake and exhaust flow. Chevrolet made its anti-lock braking system standard equipment on the Corvette in 1986. GM also fitted mandatory upper brake lights, complying with federal regulations.

New Jersey dealer Malcolm Konner created his own commemorative with a limited run of 50 coupes painted silver-beige over black. This was the first of many issues of limited editions and commemoratives. These addressed a special marketing niche that Chevrolet recognized and serviced.

Opposite, top: *Car & Driver* magazine named the 1987 Corvette one of the 10 best automobiles in the world in its January 1987 issue. *Motor Trend* gave it best braking and skid pad performance acknowledgement eight months later. *GM Media Archive*

Opposite, bottom: White leather seats, steering wheel, and white door panels contrast dramatically with the black trim in the anniversary coupe. Bowling Green assembled 22,789 coupes and convertibles during 1988. *David Newhardt © 2012*

Below: To commemorate the 35th anniversary of the Corvette, Chevrolet created a 1988 special edition coupe in solid white with a black roof band. The company sold 2,050 as a $4,795 option. *David Newhardt © 2012*

ABORTED TURBOS AND U-6S

Dave McLellan's engineering group had begun developing a turbocharged Corvette engine while the C4 was in development. This work started with V-6 engines, but these soon proved to be impractical. By 1985, the engineers had turbo V-8s in tests that produced more than 400 horsepower. Then Lloyd Reuss proposed that engineers take a different direction in their search for more power for the Corvette. GM had acquired 60 percent of Lotus Engineering in England in January 1986, and Reuss's suggestion led to the collaboration that developed a dual overhead camshaft four-valve per cylinder 400-horsepower engine for the Corvette, designated the LT5. Reuss encouraged this project even though this relegated engineering's turbo research to "also ran" status.

Sympathetic to McLellan's desire to get more performance to Corvette buyers, Chevrolet's market planning director Don Runkle recommended that Chevrolet share its turbo development results with outsider Reeves Callaway, who had a history of successfully developing, certifying, and producing turbo projects for other automakers. While Lotus pressed ahead with the LT5 high-performance development, Callaway worked on his approach to the same goal. After testing and development, Runkle gave Callaway's finished product a factory regular production option code, B2K.

Callaway's Turbo Corvette was given to just 20 Chevrolet dealers to sell and service. When a buyer checked RPO B2K, Bowling Green made some minor production changes and shipped an otherwise standard production Corvette to Callaway's shops in Old Lyme, Connecticut, where Callaway's staff completed the car. It was an expensive proposition, adding $19,995 to the price of the car. Despite the cost, Callaway and Runkle seriously underestimated the interest in a 345-horsepower Corvette with a warranty. Hoping to sell as many as 50, they introduced the car as a 1987 model; by year-end Chevrolet and Callaway delivered 188 cars to anxious buyers. For Corvette owners who missed "bragging rights" over the performance of their cars, Callaway gave it back to them, providing 1960s muscle-car horsepower figures with 1980s supercar top speeds. The Callaway reached 177 miles per hour.

Above: For many owners, the subtle badge on the rear, visible as the car thundered away from those it passed, was enough distinction. Here, Indy racing champion Rick Mears stirs up the Road America racetrack leaves for photographer Pete Biro as they lap the circuit in Elkhart Lake, Wisconsin. *GM Media Archive*

Opposite, top: While Chevrolet delayed introducing the ZR1 to the buying public until 1990, it got a few dozen cars to a few hundred journalists for evaluation late in 1989. Its understated appearance disguised its performance capabilities. *Randy Leffingwell © 2012*

Opposite, bottom: With 375 horsepower available from the new LT5 V-8 engine, these 1989 ZR1 pilot-production cars were the most powerful Corvettes since 1971. State-of-the-art engineering provided much better fuel economy than the older version as well. *Randy Leffingwell © 2012*

Secret Steps into the Future with the CERV IV(a) and CERV IV(b)

While the striking and radical Corvette INDY and CERV III never reached production, one of its most significant innovations became the backbone, literally, of the fifth-generation Corvette. The central tunnel structure, created by Lotus Engineering and adopted for the INDY and CERV III, had new adherents as engineers and designers plotted and schemed as to what the new Corvette would be. Sales figures told them there always had been a market for convertibles, but engineering an open car to be as stiff as a coupe presented enormous challenges. The central tunnel fixture, mated to side rails formed through another new technology, delivered the rigidity and strength that chief engineer Dave Hill had in mind.

A process called hydroforming reshaped steel tubing by injecting liquids—in this case water—at 7,000 pounds per square inch (psi) pressure. By not using high heat to bend the metal to conform to its molds, the steel kept its original strength. This allowed engineers to develop thinner side rails, making occupant ingress and egress much less of a stretch. These side rails also allowed the fifth-generation car to come in more than 100 pounds lighter than C4 while maintaining much higher side impact resistance in a crash.

New computer-aided modeling programs enabled engineers to confirm their ideas, but nothing brings home the truth like a real model that is

drivable. To that end, in December 1992, Hill and his team contracted an outside fabricator, TDM Inc., in Livonia, Michigan, to create a C5 chassis and suspension inside a C4 body shell. They dubbed the car CERV IV. TDM's Madison Heights operations took on the task of modifying the body to fit the new running gear without betraying what it was. It did offer some surprises, however. Unlike CERV III or even previous production models since 1962, this prototype had a trunk.

All this took money, and that was in scarce supply at General Motors in the early 1990s. Jim Perkins, Chevrolet's general manager, skimmed from some budgets and fattened others to come up with funding that remained below corporate radar. Designer Jon Moss modified one black C4 convertible and then a second to accommodate the C5's 8.3-inch longer wheelbase. These became CERV IV(a) and CERV IV(b), the Alpha and Beta of the C5 prototype world. Together, these "mules" and their more numerous clones rolled on hundreds of thousands of test miles from Alaska in the winter to Australia's outback during its summer.

Two years after C5 introduction, Chevrolet put the CERV IV cars up for auction. Both ended up with Mid America Motorworks founder and Corvette collector Mike Yager as part of his MY Garage museum in Effingham, Illinois.

Opposite: In early 1993, engineers inside the Corvette group created test mules to develop running gear and systems for the next-generation car. Secretly, an outside contractor assembled C5 prototype running gear under a C4 body, known as CERV IV, and then months later created this updated twin, CERV IV(b). *Ed Baumgarten © 2012, courtesy Mid America Motorworks*

Above: In early 1992, Corvette engineers found the funds—$1.2 million—to have the prototypes fabricated, essentially creating a C5 inside a C4. The project remained a secret for more than a year for fear GM management would veto the expenditure. *Ed Baumgarten © 2012, courtesy Mid America Motorworks*

Above: In the two decades since the C4 ZR1, some people have criticized Chevrolet and others have praised the company for not making the car look more flamboyant. The car sold 3,049 copies in its first year. *GM Media Archive*

Opposite, top: On March 1, 1990, this ZR1 set a collection of 24-hour endurance records on Firestone Tire's 7.7-mile test track at Fort Stockton, Texas, including 24 hours averaging 175.885 miles per hour. Behind it, the L98 established an equally impressive number of 12-hour records. *GM Media Archive*

Opposite, bottom: In auto assembly parlance, the moment at which the car body joins the chassis and running gear is called "the marriage." At Bowling Green, the chassis on these 1991 models rose and the body descended, making the connections easier on assemblers' backs and arms. *GM Media Archive*

Base Corvette coupes went for $27,999 and convertibles for $33,172. (The Callaway option was added to this base price.) Chevrolet offered its standard 240-horsepower 350 V-8, up another 5 horsepower gained by switching to roller valve lifters for 1987. Nearly every car sold went out of Bowling Green factory with the power driver seat, door locks, cruise control, and the Bose sound system that had become the required litany of RPO code numbers for any Chevrolet dealer. Bright Red again led the color charts, followed by Dark Metallic Red, and then black. The rarest color for 1987 was Copper Metallic with just 87 cars produced.

For 1988, Chevrolet gave the Corvette coupes less restrictive mufflers that added another 5 horsepower, bringing the total to 245. Fearing backlash from convertible buyers over the louder engine, the open cars used the previous exhaust system that kept power at 240. The division assembled 15,382 of the coupes at $29,489 base price, and 7,407 convertibles priced at $34,820. Callaway production reached 125 units; the B2K option listed at $25,895 and provided buyers with 382 horsepower and 582 foot-pounds of torque.

This model year represented the 35th anniversary of Corvette production and Chevrolet offered a commemorative coupe in two-tone white. As a $4,795 option, 2,050 buyers took advantage of the opportunity. Proving once again it was the must-have option, the Bose stereo system ranked second on order lists, slightly behind the power driver seat but at 20,304 units installed, ahead of everything else. Music clearly was important to Corvette owners; the least popular option was UL5: radio delete. Just 179 individuals, presumably racers, made that selection. Bright Red, then white, then black made up the most popular color choices, taking 12,380 of the total 22,789 production for 1988. Silver Metallic proved too subtle for all but 385 buyers.

Right: Chevrolet sponsorship of the 1992 America's Cup yacht America³ gave red convertibles the designation "Official Vehicle of America³." America³ went on to win the America's Cup, contested offshore from San Diego, California, in early May 1992. *GM Media Archive*

Below: Styling differences between regular production models and ZR1 options merged in 1991 as all models adopted the ZR1 rear fascia and four rectangular taillights. All models got new side-panel louvers and wraparound lamps for parking, cornering, and fog. *GM Media Archive*

CORVETTE CHALLENGE

Among the total production run was a series of 56 coupes that Bowling Green assembled for a new racing series, the Corvette Challenge. Sanctioned by the Sports Car Club of America, this match race program ran in support of other events during SCCA weekends. Racers used stock engines matched by the factory for their power output.

For 1989, the Corvette Challenge continued with another 60 cars emerging from Bowling Green's factory doors. For this second year, racers received slightly higher performance engines, installed after purchase. At the end of the racing season, the series ended, and Chevrolet reinstalled the original-production lower output engines and sold any cars the racers chose not to keep.

Production increased slightly for 1989, reaching 16,663 coupes and 9,749 convertibles for a total of 26,412 Corvettes. Coupe base price was $31,545 for the 245-horsepower V-8, while convertibles again ran 240-horsepower engines and cost $36,785. Callaway production dropped to 67, still exceeding initial projections of 50 cars per year. The B2K option went for $25,895 in addition to the base coupe. A new electronic climate-control air conditioning system barely edged out the Bose system for most-wanted option at 24,675 delivered (for $150) compared with 24,145 Bose installed at $773.

Equipping 24,412 total cars produced with 24,675 optional climate-control systems seems a little odd. When you add in the 84 ZR1 models built but not sold to the public (see page 144), the total number of cars built is still only 24,496. This leads to two possible conclusions: either there has been some sort of a mix-up in the record keeping regarding the installation of this system, or 179 cars were equipped with not one but two climate-control systems, ostensibly one for the driver and one for the passenger, though odds favor a bookkeeping error, since no such car has ever been seen. Either way, this again brings into question the concept of "optional equipment."

Below: The base LT1 350-cubic-inch V-8 for 1993 developed 300 horsepower. Base coupes sold for $34,595, while the convertibles went for $41,195.
GM Media Archive

Hammers and Sledgehammers

When fast is good and faster is better, *fastest* silences the opposition.

Such was the case when Reeves Callaway joined forces with Dave McLellan to create the Callaway Twin Turbo Corvette, regular production option B2K, introduced for the 1987 model year. Capable of 177 miles per hour with acceleration that resembled a large missile launch, the Callaway restored bragging rights to Corvette buyers, a personal goal of Dave McLellan's. His other goal was to gain the respect of the Europeans. Callaway, a shrewd engineer and sharp marketer, knew the way to get to European markets was to take the car to them. He helped his German distributor to prepare a car for *AutoMotor und Sport* magazine for review. Mercedes-Benz performance arm AMG had just introduced a high-performance sedan nicknamed *Das Hammer*. After the German magazine test of Callaway's Corvette, the magazine's headline over a photo of the red 1987 Twin Turbo read, "This is The Hammer!"

That led *Car and Driver* magazine to stage "The Gathering of Eagles," assembling in one place every car that expected to go really fast. Reeves created his top gun, which humbled all competitors with a top speed of 231.1 miles per hour. But that set him and McLellan thinking about the next test. Reeves knew surely there would be another.

Over the next year, they created a car with a top speed faster than many aircraft. Callaway and his chief engineer, Tim Good, called the project a rolling laboratory. Under their breath, they admitted if their 1987 car had been the hammer, this would be a sledgehammer. "It's not just a statement about top speed," Good explained. "It has to be able to be driven to the store by your mom as well as go 250 miles an hour." Although few people would want their mothers driving to the store at 250 miles per hour, performance fans appreciated the sentiment.

On October 19, 1988, when they had finished their shop work on the car, they climbed in and drove it from Callaway's shops in West Lyme, Connecticut, through rain and shine, to the Transportation Research Center in East Liberty, Ohio. TRC had a 7.5-mile high-speed test track. By the time the Callaway team wrapped up tests and tweaks, the silver sledgehammer ran a timed 254.76 miles per hour.

"We weren't thinking about setting a record in that car," Callaway said. "We were testing our calculations. We didn't do too well." He paused for effect. "We had figured the car would go two-fifty-two. It went two-fifty-four and three quarters. We screwed up somewhere."

Reeves followed the B2K coupes with a limited-edition Speedster that first appeared in 1991. Based on the Callaway Corvette modifications, the 350-cubic-inch engine developed 450 horsepower. With a top speed quoted at 188 miles per hour, each new car Reeves Callaway created became a target for every other carmaker.

Callaway followed the production Twin Turbo B2K and the one-off Sledgehammer with the 1992 SuperNatural Corvette. The fifth-generation Corvette yielded Callaway C12 models for street and track, one of which took pole position for the 2001 24 Hours of Le Mans.

Callaway continued developing and stretching Corvettes for public road use and international track competition with an FIA GT3 team or driver championships from 2007 through 2010 using C6-based platforms. His latest production cars, the C16, are primarily made-to-order coupes, convertibles, or speedsters, meant to compete in performance and price with supercars such as the high-end Porsches, Lamborghinis, and Ferraris. SC560 and SC616 models (the numbers reflect horsepower output) are the current-generation Callaway Corvettes, still available through select Chevrolet dealers.

Opposite, top: When Dave McLellan phoned Reeves Callaway and asked him to come on board to develop, produce, and sell a turbocharged Corvette, neither man knew where it would take them. Ultimately, it took Callaway and this 1988 "Sledgehammer" to 254.76 miles per hour. *Randy Leffingwell © 2012*

Opposite, middle: Reeves Callaway launched the Speedster at the Los Angeles Auto Show in January 1991, with this car. The chopped windshield permitted no top but Callaway joked that above certain speeds, rain just skipped over the 450-horsepower open car. *Randy Leffingwell © 2012*

Opposite, bottom: Once again Reeves Callaway chose the Los Angeles Auto Show in November 2006 to introduce his newest automobile, the C16 (6th generation) that he and his staff assembled. Priced at $119,865, the 650-horsepower coupe accelerated from 0 to 60 miles per hour in 3.3 seconds. *David Newhardt © 2012*

Below: On August 18, 2007, Callaway unveiled this 700-horsepower third-iteration Speedster no. 1 at Pebble Beach Concours d'Elegance. Because of its dual ultra-low windscreens, Callaway equipped the car with a pair of Stand 21 carbon-fiber racing helmets and sold it for $305,000. *David Newhardt*

The bargain of the option list was not the $22 performance rear-axle ratio or the $20 engine block heater. It was Corvette's no-extra-charge six-speed manual transmission designed and built (initially) by ZF (Zahnradfabrick Friedrichshafen) in Germany. A computer sensed driving style and, to preserve fuel economy, detoured upshifts from first to fourth gear, a workload the strong torque of the base engine handled easily.

Following its midyear press introduction, Chevrolet rescheduled the public launch of the heavily anticipated ZR1 package with the LT5 engine. Mike Antonick reported in his *Corvette Black Book* that Chevrolet assembled 84 vehicles, used for photography, media testing, and engineering development before determining that a few additional changes should delay sales until the 1990 model year. Many of these cars suffered damage during media introductions; others were crushed following the testing and final development cycle. A few survived as test mules for later projects and as executive cars for a fortunate group of GM designers, engineers, and managers.

Every ZR1 owner in the United States knew this Corvette had only the B2K as its nearest competition on these shores. That left the rest of the world as the target for Corvette's engineers. The extensive media attention this car received in the United States and abroad might lead someone to believe that Chevrolet manufactured only 3,049 Corvettes in 1990 and all of them were ZR1 models. The other 20,597 coupes and convertibles didn't count. All that mattered were these long-awaited 385-horsepower ZR1s available at an option price of $27,016 over the base coupe cost of $31,979. Chevrolet's PR machine worked magnificently promoting the car. Magazines and newspapers that seldom covered automobiles wrote endlessly about the new "King of the Hill" as *Car & Driver* magazine named it. Enthusiast magazines put it on their covers and given any chance to drive one a second time, wrote again and again about its sound and fury. It accelerated from 0 to 60 miles per hour in 4.2 seconds and reached a top speed of 175 miles per hour. It looked subtly different, a fact that some say helped sales and others suggest hurt the numbers. The wider back end was distinctive, enlarged to make room for massive 315/35ZR-17 Goodyear rear tires on 11-inch-wide wheels.

Below: For the 40th Anniversary, Chevrolet designed a $1,455 package that included Ruby Red metallic exterior paint, Ruby Red leather sports seats, and other trim. Bowling Green assembled 6,749 of the commemorative coupes and convertibles. *GM Media Archive*

Left: ZR1 production had settled into a steady pace through 1993, 1994, and 1995 at 448 units per year. That was the maximum number of engines Mercury Marine in Stillwater, Oklahoma, could assemble for installation at Bowling Green. *GM Media Archive*

Below: Chevrolet assembled 527 of these 1995 Indianapolis 500 replica pace cars as convertibles only. It was a $2,816 option on top of the $43,665 base price. *GM Media Archive*

Bowling Green did manufacture a full run of cars for 1990, including 16,016 coupes and 7,630 convertibles for a total of 23,646 cars. Coupe base price with slight engine improvements boosting horsepower output to 250 from the V-8 was $31,979. The convertible started at $37,264 with a base 245-horsepower engine. Standard transmission remained the four-speed automatic, and Chevrolet continued to offer the ZF six-speed as a no-cost choice. The Callaway Turbo B2K, still at 382 horsepower listed for $26,895, was an option selected by 58 buyers.

A new Delco-Bose variation incorporated a CD player, a choice made more than two-to-one over the non-CD version despite its nearly 50 percent additional cost, $1,219 compared to $829. A power driver seat, electronic air conditioning, and a power passenger seat adjustment made the top-three options list, each appearing on nine out of ten cars.

MOST CORVETTES REALLY ARE RED

Since 1954, when Chevrolet introduced red as a color choice, it often was the customers' favorite. This year was no different with nearly a third of the cars (6,956) delivered painted in Bright Red and another 10 percent (2,353) in Dark Red Metallic. White and black ended the year in a virtual photo finish for second and third at 4,872 and 4,759, respectively. Competition Yellow proved the least popular color (278) despite its selection as one of two colors for the 80 "Indy Festival" commemoratives Chevrolet produced. The other Festival choice, Turquoise Metallic, sold twice as well, at 589 copies.

Following the end of the Corvette Challenge match-racing series, Corvette entered and developed cars for the World Challenge race. Selecting option R9G designated several small but significant changes to a production coupe. According to Mike Antonick, customers then purchased "sealed" racing engines directly from Chevrolet. Bowling Green assembled 23 of the cars for 1990.

The crumbling economy brought on by the start of the first Gulf War and a corresponding spike in oil prices, as well as rumblings of problems in the savings and loan industry, affected consumer confidence, and 1991 model-year Corvette sales and production suffered. Totals slipped to 14,967 coupes (at $32,455 base price) and 5,672 convertibles (at $38,770). Add to that a 10 percent luxury tax on vehicles costing more than $30,000 that started in 1991, and it was easy to understand the depressed numbers. Base horsepower output remained at 250 for the coupes and 245 for the convertibles, coupled either to the four-speed automatic or six-speed manual. The ZR1 option climbed to $31,683, with production of 2,044 units and Callaway B2K option rose to $33,000. Chevrolet delivered 71 B2K cars for the 1991 model year. It was the final year for the Callaway. (CONTINUED ON PAGE 152)

Left: The Grand Sport returned in 1996 as a production model to wrap up more than a decade of success as the fourth-generation Corvette. Available as a coupe or convertible, Chevrolet limited production to 1,000 copies. *GM Media Archive*

Opposite, top: Model year 1995 was the last year for the fourth-generation ZR1 model. Horsepower output leveled off at 405 since 1993. In all, Chevrolet assembled 6,939 of the high-performance coupes. *GM Media Archive*

Opposite, bottom: The Grand Sport option included the new LT4 engine with 350 cubic inches displacement and 330 horsepower. The option, including paint, trim, and special wheels, added $2,880 to the base $45,060 convertible. *GM Media Archive*

How Many Are There?

Corvette ended seventh-generation assembly on November 14, 2019, when the final Z06 left the production line at 3:10 p.m. That closed the books on C7 production and allowed for reporting accurate totals.

Chevrolet Division made data available for authorized publications such as this book. But these numbers provided production totals, not numbers of cars that dealers sold. As happened before, sometimes more information is available than there is room to reproduce.

For enthusiasts desiring especially detailed production information, one source consistently has outshined the rest: Corvette historian and National Corvette Restorers Society cofounder Mike Antonick has published and continually updated the *Corvette Black Book* since 1978. This is a unique and important historical resource. For information, see www.corvetteblackbook.com.

Note: Eighth-generation production figures were unavailable as this edition went to press.

FIRST-GENERATION PRODUCTION	
1953	300
1954	3,640
1955	700
1956	3,467
1957	6,339
1958	9,168
1959	9,670
1960	10,261
1961	10,939
1962	14,531
Total Generation I	**69,015**

SECOND-GENERATION PRODUCTION		
1963	Coupe	10,594
	Convertible	10,919
	Total	**21,513**
1964	Coupe	8,304
	Convertible	13,925
	Total	**22,229**
1965	Coupe	8,186
	Convertible	15,378
	Total	**23,564**
1966	Coupe	9,958
	Convertible	17,762
	Total	**27,720**
1967	Coupe	8,504
	Convertible	14,436
	Total	**22,940**
Total Generation II		**117,966**

THIRD-GENERATION PRODUCTION		
1968	Coupe	9,936
	Convertible	18,630
	Total	**28,566**
1969	Coupe	22,129
	Convertible	6,633
	Total	**28,762**
1970	Coupe	10,668
	Convertible	6,648
	Total	**17,316**
1971	Coupe	14,680
	Convertible	7,121
	Total	**21,801**
1972	Coupe	20,496
	Convertible	6,508
	Total	**27,004**
1973	Coupe	25,521
	Convertible	4,943
	Total	**30,464**
1974	Coupe	32,028
	Convertible	5,474
	Total	**37,502**
1975	Coupe	33,836
	Convertible	4,629
	Total	**38,465**
1976	Coupe	46,558
1977	Coupe	49,213
1978	Coupe	40,274
	(Indy Pace Car replica)	(6,502)
	Total	**46,776**
1979	Coupe	53,807
1980	Coupe	40,614
1981	Coupe	40,606
1982	Coupe	18,648
	(Collector Hatchback Coupe)	(6,759)
	Total	**25,407**
Total Generation III		**542,861**

FOURTH-GENERATION PRODUCTION		
1984	Coupe	51,547
1985	Coupe	39,729
1986	Coupe	27,794
1986	Convertible	7,315
	Total	**35,109**
1987	Coupe	20,007
	Convertible	10,625
	Total	**30,632**
1988	Coupe	15,382
	Convertible	7,407
	(Callaway B2K)	(125)
	(35th Anniversary)	(2,050)
	Total	**22,789**
1989	Coupe	16,663
	(Callaway B2K)	(67)
	Convertible	9,749
	Total	**26,412**
1990	Coupe	16,016
	(Callaway B2K)	(58)
	(ZR1)	(3,049)
	Convertible	7,630
	Total	**23,646**
1991	Coupe	14,967
	(Callaway B2K)	(71)
	(ZR1)	(2,044)
	Convertible	5,672
	Total	**20,639**

1992	Coupe	14,604
	(ZR1)	(502)
	Convertible	5,875
	Total	**20,479**
1993	Coupe	15,898
	(ZR1)	(448)
	Convertible	5,692
	(40th Anniversary)	(6,749)
	Total	**21,590**
1994	Coupe	17,984
	(ZR1)	(448)
	Convertible	5,346
	Total	**23,330**
1995	Coupe	15,771
	(ZR1)	(448)
	Convertible	4,971
	(Indy Pace Car replica)	(527)
	Total	**20,742**
1996	Coupe	17,167
	Convertible	4,369
	(Collector Edition)	(5,412)
	(Grand Sport)	(1,000)
	Total	**21,536**
Total Generation IV		**358,180**

FIFTH-GENERATION PRODUCTION		
1997	Coupe	9,752
1998	Coupe	19,235
	Convertible	11,849
	(Indy Pace Car replica)	(1,163)
	Total	**31,084**
1999	Coupe	18,078
	Convertible	11,161
	Hardtop	4,031
	Total	**33,270**
2000	Coupe	18,113
	Convertible	13,479
	Hardtop	2,090
	Total	**33,682**
2001	Coupe	15,681
	Convertible	14,173
	Hardtop Z06	5,773
	Total	**35,267**
2002	Coupe	14,760
	Convertible	12,710
	Hardtop Z06	8,297
	Total	**35,767**
2003	Coupe	12,812
	(50th Anniversary coupe)	(7,310)
	Convertible	14,022
	(50th Anniversary convertible)	(7,547)
	Hardtop Z06	8,635
	Total	**35,469**
2004	Coupe	16,165
	(C5R Commemorative)	(2,215)
	Convertible	12,216
	(C5R Commemorative)	(2,659)
	Hardtop Z06	5,683
	(C5R Commemorative)	(2,025)
	Total	**34,064**
Total Generation V		**248,355**

Above: Some of the 39,729 coupes that Bowling Green Assembly manufactured during 1985 are lined up outside the plant in Kentucky. Its peak production year, 1984, saw 51,547 cars assembled at the plant. *GM Media Archive*

2005	Coupe	26,728
	Convertible	10,644
	Total	**37,372**
2006	Coupe	16,598
	Convertible	11,151
	Z06	6,272
	Total	**34,021**
2007	Coupe	21,484
	Convertible	10,918
	(Indy Pace Car replica)	*(500)*
	Z06	8,159
	(Ron Fellows Z06)	*(399)*
	Total	**40,561**
2008	Coupe	20,030
	(Indy Pace Car replica coupe)	*(234)*
	Convertible	7,549
	(Indy Pace Car replica convertible)	*(266)*
	Z06	7,731
	(427 Z06 505)	
	Total	**35,310**
2009	Coupe	8,737
	(GT1 Championship)	*(53)*
	Convertible	3,343
	(GT1 Championship)	*(17)*
	Z06	3,461
	(Competition Sport)	*(20)*
	(GT1 Championship)	*(55)*
	ZR1	1,415
	Total	**16,956**

2010	Coupe	6,761
	(Grand Sport coupe)	*(3,707)*
	Convertible	3,338
	(Grand Sport convertible)	*(2,335)*
	Z06	518
	ZR1	1,577
	Total	**12,194**
2011	Coupe	8,324
	(Grand Sport coupe)	*(5,212)*
	Convertible	3,562
	(Grand Sport convertible)	*(2,782)*
	Z06 (incl. Carbon Ltd. Ed)	1,156
	ZR1	806
	Total	**13,596**
2012	Coupe	7,876
	(Grand Sport coupe)	*(5,056)*
	Convertible	2,889
	(Grand Sport convertible)	*(2,268)*
	Z06	478
	ZR1	404
	Total	**11,647**
2013	Coupe	7,505
	(Grand Sport coupe)	*(4,908)*
	Convertible	5,008
	(Grand Sport convertible)	*(1,736)*
	(427 convertible)	*(2,552)*
	Z06	471
	ZR1	482
	Total	**13,466**
Total Generation VI		**215,123**

2014	Stingray coupe (base)	11,134
	Stingray coupe with Z51	14,931
	Stingray coupe Premier Edition	500
	Stingray convertible (base)	4,493
	Stingray convertible with Z51	5,680
	Stingray coupe Premier Edition	550
	Total	**37,288**
2015	Stingray coupe (base)	9,667
	Stingray coupe with Z51	11,090
	Z06 coupe	6,980
	Stingray convertible (base)	2,397
	Convertible with Z51	2,433
	Z06 convertible	1,673
	Total	**34,240**
2016	Stingray coupe (base)	10,972
	Stingray coupe with Z51	10,415
	Z06 coupe	11,543
	Stingray convertible (base)	2,705
	Convertible with Z51	2,322
	Z06 convertible	2,732
	Total	**40,689**
2017	Stingray coupe (base)	7,548
	Stingray coupe with Z51	3,705
	Z06 coupe	6,197
	Grand Sport coupe	9,912
	Stingray convertible (base)	1,571
	Convertible with Z51	727
	Z06 convertible	6,197
	Grand Sport convertible	1,076
	Total	**32,782**
2018	Stingray coupe (base)	2,352
	Stingray coupe with Z51	716
	Z06 coupe	2,353
	Grand Sport coupe	2,569
	Stingray convertible (base)	537
	Convertible with Z51	198
	Z06 convertible	499
	Grand Sport convertible	512
	Total	**9,686**

2019	Stingray coupe (base)	9,771
	Stingray coupe with Z51	1,728
	Z06 coupe	5,965
	Grand Sport coupe	9,496
	ZR1 coupe	2,441
	Stingray convertible (base)	1,868
	Convertible with Z51	324
	Z06 convertible	972
	Grand Sport convertible	1,745
	ZR1 convertible	512
	Total	**34,822**
Total Generation VII		**189,507**

EIGHTH-GENERATION PRODUCTION

2020	(n.a.)

GRAND TOTAL CORVETTE SEVEN GENERATIONS

Generation I	69,015
Generation II	117,966
Generation III	542,861
Generation IV	358,180
Generation V	248,355
Generation VI	215,123
Generation VII	189,507
Generation VIII	(n.a.)
TOTAL	**1,741,037**

The Great Recession affected C6 production in 2011 and afterward. The C7 delivered the anticipated surge from last-year C6 in 2013 at 13,466 to first-year C7 at 37,288. Building a new paint shop between July and October 2018 shortened the production year and drastically reduced output. A six-week labor strike from September to October 2019 delayed completion of 2019 C7 assembly and pushed back C8 start up. Change-over for the new car manufacture shuttered the plant for three more weeks beginning November 18, 2019.

Above: As Chevrolet considered design and engineering directions for the C4, originally intended to debut in 1983, the company created a small number of engineering mules to run the twin-turbocharged 350-cubic-inch V-8. None were produced. *GM Media Archive*

(CONTINUED FROM PAGE 147)

A new handling package Z07 blended the best of the revised Z51 Performance Handling option with the FX3 electronic selective ride/handling feature. While it was possible to order each option individually, this option combined parts, bringing a firm ride to the cars. Chevrolet offered it for coupes only. It had 733 takers at $2,155. With total production reaching 20,639 in both body styles, the three consistently most popular options held their respective order: AC3, the power driver seat sold 19,937 units and $290; C68, the electronic air conditioning control, sold 19,233 at $180; and the two Bose stereo systems, with CD and without, saw 19,131 installed, ranging in price from $823 to $1,219 with the CD player. Yet again, Bright Red held the color lead, followed by white and then black. Least popular was Charcoal Metallic.

For racers, Chevrolet again supported the World Challenge, but the company no longer offered an R9G option. Participants built their own cars.

Production remained near the same level for 1992, down just 160 cars to 20,479 coupes and convertibles, even with the new 300-horsepower LT1 base engine. Engineers who had developed the LT5 for the ZR1 applied some of those insights to the sibling. This output was enough to accelerate the new coupe from 0 to 60 miles per hour in 4.9 seconds, just 0.6 behind the ZR1. To get this performance and the LT5's output efficiently on the ground, Corvette worked again with Bosch to develop Acceleration Slip Regulation (ASR), a euphemism for traction control.

Chevrolet manufactured 14,604 Corvette coupes and 5,875 convertibles. Base prices increased again to $33,635 and $40,145, respectively, plus luxury tax. Bowling Green also turned out 502 of the ZR1 packages priced at $31,683. Most prized options kept their sequence for another year, but the proportion of CD-equipped Bose units to those without was five-to-one. The least popular option was AQ9 Sports Seats in White Leather. The factory delivered just 709 cars with this $1,180 option. White exterior paint closed on Bright Red, coming within 10 percent of production numbers for red cars. Barely 3 percent of all Corvettes manufactured were yellow in 1992.

For those who watched such things, another milestone occurred in September 1992. Accepting early retirement at age 55, Dave McLellan took advantage of a GM corporation-wide offer and left Chevrolet and Corvette. He was besieged with offers for consulting work for former competitors who knew his talents and had seen his Corvettes get

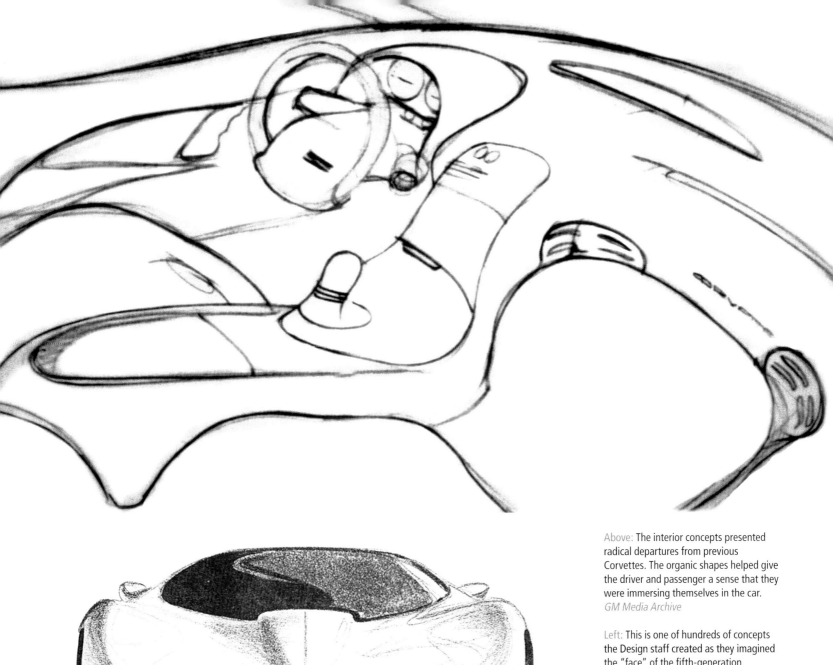

Above: The interior concepts presented radical departures from previous Corvettes. The organic shapes helped give the driver and passenger a sense that they were immersing themselves in the car. *GM Media Archive*

Left: This is one of hundreds of concepts the Design staff created as they imagined the "face" of the fifth-generation Corvette. This version recalls the dramatic fenders of the third-generation models introduced in 1968. *GM Media Archive*

Left, bottom: Following mountains of sketches and renderings on paper, clay modelers began to give form to some of the most promising ideas. Financial issues and economic concerns slipped the introduction back a year at a time. *GM Media Archive*

Right: In early 1994, Corvette engineering created a series of running prototypes of the fifth-generation car. Painted flat black and "camouflaged" with mismatched panels and odd coverings, these "Alpha" cars took to public roads, mostly at night, to provide real-world driving feedback to its creators. *Ed Baumgarten © 2012, courtesy Mid America Motorworks*

Below: By April 1995, engineers had learned enough for the black Alpha series cars to move forward with less-disguised C5 Beta vehicles. Development crews continued to update both Alpha and Beta vehicles through the test process. *Ed Baumgarten © 2012, courtesy Mid America Motorworks*

better and stronger. Dave Hill, just five years younger than McLellan, moved into Corvette from Cadillac, an alarm to enthusiasts but a comfort to board members. Hill dove into work on the next-generation Corvette.

Corvette introduced a Ruby Red Metallic commemorative model in 1993 for the 40th anniversary. To help celebrate the occasion, engineers made several changes inside the LT5 that boosted horsepower from 375 to 405. For the third year in a row, Chevrolet held the ZR1 option price to $31,683, even with the improvements. The company produced 488 of them in 1993, a number fixed by the manufacturing capabilities of outside engine assembler Mercury Marine.

Overall Corvette production inched up from 20,479 total in 1992 to 21,590 for the anniversary year. Coupes again outsold convertibles, 15,898 to 5,692. Base prices rose to $34,595 for the coupe and $41,195 for the convertible. The 40th Anniversary package, RPO Z25, sold for $1,455 and 6,749 copies left Bowling Green's factory floors. Not surprisingly, Torch Red was second in color choice behind the commemorative, at 3,172 cars produced. A new passive keyless entry system allowed owners to lock and unlock their cars by proximity to their vehicles.

As is typical among Corvette enthusiasts and journalists, rumors spread widely by 1994 that the C5 was coming. Insiders suggested the tight economy had forced General Motors to let the project slip back one year, then two. Meanwhile, Chevrolet produced cars to sell.

Federal safety laws required air bags for passengers forcing all automakers to redesign interiors. This provided yet another reason for the C5 introduction delay. Chevrolet used this opportunity to upgrade materials as well. Leather seats were standard (cloth was not even an option) and a new steering wheel, switches, trim panels, and carpet led to a richer interior cabin feel. Convertibles got glass rear windows. Production reached 17,984 coupes, listed at $36,185 base price, and 5,346 convertibles at $42,960 base. Bowling Green again assembled 448 ZR1 packages, adding $31,285 to the price of the coupe. Torch Red and Copper Metallic held their own as the most and least popular color choices, selling at 5,073 and 116 each, respectively.

ANOTHER PACE CAR

Chevrolet provided 25 convertibles to the Indianapolis Motor Speedway for use as "official cars" for the debut of the NASCAR-sanctioned Brickyard 400. According to Mike Antonick, Chevrolet then sold some of these vehicles to private customers.

For 1995, Corvette was the official Indy 500 pace car. Production stopped at 527 units of the Dark Purple and white convertible. The speedway used 87 of them for festival and public relations needs. The rest went directly to Corvette's top-performing dealers for sales.

Next-generation antilock braking (ABS) included larger diameter rotors for all models; previously these only were available with ZR1 and Z07 packages. Production reached 20,472 cars, with 15,771 coupes and 4,971 convertibles making the total. The Indy Pace Car replica package added $2,816 to the convertible base price of $43,665. The ZR1, in its final year, hit its pre-set 448-car production limit and added $31,258 on top of the base $36,785 coupe.

Left: After Chevrolet management committed to the body design for 1997, engineering fabricated functional running prototypes that they tested in all weather conditions from summer heat in Australia to winter cold in Michigan's Upper Peninsula. *GM Media Archive*

The Corvette In Culture

Actor Jim Caviezel earned the nomination to drive the Indianapolis 500 pace car on May 26, 2002. Chevrolet gave customers and enthusiasts a sneak peek at the coming 50th Anniversary 2003 color scheme for the Memorial Day race. *GM Media Archive*

As the Corvette matured, its appeal grew larger and stronger. In music, on television, and at the movie theater, the car continued to evolve from sporty transportation to cultural icon, representative not only of how people lived and behaved but also of who they wanted to be and what they wanted from life.

All genres of popular music embraced the Corvette. Country singer George Jones featured a Corvette in his song "The One I Loved Back Then." In it, the owner of a quick-shop market reminisced about how the passenger in a customer's '63 Sting Ray reminded him of one that got away. He meant the passenger, not the car, which became the vehicle for his memories.

In 1983, singer/songwriter Prince released a song on his album *1999*, titled "Little Red Corvette." While there were several automotive metaphors in the lyrics, it had little to do with Chevrolet's sports car. It had much to do with human relations, specifically of the carnal variety. (I'll leave it to the reader to guess as to what, exactly, the "little red Corvette" allegorically refers.) It might not have been about America's beloved sports car, but "Little Red Corvette" was the song that broke Prince on the national music scene and made him one of the most popular singers of the 1980s.

The Corvette also made its mark on television and in movie theaters. In summer 1985, Stephen Cannell produced a 90-minute television pilot titled

"Stingray" for a series he hoped to sell. In the film, a do-gooder named Ray, played by Nick Mancuso, helps a district attorney in exchange for a promise to return the favor sometime in the future. From spring of 1986 through the following spring, the series ran 23 episodes, during which Ray helps people change their lives in exchange for calling on them for their help in the future. The name came from Ray's 1965 black Stingray that he drives throughout the single season. As a tie-in for this show, Monogram Models made a plastic kit of Ray's black Corvette. Shortly after the kit's release, the show was canceled, so Monogram re-released it as Item no. 2724, '65 Corvette Street Machine.

A film called *Wanted* examined the training of assassins. One of them, Angelina Jolie, positions her silver 1986 C4 in such a way that her partner flips his car in order to shoot into the open sunroof of his target's bullet-proof limousine. Few other cars offer the perfect wedge shape to launch the killer's more mundane Mustang mid-1960s notchback coupe.

The Corvette continued to inspire filmmakers into the twenty-first century. The 2009 film *Transformers: Revenge of the Fallen* gave Corvette enthusiasts what they thought was a glimpse of the C7 concept. That turned out not to be the case; instead, a fantastical creation from GM Styling to honor the General Motors 100th, called the Corvette Centennial Design Concept (and then the Corvette Stingray Concept) earned a co-starring role in the film, playing a creature called "Sideswipe." Inspired by Corvette's history from Bill Mitchell's 1959 Stingray racer to the 1963 production coupe, and pulling in cues from later variations on the Corvette theme, the car debuted at the Chicago Auto Show. In mid-2010, rumors placed a roadster version of Sideswipe on the streets of L.A. in close proximity to where a Camaro and other Transformers were fighting to save the world. *Transformers: Dark of the Moon* was released to theaters on June 28, 2011.

Above: Popular actor and talented racer Patrick Dempsey agreed to drive the 2007 Indy 500 pace car at the start of the event. Bowling Green manufactured 500 pace car replicas in Atomic Orange with Ebony black leather seats. *GM Media Archive*

Below: "Sideswipe" was created for the Transformer film series. When the car first appeared on film sets, film groupies wondered if the car hinted at the appearance of Chevrolet's seventh-generation Corvette. *GM Media Archive*

Model year 1996 was the 13th for the C4 and the last under Dave McLellan's influence. Anyone in the United States and most people around the world who followed Corvette rumors knew the C5 was due to arrive as a 1997 model. What many wise buyers recognized was that, traditionally, Chevrolet introduced many of the technical advances the year before the new body appeared. So 1996 was no different.

The LT4 optional engine showed up on order sheets. This redesign of the traditional 350-cubic-inch V-8 developed 330 horsepower at 5,800 rpm. Crane roller rocker arms, new camshafts, and aluminum heads made the engine lighter and stronger. Chevrolet offered it only with the six-speed manual gearbox and only for a single year.

In the absence of the ZR1, Chevrolet created the Grand Sport package, limited to 1,000 coupes or convertibles. The LT4 came standard in this $3,250 package for coupes. The convertible charge was lower: $2,880. The differences accounted for tire sizes and bodywork variations. Admiral Blue paint, a white center stripe, and red slashes over the front fenders differentiated the cars.

For those who missed the Grand Sport, Chevrolet offered a Collector Edition in Sebring Silver for $1,250. The LT4 engine was optional at a $1,450 additional cost. Bowling Green assembled 5,412 of these.

One feature coming to the C5 appeared in 1996, the F45 Selective Real Time Damping. This system evaluated road shock and load inputs 80 to 100 times a second, adjusting individual shock absorbers to conditions nearly instantly. A $1,695 option, Chevrolet delivered 2,896 cars equipped with this new system.

Production settled at 17,167 coupes and 4,369 convertibles, for a total of 21,536 cars. Base prices ranged from $37,225 for the coupe to $45,060 for the convertible. With silver in the Commemorative package specification, it was the most popular color selection for the first time in Corvette sales history.

RAISING THE BAR

The ZR1 and Callaway's Turbo set benchmarks that Dave McLellan and his successor Dave Hill knew they had to match to keep Corvette buyers interested. As early as 1989, they brainstormed engineering methods to make the next Corvette

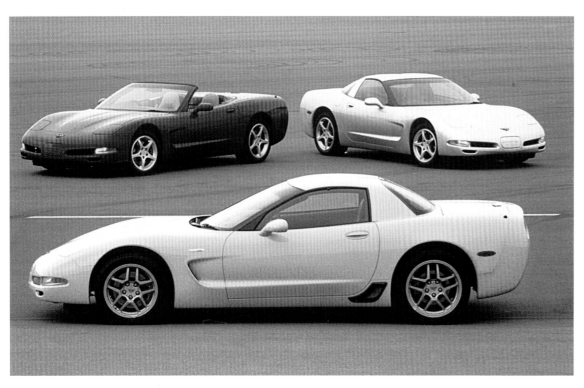

Left: From the earliest days, Corvette planners considered a third body style for the C5; for 1999, the hardtop appeared. It provided greater rigidity and less weight than the glass-window coupe, and offered owners the same trunk as in the convertible bodies. *GM Media Archive*

Below: The convertible, introduced in 1998, gave Corvette owners the first rear trunk compartment they had since 1962. Bowling Green manufactured 11,161 convertibles, 18,078 coupes, and 4,031 of the new hardtops in 1998. *GM Media Archive*

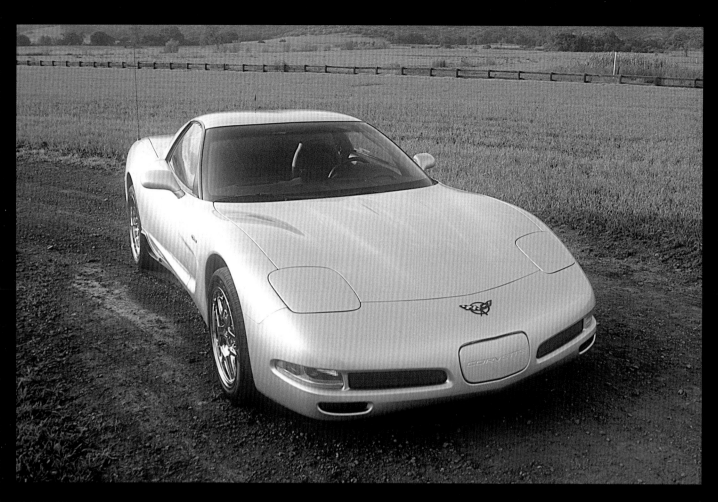

handle and perform better. To them, this meant giving it a stiffer platform on which to operate. During their design process with Lotus for the LT5 engine for the ZR1, McLellan asked them if they would join the thinking process. As McLellan explained in his book *Corvette from the Inside*, Lotus told him they felt the Corvette needed a "torsionally-stiff backbone." Lotus knew this one well, having introduced a compact fiberglass-body Elan with a steel backbone initially as a roadster in 1962. The Elan coupe followed in 1965. According to McLellan, Chevrolet had considered this type of construction in 1964 as the company schemed ideas for the C3, though this never advanced beyond concept stages. The front-engine Elan and the successor midengine Eclat employed a kind of X-shape backbone to allow for front-engine/rear-drive layouts. Lotus's recent Esprit and its next-generation Elan used the steel backbone concept, but the Esprit was rear-midengine/rear-drive and the Elan was to be a front/front configuration. What's more, none of Lotus's cars ever dealt with 400 horsepower. In addition, the backbone concept worked best if the engine and transmission were separated, using something like the Q Corvette transaxle. The manual gearbox was no problem for the engineers, but three-quarters of Corvette buyers chose the automatic and that posed a challenge: GM had no automatic transaxles. McLellan began shopping for ideas and through Jim Minneker in GM powertrain he dovetailed onto a project for four-wheel-drive trucks that paid the development costs for what Corvette needed.

The major budget concerns that Research and Design faced to begin developing a C5 got mired in financial projections, and the car slipped a year and then another before work began. Meanwhile, stylists began sketching what the car might look like. John Schinella's Advanced Concept Center north of Los Angeles won an internal competition, and they moved forward with a design that became the Sting Ray III concept car, a strong inspiration as the C5 took form.

Following a series of marketing research surveys, Chevrolet's general manager Jim Perkins challenged designers and engineers not only to pay attention to Corvette customers but also to design the new C5, as McLellan summarized it, "the first car of the twenty-first century rather than the last car of the twentieth."

Chevrolet's manufacturing process for this new backbone frame fell under Perkins' long view. Hydroforming reshapes metal by using ultra-high-pressure water; in the C5's case this was 10,000 pounds per square inch (psi). The process started with a 15-foot-long, 6-inch-diameter steel tube with 0.08-inch walls already angled into two S-bends. Water

Opposite, top: Chevrolet offered coupe and convertible buyers two red colors for 2000. Torch Red was available at no extra cost, while Magnetic Red Metallic, introduced in 1999, added $500 to the cost of the car. *David Newhardt © 2012*

Opposite, bottom: Chevrolet made its second-generation active-handling standard equipment on 2001 model Corvettes. This added a great deal to driver security in foul weather. *GM Media Archive*

Below: The biggest news for 2001 was Corvette's reintroduction of the Z06 name, attached to a hardtop with the LS6 engine, a 385-horsepower, 346-cubic inch V-8. *GM Media Archive*

" *The first car of the twenty-first century rather than the last car of the twentieth.* **"**

Product Change Versus Model Longevity

Just about one year after Dave McLellan took over the job of Corvette chief engineer from Zora Duntov, he put his experience as an automotive engineer and his education as a Sloan Scholar at Massachusetts Institute of Technology together in a paper he wrote for the Society of Automotive Engineers (SAE). Titled "Corvette: The Buyer and the Car," it appeared in 1977, in time for the organization's national convention.

In his introduction, he pointed out that in 1976 Corvette had enjoyed its most successful year to date, with 46,558 cars manufactured. "The wholesale dollar value of this production exceeded one-third of a billion dollars," he wrote, "approximately [1 percent] of the gross sales of General Motors Corporation."

McLellan had access to market surveys that included Corvette. In 1976, the median age of the Corvette buyer was 30 years, about 10 years younger than the median age of all new-car buyers. In those days, by the time owners reached 50, they had moved on from Corvettes to intermediate or luxury cars that accommodated their family needs and their positions in business or the community. While 80 percent of all car buyers were married, only 57 percent of Corvette buyers were. Men constituted 90 percent of the car's customers. Median income was $23,166 (about $91,500 in 2011) while the figure for all Americans was $12,686 (roughly $50,100 in 2011).

In one survey McLellan cited, buyers explained why they bought the cars they purchased. The three most significant reasons Corvette customers listed were exterior styling, open-road performance, and resale value. The lowest three were fuel economy, price, and quality of workmanship (this was 1976, after all). McLellan was most interested in the disparity between purchase price and resale value.

"The higher ranking given to resale than to price is unusual," he wrote. "This is much more pronounced with Corvette buyers and reflects their willingness to pay a high new car price knowing that their Corvette has a higher than normal resale value."

Information at hand showed McLellan that Corvette buyers had accepted decreasing performance as higher insurance premiums made sports-car "sportiness" a drawback. Automatic transmissions by 1976 had outnumbered the manual gearbox four-to-one. "While the remaining 20 [percent] manual transmissions may represent a 'hard core' of sports car enthusiasts, the urban lifestyles of owners and the traffic demands of commuting seem to favor the automatic. . . .

"Comfort and convenience options have run completely opposite to the trend of optional engines. Power steering, power brakes, and interiors with leather seats have been made standard equipment as a result of this trend. Air conditioning, tilt-telescope steering wheel, power windows, and stereo radios are all in the 80 [percent] penetration range.

"The data shows in the changing character of the car that the Corvette buyer has changed over the years and is today demanding comfort and

Right: General Motors wasted little time in getting its new Corvette into European markets. Here, the GM showroom in Madrid, Spain, put the Corvette up front. *GM Media Archive*

Opposite: As Chevrolet sought to expand interest in the Corvette to European buyers, it took a number of cars to a variety of locations for advertising photo sessions. In Rome, the car draws attention from a cluster of newfound friends. *GM Media Archive*

"A long product life cycle has not hurt demand."

convenience in his Corvette." And was willing to pay for it. The base coupe in 1976 sold for $7,604.85. Adding those "standard equipment" bits to the car for 1977 increased the base price to $8,647.65, and tacking on air conditioning, power windows, tilt wheel, and stereo radio added an additional $1,228 to the sticker total price of $9,875.65 (approximately $37,200 in 2011).

Corvette's "repeat purchase rate" intrigued McLellan. "Corvette owners themselves grow older and leave the Corvette. . . . The repeat purchase rate for Corvettes is consistently below 20 percent. . . ." It related, he recognized, to buyer interest in resale value. But he drew one conclusion that, with 35 years of additional hindsight, may not hold up as well.

Corvette's first two generations had production runs of nine years and five years, respectively. Styling and Engineering proposed new Corvette models every year but sales of the sports car and corporate revenues did not justify applying Alfred Sloan's "annual model change" to the Corvette series. In some ways, this contributed to a self-fulfilling prophecy.

"The low level of repeat buyers," McLellan wrote, "has apparently reduced demand for product change that is characteristic of the passenger-car market where cyclical appearance change gives buyers added incentive to buy a new car. In fact, if the demand for the Corvette begins in the teen years and is not satisfied for 10 years, this may argue [in favor of] a very long product life cycle. This is consistent with the actual life cycle of the Corvette. A long product life cycle has not hurt demand." Or perhaps, when the 1977 model looked very much like the 1979 and 1982 cars, why did one need to update?

The median Corvette buyer's age has risen to 53 years. During the 50th Anniversary celebrations in Bowling Green in 2003, the factory and the museum reported a frenzy of 50-year-old buyers acquiring their first Corvette that year. Since introducing the C5, Corvette and Chevrolet have changed operating procedures, with new models every six or seven years. First-time buyers patiently had waited until middle age to reward themselves with the car they coveted in their teens.

McLellan's conclusion was far-sighted. "The demand is at least initiated by the image that has built up around the car—that of an exciting sports car distinctive in appearance, a car to be seen in and an exciting and sensuous car to drive. These expectations must be realized in the actual car if its market strength is to be sustained. At the same time the long cycle of demand build up and satisfaction and the low repeat purchase rate, would suggest that a long product cycle is acceptable unless repeat purchase is to be encouraged." The C5 and C6 cycles ran eight years each, creating a seemingly happy medium among its customers.

pressure reformed the tube into a rectangle. Using water instead of heat to reshape the steel maintained its strength and stiffness. Every step of the C5 production process inaugurated these levels of complexity and technical advancement.

C5 delivered many changes when it arrived in showrooms in late February 1997. The transaxle lengthened the wheelbase from 96.2 to 104.5 inches, though this added only 1.2 inches to the overall length, up from 178.5 to 179.7. Weight balanced out at 51.4 percent on the front wheels, 48.6 on the rear with the four-speed automatic transmission. Chevrolet throttled back engine displacement incrementally from 350 cubic inches to 346 with a new aluminum alloy block. This LS1 produced 345 horsepower at 5,600 rpm, and 350 foot-pounds of torque at 4,400 rpm. The car's base price was $37,495 and Chevrolet offered a Targa-top hatchback sport coupe only. Production for the abbreviated model year was modest at 9,752 units.

The convertible returned for 1998, adding 11,849 units to the coupe's 19,235 production for a full-year total of 31,084 Corvettes. The coupe base price did not change; the convertible came in at $44,425. The convertible offered a trunk for the first time since 1962. The design standard was that it had to accommodate two sets of golf clubs with the top up or down.

The Z4Z option gave customers an Indy 500 pace car replica in purple with black-and-yellow seats, and yellow wheels. Bowling Green manufactured 1,163 at a $5,039 option price for the automatic and $5,804 for the six-speed manual transmissions. A new Active Handling System, option JL4, a real-time traction control system, applied individual wheel brakes to manage understeer or oversteer.

Chevrolet introduced a hardtop body style for 1999. Product planners initially intended this to be a de-contented "entry-level Corvette," but strong sales through 1997 and 1998 changed that plan. Chevy did limit color selection to four choices instead of eight, and the only seat available was black leather. Starting with the convertible body and

Above: Convertible production slipped slightly from 2001 to 2002 model year. The Bowling Green output dropped from 14,173 to 12,710 of the open cars for 2002. *GM Media Archive*

Left: At the Paris Auto Salon in October 2002, GM showed off its 2002 Le Mans class winning C5-R. Amid a photo gallery of classic Corvette images, it suspended a 1958 Signet Red convertible as an art piece in itself. *GM Media Archive*

Above: Whether on the roads of Georgia or, in this case, Germany, the 2003 50th Anniversary color scheme—red "Xirallic Crystal" paint with Shale leather interior—was an attractive combination. Bowling Green assembled a total of 12,632 commemorative sport coupes and convertibles. *GM Media Archive*

Right: At Chevrolet's massive 50th Anniversary celebration for the Corvette, staged at Bowling Green, Kentucky, and during a weekend at Nashville, Tennessee, children got their own chance to wheel a commemorative convertible around a go-kart circuit. *GM Media Archive*

welding the hardtop roof in place made this the stiffest of all the C5 models. Priced at $38,777, the factory assembled 4,031 hardtops. Hatchback coupes sold for $39,171 and counted for 18,078 units in production, and the convertible, at $45,579, added 11,161 to the factory total of 33,270 cars. A new Head-Up Display, option UV6, adapted fighter aircraft technology to project information onto the inside of the windshield. It added $375 to the price of the car and 19,034 buyers added it to their purchases.

Subtle changes further improved the 2000 model-year Corvettes. Most upgrades were under the hood or inside the skin; however, new wheels were obvious in magnesium or polished aluminum, as well as new standard-equipment painted wheels. Total production inched up to 33,682 units, broken down to 18,113 coupes (at $39,475 base price), 2,090 hardtops (at $38,900), and 13,479 convertibles (at $45,900). Engineers fitted larger front and rear stabilizer bars to the optional performance handling package (Z51). The F45 selective real-time damping received computer program changes to enhance ride and handling.

RETURN OF THE Z06

Model year 2001 brought the new Z06 (in the hardtop body only), a long-awaited return to power and performance. The LS6 version of the 346-cubic-inch V-8 developed 385 horsepower by using higher capacity fuel injectors, new cylinder heads and valve springs, a new camshaft, and titanium exhaust, as well as other engine improvements. Engineers applied some of these to the base engine as well. With these lesser changes, base engine output inched up from 345 to 350 horsepower. Bowling Green manufactured 5,773 of the Z06 hardtops (at $47,500), as well as 14,173 convertibles (selling for $47,000), and 15,681 coupes (base priced at $40,475). Chevrolet made the active handling system standard equipment across the Corvette line. One new option, R8C, caught the imagination of 457 buyers: Corvette Museum Delivery, which also provided the customers a tour of the assembly plant.

The 2002 model year Z06 boasted 405 horsepower, an increase of 20 from 2001. New camshaft profiles and substantially reduced exhaust back-pressure accomplished the gain. Changes to catalytic converters earned the Corvette the "LEV" distinction as a Low Emissions Vehicle. Developments in 2000 and 2001 resulted in subtle weight losses all

Below: Chevrolet created a series of 2004 Le Mans commemorative coupes, Z06 hardtops, and convertibles to celebrate successive class victories at the 24-hour French race. Bowling Green assembled a total of 6,899 of the Le Mans Blue models. *GM Media Archive*

over the car, improving performance and fuel economy. Bowling Green assembled a total of 35,767 cars, of which 14,760 were coupes (starting at $41,450), 12,710 were convertibles (at $47,975), and 8,297 were Z06 hardtops with a base price of $50,150.

Chevrolet celebrated Corvette's 50th anniversary with a week of events at the National Corvette Museum near the Bowling Green Assembly plant. A weekend of concerts and other activities took celebrants down I-65 to Nashville. Cross-country caravans left Seattle, Los Angeles, Chicago, Boston, New York, Miami, Dallas, and other metropolitan areas to motorcade to the anniversary party.

To commemorate the year, the division created a 50th Anniversary package, 1SC, priced at $5,000 for coupes and convertibles (but not the Z06). An Anniversary Red Xirallic Crystal paint covered the exteriors while Chevrolet finished the interiors in Shale, a blend of beige and gray. A new F55 magnetic selective ride control was the standard upgrade for the commemoratives. This system incorporated magnetic liquid-filled shock absorbers that altered fluid flow rate through the system. Sensors monitored road inputs 1,000 times each second.

Corvette served again as Indy 500 pace car using a slightly modified 50th Anniversary coupe. For those wanting a replica, Chevrolet offered the decal package for $495. Bowling Green assembled 12,812 coupes (base priced at $43,895). Of these, 4,085 were anniversary commemoratives. The factory also manufactured 14,022 convertibles (at $50,370), with 7,547 as 50th anniversary models. In the end, Bowling Green turned out 8,637 Z06 coupes, starting at $51,155. Out of the 35,469-unit manufacturing run, 787 buyers chose to pick up their cars at the National Corvette Museum.

Following their first-class victory at Le Mans in 2001, Corvette C5.R models continued to rack up wins at a variety of venues, including again at Le Mans in 2002. For 2004, Chevrolet offered a Le Mans commemorative version of Corvette coupes, convertibles, and Z06 hardtop. Painted Le Mans Blue, Bowling Green assembled 6,899 of these commemoratives, divided nearly equally between the three body styles. The front deck lid of the Z06 was carbon fiber, the first use of the material for a regular production vehicle manufactured in North America. Coupes and convertibles got standard fiberglass hoods.

In all, Chevrolet manufactured 34,064 Corvettes for 2004. Of these, Bowling Green assembled 16,165 of the $44,535 coupes, 12,216 of the $51,535 convertibles, and 5,683 of the $52,385 hardtop Z06s. The Le Mans commemorative package added $4,355 to the price of the Z06 but $3,700 to the sticker on the coupe and convertible.

Dave McLellan

Enthusiasts who liked the 1978 Corvette must thank Dave McLellan. That was the first one on which he had direct influence. Those who liked the C4 introduced for 1984 should thank him again. Insiders suggest it reflected his personality most accurately.

McLellan was born in Michigan's upper peninsula in 1936, though soon after that his family relocated to Detroit. He graduated in mechanical engineering from Wayne State University in 1959 and joined GM at the Milford Proving Ground almost immediately. He stayed there for nearly a decade while he earned his engineering master's at Wayne. After a few years in Chevrolet division, he took another educational break, this time as a Sloan Fellow at Massachusetts Institute of Technology from 1973 to 1974. This exposed him to business, engineering, manufacturing, and problem-solving theories and experiences from auto industries around the world.

On his return to Chevrolet in 1974, he received his first Corvette assignment under Zora Duntov. Six months later, Duntov retired and McLellan became chief engineer. His and Duntov's timing were perfect: McLellan arrived when the Mitchell/Duntov-favored midengine Corvette (in the shape of the Aerovette) nearly was through design. McLellan talked to enthusiasts, owners, and customers who had looked at the Corvette but bought something else. He learned that the midengine car was an answer to a question only Mitchell and Duntov were asking.

His time as a Sloan Fellow taught him to see the Corvette in a world context, one faithful to American enthusiast ideals, but also useful and appealing to a broader market. With a stiff new frame enhanced by the capabilities of high-performance tires, McLellan's engineers recommitted to glass-fiber bodies and fully committed to supporting racing from production classes to a GT prototype with a Corvette engine right behind the driver. One of his more courageous moves was sharing technology with Reeves Callaway, who went on to develop his Twin Turbo models in advance of Corvette's own LT5/ZR1 introduction. He knew his customers wanted to get back their "bragging rights" about Corvette performance. "Competitors," he explained, "only make you stronger!"

With plenty of ideas and energy inside him, McLellan accepted early retirement from General Motors at age 55 in 1992.

In a final note on the C5, while Dave McLellan led its invention and development, Dave Hill managed its completion and introduction, in the process improving quality and encouraging the racing programs that took the car to Le Mans. As the first of the C6s appeared, cars Hill helped invent, he retired, in October 2005. He helped in the selection of his successor Tom Wallace.

With the C5 solidly profitable, Chevrolet committed to a next-generation model. The goal was a 2003 model-year launch during the 50th anniversary. But world politics changed everything on September 11, 2001, throwing many plans into chaos. Development was underway. While Hill and his engineers had introduced a steady stream of improvements and updates, "the fifth-generation Corvette had all these little things that could not be fixed without a redesign" Hill told author Phil Berg for Berg's history of the C6. "I would say we started passing notes back and forth in 1999."

Tom Peters, styling chief for the C6, remembered beginning to make sketches in late 1999. The goal of his team was to take the stylish appearance of the C5 and make it purposeful for the C6. One purpose was a higher top speed capability, resulting in nearly a thousand hours of wind tunnel time to develop a Cd of 0.28. To achieve that number, stylists exposed the headlights for the first time since 1962.

Engineers continued the C5's hydroformed frame side rails. Dimensions changed. The wheelbase grew from 104.5 inches to 105.7. Despite this, overall length shrunk by 5.1 inches, from 179.7 to 174.6 inches. This pushed the wheels closer to the corners, improving balance and handling.

Below: By the 2004 model year, these sixth-generation Corvette sketches had become near-reality. The new design represented an evolution from fifth-generation models. *GM Media Archive*

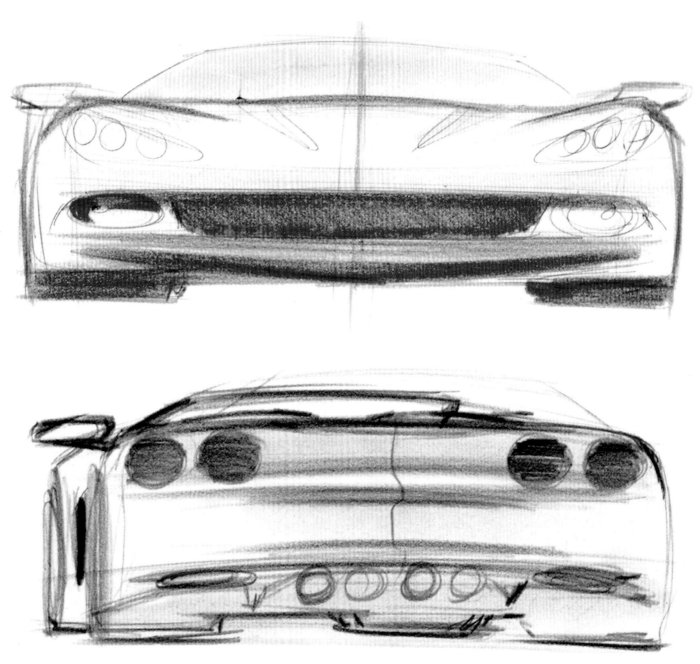

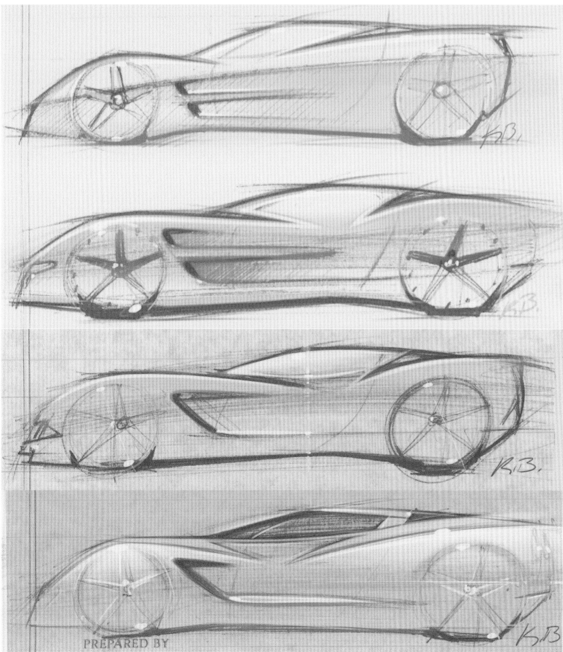

Above: The lineage and evolution from the 2004 fifth-generation Corvette to the 2005 sixth-generation car was easy to follow. While engineers added 1.2 inches to the wheelbase, they shortened the car 5.1 inches in overall length. *GM Media Archive*

Left: A series of side-elevation concepts experimented with side coves and where front and rear fender arcs met in the doors. The finished product took a little from each of these ideas. *GM Media Archive*

Hill's engineering group set the Z06's 405-horsepower output as the standard output for the new C6. They wanted the identical fuel economy that C5 provided C6 customers. They toyed with simply installing the C5's 405-horsepower LS6, but they reasoned that its camshaft was a little too aggressive for idling in traffic on the way to the market. The torque curve was great for open roads or track days, but something more even-tempered became their goal. The new LS2 delivered 400 horsepower at 6,000 rpm and 400 foot-pounds of torque at 4,400 rpm through a number of means, including bumping displacement from 346 to 364 cubic inches. The updated Tremec six-speed manual transmission introduced new synchronizer technology that let engineers shorten the gearshift lever and its travel. Shifting got faster and became more precise.

BETTER CAR, LOWER PRICE

Despite the improvements—greater horsepower, lighter weight, better handling and steering performance—Corvette's C6 team brought the 2005 coupe in for a base price $290 below the 2004 C5: $44,245 for the new model compared to $44,535 for its predecessor. Reflecting its great value, customers pulled 26,728 of them out of Bowling Green assembly. The price of the convertible went up slightly, from $51,535 to $52,245, and the factory manufactured 10,644 of these. There was no hardtop version of the new car; total production settled at 37,372, up nearly 10 percent from the previous year, with either six-speed manual or four-speed automatic included in the price, along with leather seats, active handling, traction control, keyless entry and start features, and a stereo CD with MP3 capability.

For 2006, prices inched up and production slipped back. Base coupes went for $44,600 and the plant assembled 16,598; convertibles sold for $52,335 and 11,151 went out of Bowling Green's doors. A new six-speed automatic transmission offered paddle shift, a $1,250 option that 19,094 buyers selected. If that wasn't enough to get pulse rates up, Chevrolet brought back the Z06, providing customers 505 horsepower out of a new 427-cubic-inch V-8. The car was capable of acceleration from 0 to 60 miles per hour in 3.7 seconds. Cycling champion Lance Armstrong drove a red-white-and-blue Z06 pace car at the Indianapolis 500. The Z06 carried a base price of $65,800, and the factory assembled 6,272.

Opposite, top: With the sixth-generation coupe and convertible out the door, designers and modelers put their finishing touches on the prototype Z06 body in the Design Center. Chevrolet discontinued the C5 hardtop body so high-performance models appeared only as fastback coupes. *GM Media Archive*

Opposite, bottom: During the production run of fifth-generation Corvettes, GM decided not to export Z06 models outside the United States. That changed with the introduction of the 2006 Z06, as seen by this Velocity Yellow coupe with license tags from Dubai. *GM Media Archive*

Below: At the 2006 Bologna, Italy, motor show, Italian visitors got their first view of the new Z06 in coupe form. In all, Bowling Green assembled 6,272 of the Z06 models for consumption in GM's growing worldwide markets. *GM Media Archive*

Models proliferated, prices jumped, and so did production for 2007. An Atomic Orange Indy 500 Pace car convertible replica, limited to 500 copies, sold for $66,995. Actor/racer Patrick Dempsey fulfilled pace car driving duties as Corvette enjoyed the first back-to-back selection. Racing prominence was a theme Chevrolet explored, celebrating international victories with a Ron Fellows Z06 Special Edition. This Arctic White coupe commemorated Corvette's successes in the American Le Mans Series (ALMS). Limited to 399 copies, the car hit order books at $77,500.

These two commemoratives made base coupes and convertibles seem a bargain and customers again recognized a good deal when they saw it. Bowling Green assembled 21,484 base coupes at $44,995 and 10,418 base convertibles at $52,910. Base cars came with the six-speed manual while the six-speed paddle-shift automatic remained an option at $1,250.

For 2008, the model lineup again counted six variations: coupe, convertible, Indy 500 Pace coupe, Pace convertible, Z06, and a new 427 Limited Edition. Displacement of the base model engine grew from 364 to 376 cubic inches, taking horsepower up from 400 to 430. An optional Dual Mode Exhaust System boosted output by another 6 horsepower using vacuum-operated outlet valves to deliver a more enthusiastic sound. Understandably, 13,454 roared out of the Bowling Green factory after buyers paid the $1,195 premium. Base coupes (19,796 manufactured) went for $45,995; convertibles (all 7,283 of them) listed for $54,335. Indy commemoratives jumped to $59,090 for the 234 coupes assembled, and $68,190 for the 266 convertibles. The 7,226 examples of the Z06 were listed for $71,000 and the "427 Limited Edition," set at 505 copies, one for each horsepower produced, sold for $84,195 and featured Bowling Green assembly plant manager Will Cooksey's autograph on each car.

In 2009, Corvette verged on becoming its own division with nine models vying for buyer attention. From the base Corvette coupe, at $47,895, up to the record-price-setting ZR1 coupe at $103,300, Chevrolet had taken early chairman Alfred Sloan's motto to heart: Offer a Corvette for every purse and purpose.

Below: Corvette designers introduced Atomic Orange as a $750 option for the 2007 model year. Bowling Green assembled 3,790 coupes and convertibles in the new color, one that replaced Sunset Orange, the least popular color choice from 2006. *GM Media Archive*

Opposite, top: The 2007 Ron Fellows American Le Mans Series (ALMS) GT1 Z06 commemorative represented a new step for Corvette marketing. While it honored ALMS racer Fellows, it also was Corvette's first signed-edition automobile and was limited to 399 examples.
GM Media Archive

Opposite, bottom: The Design Center's mock up for the 2009 ZR1 appeared for design review in mid-2006 as a nearly complete project. It debuted as the highest-priced production model General Motors ever had introduced, at $103,300.
GM Media Archive

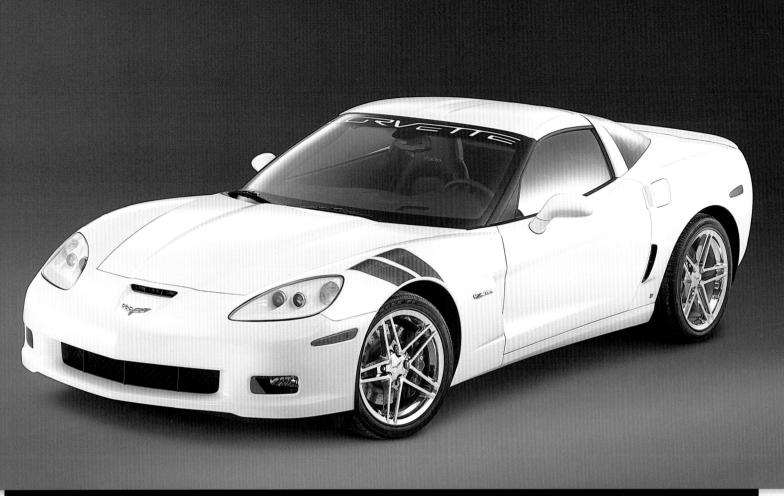

MOST POWERFUL CORVETTE EVER

The purpose of the new ZR1 simply was to put every other automaker on notice. With its Root-type supercharger, the 427-cubic-inch V-8 beneath the see-through hood developed 638 horsepower. No vehicle General Motors ever had sold offered more. Fittingly, the first production model, auctioned for charity, went for $1 million. The buyer, Dave Ressler, a longtime Chevrolet dealer and Corvette collector, paid the generous premium on top of its already considerable base price. It was the only one with its vehicle identification number sequence and the only 2009 Corvette painted Le Mans Blue. The sale price of every ZR1 included time at a high-performance driving school.

Because of the economic crash of 2009, and despite this proliferation of choices, production barely reached half of 2008 numbers. Just 16,956 cars moved out of the Bowling Green assembly. Of those, 1,415 were the new ZR1, 3,326 were base convertibles, 3,386 were Z06 models, 8,632 were base coupes, and an interesting assortment of cars labeled GT1 Championship Edition coupes and convertibles, and Competition Sport Special Edition coupes and Z06s added another 152 cars to production totals. Chevrolet painted the GT1 commemoratives either in black or yellow to match the ALMS class champions racing livery. Competition sport coupes were white or black with gray stripes (although 55 cars assembled as Z06 versions were silver or black).

Corvette's 2010 model-year performance demonstrated the continued fragility of the economy. Bowling Green production reached only 12,194, a figure not seen on assembly totals since the 1997 abbreviated manufacturing year where only 9,752 coupes were built. Before that, historians looked back to 1961 for a similarly small output and in those days, the production of 10,939 cars provided the corporation with encouragement.

Chevrolet moved ahead with planned new variations, reintroducing the Grand Sport last seen in 1996. Equipped with the same LS3 430-horsepower engine and transmission packages available in base coupes and convertibles, the GS gave buyers better suspension, brakes, wheels and tires, the dry-sump engine lubrication system from the ZR1, and slightly different bodywork from base cars. The 3,054 base coupes sold for $49,880; the 1,003 base convertibles

Above: In production, designers and engineers cleaned up excessive styling cues. The front deck lid with its power bulge offered a transparent cover to tantalize observers with the power under the hood. *GM Media Archive*

Opposite, top: Pratt and Miller got its hand in limited-production models with the 2009 C6RS model based on the production Corvette Z06 but covered entirely in carbon fiber. Their supercharged 427-cubic-inch V-8 developed 750 horsepower, and the package cost $178,500 on top of the Z06. *GM Media Archive*

Opposite, bottom: With 638 horsepower available, it was impossible to resist seeing what the 376-cubic-inch engine could do. Brembo 15.5-inch disc brakes and Michelin Pilot Sport 2 tires helped keep this potential on the ground and in control. *GM Media Archive*

Above: "Stingray" was a design center concept that appeared in 2009. It explored a number of styling and appearance features that designers were interested in for the seventh-generation Corvette. *GM Media Archive*

Right: Base coupe and convertible models—as well as the returning Grand Sport versions—ran with a standard 430-horsepower 376-cubic-inch V-8. Corvette included "Launch Control" with all six-speed manual transmissions. *GM Media Archive*

were listed at $54,530. Published price of the 3,707 Grand Sport coupes was $55,720, while the 2,335 Grand Sport convertibles went for $59,530. The 505-horsepower Z06 sold at $75,235 (518 assembled), and the 1,577 copies of the ZR1 commanded $107,830.

For manual transmission drivers, the exciting change in their gearbox was the addition of "launch control." This computer-monitored system allowed the driver to push the gas pedal to the floor and release the clutch while the computer varied torque 100 times per second to ensure maximum traction and acceleration.

In some sectors the economy showed signs of recovering as the 2011 model year rolled around. Chevrolet kept the Grand Sport models in the Corvette lineup and added a Z06 Carbon limited edition so the lineup stepped back up to seven models. The division priced the base coupe at $49,900, and the convertible went for $54,550. Grand Sport coupes went for $55,740, and convertibles were listed at $59,950. The normal Z06 was priced at $75,255, while the Carbon edition went for $90,960. Again, the ZR1 topped the lists at $110,750.

In an effort to personalize the Z06 and ZR1 models and further engage their customers, Chevrolet introduced RPO PBC. For an additional $5,800, this option allowed buyers to assist in assembling the engine that went in their car at the Performance Build Center in Wixom, Michigan.

Below: Torch Red paint returned to the 2010 model year color lineup after being absent since 2004. It was a no-extra-cost color option. *GM Media Archive*

Above: **The Grand Sport returned to Corvette models as a 2010. Both convertible and coupe versions came with the base 430-horsepower 376-cubic-inch engine as standard equipment.** *David Newhardt © 2012*

Opposite: **Grand Sports used the Corvette "wide body" along with wider wheels and tires. Manual transmission versions mounted the battery in the rear and employed a dry-sump oil-lubrication system.** *David Newhardt © 2012*

If Corvette's past is any predictor of its future, model year 2012 meant that Chevrolet introduced another significant commemorative package to celebrate what customers, enthusiasts, observers, and journalists expected was the last year of the C6. In past generations, GM had let the Corvette introductions slip behind as the economy affected overall corporate health. The C7's final development and testing years, 2009 and 2010, fell under the worst economic recession since the 1930s. Management changed, the federal government stepped in and then back out. Yet hope remained: During the fifth and sixth generations, the Corvette transitioned from GM's stepchild to its corporation pacesetter with 200-mile-per-hour top speeds, $100,000-plus price tags, and 638-horsepower V-8s. Design engineers at sports car companies in Europe complimented the car, regularly benchmarking it against their own products. They were impressed by its value per dollar and performance per pound.

Recalling the darkest days during the lifespan of the C3, the engineering, design, and materials technologies improved greatly. Couple this with the motivation of the small group of dedicated individuals responsible for the Corvette. They remained devoted and energized. No one doubted the seventh-generation Corvette would be better. But no one outside had guessed just how much better it became.

Open-top Power Returned and Honored

Z06, ZR1, LS7, GT1. The 2013 Corvette 427 Convertible Collector Edition had so many significant initials in its DNA origin codes that it was as complicated and sublime as the human body. It certainly was as desirable—think back to the glory days of 1969, 1970, when the L88 convertible was the most outrageous, quickest, rarest open car in the world. Factory specs suggested it had 425 horsepower. The 2013 Collector convertible came from Bowling Green with 505 horsepower from the 427 CID LS7 from the Z06 (co-developed with the Le Mans class-winning GT1 engine) as its only power plant and, similar to the Z06, it only was available with the manual 6-speed gear box.

Carbon fiber panels—hood, fenders, and floor—helped hold overall weight to 3,355 pounds. This gave the convertible a power-to-weight ratio of 1 hp to 6.64 pounds of car. These specs beat Porsche's Turbo S Cabriolet, the performance standard setter at 1:6.90. Writers joked that the Porsche could halt the rotation of the earth; the 2013 427 Convertible had the potential to reverse it.

Chevrolet division offered the 427 convertible and all 2013 models with a 60th Anniversary Package that gave buyers the Artic White exterior and a Blue Diamond leather interior with suede accents. Anniversary Convertibles had a blue cloth top. Corvette engineers and stylists added the ZR1-style rear spoiler, special badges, gray-pained brake calipers, and other graphics. C6 production for its final year came to 13,466 cars (7,505 coupes, 5,008 convertibles, 471 Z06s, and 482 ZR1s). Total C6 production between 2005 and 2013 reached 215,123 cars. After four strong years, production tumbled because of the recession.

All GM Media Archive

4 RACING

BEATING THE WORLD'S BEST

Above: After finishing a few laps around the Indianapolis track, Mauri Rose pulls into the garage area to show off the 1953 Corvette. Rose joined GM as an engineer when he stopped racing in 1951.
GM Media Archive

Opposite: GM Engineer Mauri Rose takes an early production 1953 convertible back to his old haunts at the Indianapolis Motor Speedway. He won the 500-mile race three times: in 1941, 1947, and 1948.
GM Media Archive

Briggs Cunningham thought any American-made sports car should race, and he challenged Harley Earl to build one that was up to the task. General Curtis LeMay agreed with Cunningham, and he already had made his Air Force bases available as suitable venues for speed events. What Harley Earl made of all this, beyond creating the Corvette, is open to conjecture, but what Zora Arkus-Duntov believed was that Earl's Corvette *should* race. And it was his goal to make that happen.

Competition was not in the Corvette's initial DNA (although it was, ironically, in Harley Earl's; his son Jerry was an avid racer). Engineers such as Duntov, Mauri Rose, and Russ Sanders, along with outsiders such John Fitch, surgically added to its racing capabilities later. There were halting first steps, such as ghost reports of 1954 Corvettes racing on dirt as part of a NASCAR effort to broaden their entry lists and their audiences.

For certain, Chicago speed shop owner Bill von Esser and his partner and buddy Ernie Pultz entered a 1954 convertible in the Carrera Panamericana. But speed along suburban drag strips or Chicago's Lake Shore Drive didn't prepare von Esser and Pultz for the potholes, rocks, and bad gas of the great Mexican road race. The car failed to complete the first leg when a connecting rod failed in its six-cylinder Blue Flame engine.

Duntov waited impatiently for the V-8 and manual transmission he knew was coming. With it, he launched a campaign to publicize and legitimize the car, starting with speed trials at Daytona Beach. Whatever was the impression the Corvette had made on sports car enthusiasts in its first two years, Duntov believed that all could be changed if he demonstrated that it was as fast as the cars that traditionalists respected. With a variety of modifications, he set out to show "his" Corvette could reach 150 miles per hour. A driving team comprised of Le Mans veteran John Fitch, woman stunt flier

Betty Skelton, and Duntov took two 1956 pre-production convertibles and a third heavily revised open car to Florida in January 1956. When they quit, Skelton had set a record in the Ladies Sports Car Class at 137.77 miles per hour; Fitch had done the same in the Production Class at 145.54; and Duntov had reached 150.58 miles per hour. This was news that Chevrolet waited to release until the public launch of the 1956 production models at the New York Auto Show.

Ford's Thunderbird had raced the Corvette into international competition. Fred Scherer and Don Davis campaigned a T-Bird in the 1955 12 Hours of Sebring, finishing the race in 37th place out of the 48 cars that took the checkered flag. These privateers had gutted their car, and they launched a factory-supported rivalry. On the beach in 1956, however, Chuck Daigh, while winning his class in a T-Bird, went no faster than 136 miles per hour.

SEBRING RACER

Flush with naïve confidence, Chevrolet division chief Ed Cole sent a four-car racing team back to Florida for the 12 Hours of Sebring in March. Duntov balked at the idea; he knew brief top speed runs on a beach did not mean the cars could survive 12 hours of racing on a tattered airport just five weeks later. Undeterred, Cole hired Fitch to run the effort and lead the team, and Cole supported him when one of their greatest challenges came from the rules themselves. Any parts Fitch or his engineers put on the car had to be available over the counter to outsiders for these cars to remain "production" class entries. Cole quickly created a new "option," the SR model that stood for Sebring Racer. They modified one "prototype" with an engine bored out to 307 cubic inches. They mated this to a German-made four-speed transmission. By the end of 12 hours, Fitch and his co-driver, Walt Hansgen, had struggled into a ninth place overall finish that put them first in the Sports 8000 class. Two of their production cars failed to finish, but the team's fourth car came in 15th overall. This accomplishment earned Corvette the Sebring Team Prize, a moral victory against the likes of Ferrari and Jaguar.

A season of actual wins followed quickly. A Duntov-prepared car arrived at Pebble Beach, California, in April for Walt Hansgen to race the annual meet there. As a professional, Hansgen couldn't get compete in this SCCA amateur race, so his friend Dr. Dick Thompson, a soft-spoken understated dentist from Washington, DC, climbed into the car and ran

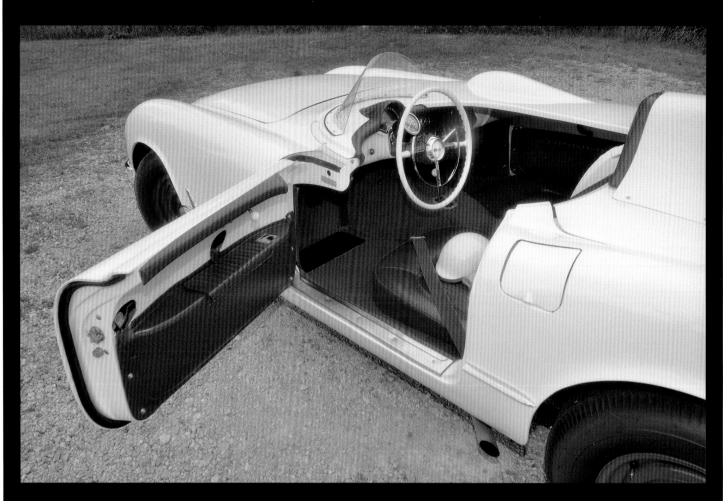

away from Jaguar XK120s and Mercedes-Benz 300SLs until the Corvette's brakes failed. From then on, he simply threw the car sideways to scrub off speed in the turns and he finished second overall with another class win. With cars prepared for Thompson on the East and the West Coasts, the Flying Dentist won the 1956 SCCA C-Production championship for Corvette. It was the first of five he captured.

Harley Earl stepped back into the picture, telling his "fellahs" he wanted to put a Corvette engine in a D-Type Jaguar chassis and body shell he'd acquired from a friend. He intended to provoke management and it worked. Instead of the tired-and-trashed Jaguar, Earl and Duntov bought and brought a new Mercedes-Benz 300SL into a secret styling studio. There, designers and engineers removed the body and duplicated the tube-frame chassis, adjusting it to fit Corvette racing gear. Bob Cumberford and Tony Lapine created the lines of the completed car named the Corvette SS. Authorized to assemble one car, Duntov cleverly ordered parts sufficient to make several; one of them Earl's staff finished in blue-painted magnesium and the other was a hurriedly finished working prototype they clad in fiberglass. Destined for Sebring 1957, the SS got nowhere near enough development time. The beautifully finished racer retired after only 23 laps. (However, another John Fitch "team" entry with Dick Thompson and Gaston Andre sharing driving duties in a 1957 "production" convertible won the Grand Touring 5000 class, finishing 12th overall.)

Cole, who got a ride in the blue SS before the race, was an enthusiast. He hinted to reporters that Chevrolet might take a team of SS cars to Le Mans three months later; however, the race showed him, Duntov, and Fitch that this might be a big challenge. The battle became impossible on June 7, two weeks before the 24 hours race.

A tragic crash at Le Mans in 1955 had killed a driver and 83 spectators and injured 120 more. It was motorsports' darkest moment, and organizations such as the American Automobile Manufacturers Association (AAMA) and the

Above: **With his target in mind, Zora Duntov begins the first of his two-way runs at Ormond Beach, near Daytona, Florida. His mule, cleaned up and repainted after its Arizona sessions, averaged 150.583 over two directions.** *GM Media Archive*

Opposite, top: **Because open cockpits allowed air turbulence that could slow a car, Duntov adopted another Jaguar idea for a hard tonneau to cover the passenger area. The hump accommodated the radio speaker in the otherwise stock dashboard.** *Randy Leffingwell © 2012*

Opposite, bottom: **GM engineering initially resisted Duntov's request to build a new camshaft. Once the cam was in, Zora ran it at GM's Arizona proving ground and set a new record of 163 miles per hour. Later at Daytona Beach, the car averaged 150.583 miles per hour.** *Randy Leffingwell © 2012*

CERV I

Zora Duntov learned from past experience. Everyone who had driven the handsome SS Corvette magnesium race car complained about engine heat scorching their feet and legs. To avoid this risk, Duntov considered putting the engine behind the driver. Chevrolet had introduced its Corvair for the 1959 model year, with plans to enhance its performance and its image into something more sporty.

After Maurice Olley retired as head of GM Research and Development, Robert Schilling replaced him. In January 1959, he imported Duntov to solve vexing chassis and handling problems, and he brought in Frank Winchell to deal with powertrain and transmission issues. Winchell supervised development of the Corvair's transaxle, and Schilling assigned both men to create a transaxle for a new front-engined car code named the Q.

Duntov looked at every project and saw applicability to his beloved Corvette. A transaxle fit comfortably in his imagination.

In his time away from Schilling, he worked with his own senior engineers, Harold Krieger and Walt Zetye, to mate a V-8 engine to the

Right, top: In late 1960, after Duntov debuted the CERV I at Riverside International Raceway in California, he took the car to Daytona Speedway in Florida to try to beat Bill France's challenge to lap the track at 180 miles per hour. Duntov didn't reach his goal. *GM Media Archive*

Right, bottom: In September 1960, Zora Duntov got his "hillclimber" to Pikes Peak. But early snows had closed the summit, so Duntov only could run segments, giving him times he couldn't compare to past performances. *GM Media Archive*

Opposite, top: Duntov ran laps around the banked speedway at Daytona Beach, Florida, but was unable to meet his 180-mile-per-hour target. He took CERV I back to Michigan and continued working on it for another two years. *GM Media Archive*

Opposite, bottom: Duntov converses with another engineer at the Milford engineering center. In March 1964, with this new nose and a larger more powerful engine behind his seat, Duntov lapped the 4.5-mile Milford banked circle at 206 miles per hour. *GM Media Archive*

prototype transaxle. The three men packaged it in a vehicle that, not accidentally, bore strong resemblance to an Indianapolis 500 racer, even to its 96-inch wheelbase, 56-inch body width, and 172-inch overall length. Stylists Larry Shinoda and Tony Lapine created a minimalist cigar shape that encased the tube frame and running gear.

When it all was assembled with an experimental 283-cubic-inch alloy block with aluminum cylinder heads, the engine put out 353 horsepower and the car weighed just 1,450 pounds. Duntov carried over the front suspension concept he'd created for the SS, but he developed a fully independent rear using the half-shafts as upper links in a multi-link configuration. This idea, with some changes, went into production as the independent rear suspension for the 1963 Sting Ray.

Duntov used the car for wheel and tire development work, but he had another goal. In 1961, Bill France offered a $10,000 "reward" to the first vehicle that could lap his banked Daytona Speedway at 180 miles per hour. Duntov already had seen his car run 170 with Dan Gurney and Stirling Moss at the wheel. He took the car to Daytona but could not meet France's target. Through 1962, he experimented with superchargers and then turbochargers, ultimately raising output to 500 horsepower. Shinoda and Lapine refined their shape with the help of Duntov's engineers. The 283 V-8 became a 377. Hilborn fuel injection sat on top of a new cross-ram intake manifold. In March 1964, Duntov took the car to the GM proving ground at Milford, Michigan. France's offer no longer mattered to him. Curiosity was his driving force. And when he finished his drive, he had lapped Milford's five-lane wide banked 4.5-mile circle at 206 miles per hour.

National Safety Council seized on it to condemn speed events as marketing tools for automobile sales. GM president Jack Gordon served on the board and he may have helped delay the inevitable, but in two years it percolated through the AAMA board and emerged in the form of a recommendation that its members "Not participate or engage in any public contest, competitive event, or test of passenger cars involving or suggesting racing or speed. . . ." Much the way the 18th Amendment to the Constitution failed to end alcohol consumption, the AAMA recommendation merely moved racing support from something provided openly through the front doors to activities done surreptitiously through rear loading docks.

END OF FACTORY RACING

The effect on the SS project, however, was terminal. The blue racer and the white fiberglass mule retired to a warehouse. Through a rear door, Bill Mitchell, still number two to Harley Earl at this point, asked Ed Cole if he could buy one of the SS cars. Mitchell told interviewer Dave Crippen in 1984 that Cole responded, "Well, I'll sell it to you for $500." Mitchell explained to Crippen that, "It was [worth] $500,000—tubular frame, de Dion suspension, inboard brakes, everything!"

Mitchell moved the chassis down to the "hammer room," a secret workshop a group of conspiratorial designers occupied, and he asked Larry Shinoda to adapt the shapes Chuck Pohlmann and Peter Brock had developed for a new convertible and coupe, and make it into a race car. He named the sleek body the Stingray. Then soon after its debut at Marlborough in Maryland, Mitchell heard from GM president Jack Gordon again.

"I was on the engineering policy committee…," Mitchell told Crippen. "So in that meeting, Gordon said, 'I thought everybody knew we were out of racing.' After the meeting I said, 'Jack, were you talking about me?' He said, 'You're damn right I was.' I said, 'Do I have to quit?' He said, 'You've got to quit right now!' And it just made me feel terrible."

Mitchell drafted a letter to Gordon, explaining his background with racing and the effect he believed his car could have on sales. Gordon acquiesced but ordered Mitchell to get it off GM property and off the books, to pay all expenses himself, a strategy Mitchell willingly followed. Shinoda and Tony Lapine became part of the pit crew and John Fitch

> **"** So in that meeting, Gordon said, 'I thought everybody knew we were out of racing.' After the meeting I said, 'Jack, were you talking about me?' He said, 'You're damn right I was.' **"**

Opposite, top: While Zora Duntov was in Arizona developing his Daytona record car, engineer/racer Mauri Rose and veteran competitor John Fitch worked in Sebring, Florida, at Ed Cole's direction to create a set of endurance racers to last 12 hours. In 1956, this SR-2 finished ninth overall, winning its class. *Randy Leffingwell © 2012*

Opposite, bottom: At Sebring in 1957, Corvette no. 4 finished 12th overall, first in class. The SR-2 behind it, no. 2, updated since its introduction in 1956, finished 16th, but an edict from GM chairman Frederick Donner soon outlawed racing by any GM division. *GM Media Archive*

Left: Harley Earl put his own name behind this project, ensuring it plenty of manpower. His purpose-built 1957 Corvette racer, the SS, comes to life in a basement workshop in the Styling center. *GM Media Archive*

Above: The SS mule, formed in fiberglass, awaits its moment on the wind tunnel stage. While rear lift was a problem, wind tunnel tests did not indicate how seriously engine heat affected the drivers.
GM Media Archive

drove the car, painted red, as number 8 through 1959. For 1960, Dick Thompson stepped in; the Stingray raced in silver wearing number 11 or 111, depending on the event. Despite poor brakes and virtually pure production parts, Thompson won a national championship in the car. They often competed alongside more normal-looking Corvettes entered by successful racers such as Dave MacDonald and Bob Bondurant on the West Coast. Back east they raced Jim Jeffords and his successful "Purple People Eater," named after a popular song at the time and sponsored by Chicago's Nickey Chevrolet, who won B-production championships in 1958 and 1959.

Among privateers, Bill Fritts and Chuck Hall brought home their 1960 Corvette first in the Grand Touring 5000 class at Sebring, racing against a number of Ferrari and Porsche entries. As Thompson campaigned Mitchell's Stingray, Briggs Cunningham finally got his chance to take an American-made sports car to race at Le Mans. Together with Lloyd "Lucky" Casner, the two entrants took four race-prepared 1960 hardtops to France. As is typical of Le Mans, drama always accompanies speed in the 24-hour race. After a mechanic failed to close John Fitch's radiator cap completely, the engine began to overheat, threatening their finish. (One Cunningham car had failed by this time, the other expired as the third car struggled for survival.) Le Mans rules required any car finishing the race to complete a prescribed number of laps in its last hour without taking on additional oil or water. A quick-thinking mechanic raided Cunningham's luxurious camper parked behind the pit boxes and packed Fitch's engine compartment with ice. After each lap run at the minimum pace, the car pitted for more ice, drawing huge cheers of support from the crowd. By the end of 24 hours, Fitch and co-driver Bob Grossman, who had been as high as third overall during the night ahead of a fleet of Ferraris and Aston Martins, eased the steaming number 3 across the finish line in eighth place, first in Grand Touring 5000. It was Corvette's first international class win.

Above: On a cold January day, the fiberglass SS mule circulates GM's test track as engineers monitor instruments. They already had opened a large cooling vent in the front deck lid. *GM Media Archive*

Left: Chevrolet chief Ed Cole became excited enough about the SS that he proposed taking a team of them to the 24-hour race in Le Mans, France. Engineers spent the day after Christmas 1956 testing a variety of auxiliary lights for the SS in an overnight event. *GM Media Archive*

TOTAL DOMINANCE

Through the 1960s, Corvettes owned B-production racing across the United States. Pennsylvanian Don Yenko joined Texan Delmo Johnson with wins along the eastern and southern coasts, while west of the Rocky Mountains, MacDonald and Bondurant traded victories with Doug Hooper, Dick Guldstrand, Bill Krause, Tony Settember, and Joe Freitas.

On drag strips around the nation, racers found that similar preparation to their road course colleagues gave them the fastest time through the traps. The National Hot Rod Association (NHRA) established several sports production racing categories in 1960. "Sports Cars Domestic" pitted Corvettes against Thunderbirds, and the Imported class invited Porsches, Volkswagens, and others to try their luck and skills. These were part of a group of five Sports Production classes based on a ratio of advertised horsepower-to-shipping weight. Modified sports production classes permitted racers to exchange engines, fit superchargers, and make more radical changes. Among the most successful of these was Californian "Big John" Mazmanian, whose supercharged C-Modified gasoline-fueled hardtop was capable of 0-to-60 miles-per-hour acceleration in 4.25 seconds and quarter-mile times of 11.1 seconds at 129.93 miles per hour.

Hooper, Bondurant, MacDonald, and Jerry Grant took delivery of Corvette's first real factory-produced race car, the 1963 Sting Ray Z06, in October 1962. This was just in time for a competition debut at the Los Angeles Times Grand Prix staged at Riverside International Raceway east of Los Angeles, California. Hooper won the race, but just as at Le Mans three years earlier, this win was not without drama. That came from another new race car, Carroll Shelby's Ford V-8-powered Cobra. With disc brakes in contrast to the Z06's drums, and weighing 1,000 pounds less, the Cobra's driver, Bill Krause, stayed on the power later into corners and accelerated faster coming out of them. A rear wheel bearing failed, retiring the Cobra. One of the Z06s lost a wheel bearing as well, and two others retired with blown engines. Hooper brought the Mickey Thompson–sponsored car home in first place, but not before the Cobra made it clear to Corvette racers and engineers that they still had work to do.

Above: In its second season racing, for 1960, Mitchell had the car repainted silver. Dr. Dick Thompson campaigned the car to a season championship in events across the United States. *GM Media Archive*

Opposite, top: The Corvette SS retired after just 23 laps at Sebring on March 23, 1957. Engineers parked it in basement storage until years later when it joined the collection of race cars at the Indianapolis Motor Speedway Hall of Fame Museum, where it remained in frequent demand for photo shoots. *Randy Leffingwell © 2012*

Opposite, bottom: When GM chairman Frederick Donner banned all divisions from racing, Bill Mitchell acquired the fiberglass 1957 SS Mule. He asked his designer and friend Larry Shinoda to come up with a new racer, code name XP-87, on the mule's chassis, and the 1959 Stingray was born. *GM Media Archive*

CERV II

Above: Zora Duntov's second engineering research vehicle, CERV II, grew out of his desire to win the 24-hour race at Le Mans, France. His experiments with CERV I taught him about handling and road holding and he decided to assemble CERV II as an all-wheel-drive race car. *Randy Leffingwell*

Opposite: Duntov ultimately fitted the car with an all-aluminum 427-cubic-inch ZL1 engine that developed more than 600 horsepower in the 1,500-pound car. The car accelerated from 0 to 60 miles per hour in 2.8 seconds and lapped the Milford test circle at 214 miles per hour. *Randy Leffingwell*

Personal goals are great motivating forces. Zora Duntov had been to Le Mans. He had won his class there in a car whose entire engine displacement—1,100 cubic centimeters—was about the size of one and a quarter cylinders of an L88. And it produced barely one-tenth of the horsepower. He had accompanied Briggs Cunningham when four 1960 Corvettes went to France and one finished, winning its class.

Duntov wanted the big trophy, not the smaller one that celebrated sectional wins. Duntov wanted his car to finish ahead of every other car. He wanted to win Le Mans. With that in mind, he called on Larry Shinoda and Tony Lapine, friends from the Corvette SS days and from CERV I, to style a new sports racer. They came up with a closed coupe and open roadster design. Then he sent a memo to Harry Barr in January 1962, outlining his idea. Once again, it was a little too obvious a race car for GM; he was told to put it away.

Within a year, many things changed. Ford bucked the AAMA recommendation, launching a promotion called "Total Performance: Powered by Ford." Henry Ford made a diligent effort to acquire Ferrari, and when that collapsed, he made an even greater effort to beat him on the racetrack. What's more, Ford-powered Shelby Cobras had humbled the

Z06 and Duntov's Grand Sport Corvettes and that re-energized him. Ford wanted to beat Ferrari. Duntov wanted to beat Ford.

He developed four-wheel-drive systems and earned a patent for his concept of using an engine with separate transaxles front and rear. When he assembled his low, wide sports racer—using the same 377-cubic-inch aluminum engine he had used in CERV I—he tested it at Milford again. The car accelerated from 0 to 60 miles per hour in 2.8 seconds and lapped the circle faster than CERV I had done, averaging 214.01 miles per hour.

By this time, Duntov had bucked too many systems too many times. True, Frank Winchell provided support, parts, and engineering know-how to Jim Hall in Texas. But Winchell had learned how to stay nearly invisible.

True, Vince Piggins, head of "Performance Products" for Chevrolet division, funneled many "heavy-duty, off-highway-use-only" parts to NASCAR teams. But Piggins had learned how to make the company a great deal of money in aftermarket sales. Duntov had neither of those credentials. His supporters, Ed Cole and Bunkie Knudsen, were scolded. Funding for Duntov projects disappeared. He and Winchell conducted tests with CERV II against Chaparral prototypes and the lack of development crippled Duntov's project. GM stored the car for several years, and then in 1971 the corporation gave away CERV I and CERV II. They went to a public museum operated by Briggs Cunningham, an outside racer who had learned how to work within the GM system.

Right, top: Longtime sports car competitor Thompson took three 1960 Corvettes to Le Mans, France, for the 24-hour race in June. Spectators thronged the cars before the start, and one long day later, car no. 3, with John Fitch and Bob Grossman sharing driving duties, finished eighth overall, first in class. *GM Media Archive*

Right, bottom: The preparation that Briggs Cunningham's team manager Alfred Momo performed on the three cars they entered was excellent. American-made automobiles attracted a crowd wherever they went in France, especially when they raced at Le Mans. *GM Media Archive*

A field of Corvette Z06 coupes challenged a collection of Cobra roadsters in the Grand Touring Over-4000 class at Sebring on March 23, 1963. It was a war of attrition but in the end a Cobra finished in 11th overall, first in class, 10 laps ahead of the best-placed Corvette of Delmo Johnson and Dave Morgan. A second Corvette followed them one lap behind with another Cobra 18 laps back. Three more of each model failed to finish.

Duntov already had a solution in mind. The Cobra's arrival accelerated his work pace and his determination. Unfortunately, both ran afoul of GM's very public support of the AAMA no-racing recommendation. Duntov named the car the Grand Sport. New Chevrolet division general manager Semon "Bunkie" Knudsen, the son of a former GM president, supported Duntov's idea and encouraged the engineer to consider a run of 125 "production" race cars and 1,000 series production replicas.

The specifications for the car suggested it not only would beat Cobras but anything else in the world: lightweight simple ladder frame, independent suspension front and rear, disc brakes on all four wheels, aluminum V-8 of 377-cubic-inch displacement developing 550 horsepower at 6,400 rpm, and 500 foot-pounds of torque at 5,200 rpm. The hand-laid fiberglass body was just 0.04 inches thick (about the thickness of 12 sheets of paper), helping reduce the Grand Sport's overall weight to around 2,000 pounds. This put it within striking distance of Shelby's Cobra, but with much more horsepower available.

Duntov had to work with the production Sting Ray body, a collection of forms and shapes beautiful to behold but difficult to force through the air at high speeds. The battle that Duntov waged with Bill Mitchell over the production

Below: After Cunningham brought his 1960 Le Mans team Corvettes back to the United States, he eventually sold them and this class winner was converted to street use. Decades later, Corvettes at Carlisle co-founder Chip Miller and racing enthusiast/restorer Kevin Mackay located the car and restored it to its past configuration. *Randy Leffingwell*

coupe's divided rear window dealt a further blow to Grand Sport aerodynamics. Because styling had been banned from sharing information with him, Duntov was unaware that the cockpit on the new Corvette fit down between the frame rails rather than above them as on the previous generation, so Duntov and his engineers mounted the ultra-lightweight fiberglass package on top of the tube racing frame. As a result of this lack of communication, the Grand Sport sat nearly two inches higher than the production Corvette.

AERODYNAMIC CHALLENGES

The luscious shapes that Brock, Pohlmann, and Shinoda developed were easy on the eyes, but they caused air traveling over the car to lift it. Combined with the front lip and the large radiator below, high road speeds pushed and pulled the car into the air. Zora's own strong belief in the rightness of his cause brought it crashing back to earth.

In another corner of GM's Warren, Michigan, Technical Center, a fellow chassis and engine developer named Frank Winchell, working in Research and Development, had perfected the art and science of backdoor support for racing outside the corporation. Working with a Texas racer named Jim Hall, who created his own series of race cars called the Chaparral, Winchell funneled engines, transmission prototypes, chassis developments, and funding to Hall's sports-racing cars. Winchell studiously maintained a low profile, and Hall, who had his own engineering facility and test track far away in Midland, Texas, was the beneficiary.

Duntov's car looked like a GM product. It sounded and performed like one on a cocktail of steroids and growth hormones. The Grand Sports were awesome and inspiring, loud and fast. Everywhere the Grand Sports competed,

photographers and journalists reported and recorded its every lap. Duntov even got the cars into the hands of journalists for magazine stories. The same could not be said for the Chaparral. Winchell and Hall wanted no one to understand what made their cars tick or win.

GM corporate management changed hands. While Jack Gordon remained in place as corporation president, Frederick Donner replaced a two-year interim chairman Albert Bradley who had signed onto the AAMA recommendation. Donner, who was elected in September 1958, had many concerns, but Zora Arkus-Duntov had become a consistent one.

That Chevrolet division had manufactured and sold 199 Z06 models in 1963, and continued to produce and sell options intended to convert production Sting Rays into racers, was immaterial. Ed Cole and Knudsen had kept such facts buried in balance sheets. Frank Winchell and his engineers kept their heads down and shipped parts to Texas. What Donner saw was Duntov's highly visible racers flaunting a GM policy. This time he didn't bother with Duntov; he called in division chief Bunkie Knudsen and ordered him to burn all the Grand Sports to the ground.

Right, top: It's hard to imagine drag racing in the rain, but that is exactly how the National Hot Road Association Championship Drag Races in Indianapolis ended on September 4, 1962. Bob Phelps of San Bernardino was an A Class sports car winner in his 1962 Corvette with an elapsed time of 13.0 seconds. *GM Media Archive*

Right, bottom: At car-owner Mickey Thompson's recommendation, driver Doug Hooper ran his engine to lower rpm during the three-hour race at Riverside. At the end of the event, Hooper and Thompson's 1963 black Z06 had won the first race for the brand-new model. *GM Media Archive*

Opposite: Chevrolet debuted the racing version of the 1963 Sting Ray Z06 coupes at the October 1962 Los Angeles Times Grand Prix on October 13 at Riverside, California. The black coupe under the shadow of the bridge, driven by Doug Hooper, won the event. *GM Media Archive*

The Grand Attempt

Once he got inside Chevrolet Division, Zora Duntov operated with single-minded dedication: Take the Corvette racing to win.

The car had achieved successes. But Duntov, like many race-car makers, was not satisfied with class victories. He wanted his cars to reach the checkered flag before anybody else. And he had a plan. A new division general manager had arrived in December 1961, Semon E. Knudsen. Known as Bunkie, he was the son of a former GM president, William S. Knudsen, from 1937 through 1940. Bunkie watched other carmakers ignoring the AAMA racing ban. They reaped headlines and parts sales profits. The hypocrisy frustrated him; he decided to advance his division's reputation in every type of racing. There still was a chairman, Frederick Donner, but Knudsen and Duntov attempted to avoid his scrutiny. It was not easy.

Together Bunkie and Zora planned to take on Enzo Ferrari, Carroll Shelby, and all others. Duntov already had figured that Shelby's potent new Cobra enjoyed nearly a 1,000-pound advantage on the production Corvette. He knew Ferrari regularly had distracted racing rulemakers with fine wines and great pastas. He understood he had to lighten his car and follow every rule precisely.

Duntov proposed a new "lightweight" model with a production run of 125, 25 more than necessary to ensure regulator approval. Knudsen suggested they add another 1,000 as a street-production run. The engineers working with Zora developed a strong basic ladder frame with parallel main members.

Duntov, first and foremost an engine man, had developed a new power-plant for his open-wheel CERV I. Based on the production 327 V-8, he had bored out cylinders to 4.00 inches and lengthened stroke to 3.77, yielding 377 cubic inches of total displacement. Calculations predicted 550 horsepower at 6,400 rpm and 500 foot-pounds of torque at 5,200 rpm.

For the new Duntov/Knudsen lightweight coupes, technicians in the engineering prototype shop hand-laid fiberglass just 0.04 inches thick (roughly 1.02 millimeters, about the same as 10 one-dollar bills compressed), helping reduce the overall weight to around 2,000 pounds, within striking distance of the Cobra but with much more horsepower.

Zora had ideas to improve visibility in the stock coupe, but banned from access to anyone in design, he made mistakes. Not understanding that the production frame gave room to set the seats between frame rails, his parallel tubes forced engineers to bolt the floorpan and bodies on top of his frame. The car sat nearly 2 inches higher than production cars. The effect on aerodynamics was disastrous and this helped undermine Duntov's grand attempt.

He and his staff took their first car, the GS001, to Sebring for tests in mid-December 1962. A small badge on the rear of the car identified it as Corvette Grand Sport. The tests were beneficial to development but too public for chairman Donner to miss. When he learned of Knudsen's complicity in the project he came down hard, shuttering the project in January 1963. It was another hint of the future Duntov chose to ignore.

Parts arrived for more lightweight coupes, and mechanics already had assembled others. Donner told Knudsen to produce no more, but Duntov interpreted this as saying nothing about what he did with cars already existing. There were five more. He hid two in the backrooms of engineering and loaned three to racers he trusted to keep his secret; however, Donner's

Top: In this configuration, Texas racer Delmo Johnson campaigned this Grand Sport for nearly two years. The microphone behind the center console connected to his two-way radio, one of the first in racing at the time. *Randy Leffingwell*

Opposite: Zora Duntov never stopped trying and his Grand Sport, the lightweight Corvette Sting Ray developed in 1963, was an excellent example. Engines developing 500 horsepower made the cars fast; ungainly aerodynamics made the cars handling challenges. *Randy Leffingwell*

Above: Duntov worked every consideration to lighten the Sting Ray to its 2,000-pound Grand Sport weight. An external oil cooler (under the shroud below the rear window) appeared in the first year; Johnson added the two "bullet lights" so he always would have taillights even if another racer rear-ended him. *Randy Leffingwell*

orders had an additional—and unforeseen—effect. With only five racers known, sanctioning bodies changed the car's racing classification from C-production to C-modified. Instead of racing against Carroll Shelby's Cobras, he was competing against Jim Hall, whose Chaparrals were powered by engines discretely moved out the back door of Frank Winchell's R&D department.

The Grand Sport development process paralleled that of any race car. The first year was to be experimentation, discovery, modification, and steady improvement. A victory near the end of the season would be welcome validation that work was proceeding. Wins were expected the second year. For most race-car engineers, the third year meant a championship.

The Grand Sport's aerodynamics presented an unresolvable problem. Dr. Dick Thompson, one of several who campaigned the cars in 1963, told stories of full-throttle acceleration down long straights where he could twist the steering wheel from side to side with no change in direction. The front end was off the ground. He flew over a hilltop at a Chicago suburban track called Meadowdale. Literally. When the front end crashed back to the pavement, it shattered the front suspension. "Handling was not a problem," Thompson said with a laugh. "There wasn't any." Horsepower never was a problem either, he said. "The Lightweight was fast enough to scare most every driver. It was just insanely fast."

Through the winter following the 1963 season, work with wider tires and wheels put more of that power on the ground. But this was the era before wings and spoilers. Engineers applied aerodynamic devices to airplanes and rockets, not rocket-fast race cars. Duntov commissioned data analyses; these suggested the car might be faster without its roof. He pulled GS001 and 002 from hiding and mechanics at the Tech Center hacked off their tops.

Then Donner spoke again. Furious with Cole and Knudsen, he commanded them to "dispose" of all the cars. He ordered them burnt to the ground.

In 2003, a GM retiree approached longtime Corvette racer Dick Guldstrand. He said he'd gotten the assignment to destroy Duntov's Grand Sports. In early 1964, in front of a front-office witness, the man reduced "the sixth Grand Sport" to ashes. The witness photographed the process and result. The man said he'd take care of the rest but that day. The witness accepted this. Soon after he left, the man, Duntov, and others hurriedly hid the three remaining coupes and two roadsters in a large storage facility below the Styling center auditorium.

Undaunted, and unchastened, Duntov parceled out the cars again in 1965. They achieved mixed success but somehow transformed themselves into legends: Their sound and their tail-sliding performance inspired racing fans of all loyalties. Unfortunately, technology caught up and passed Duntov and his Grand Sports. By the end of 1965, Ferrari had entirely abandoned front-engine race cars. Carroll Shelby accepted the job managing Ford Motor Company efforts with its new midengine GT40s.

Where Winchell's strategy had been to render support to a racing program that never showed up at the Tech Center, Duntov loaned out the Grand Sports for the season but called them back for year-end upgrades. By this time, Duntov, aware of the Grand Sport's aerodynamic challenges but perhaps oblivious to his own, had ordered his technicians to slice the roofs off two of the coupes that he had been hiding in engineering. He felt lower-profile roadsters might do better at Le Mans.

A man introduced himself to Dick Guldstrand many years later, during the 2003 50th Anniversary celebrations and told Guldstrand that he had burned and totally destroyed a sixth Grand Sport in front of a witness who photographed the activity as proof for chairman Donner. The man promised the witness he'd take care of the rest of the cars another time once the witness had seen how it was done. The witness left. Shortly after that, the man helped Duntov and others move the five remaining cars into a large storage facility below the Styling center auditorium.

But soon after that, ignoring Donner, Duntov shipped the three coupes to John Mecom in Houston while the roadsters briefly remained in hiding. Then the roadsters slipped out as well, one of them to Roger Penske, who campaigned it through 1966 in Sunoco oil company colors.

MIDENGINE DOMINANCE

By that time, racing technology had taken another turn toward midengine placement. Frank Winchell and Jim Hall got there in 1962 with the Chaparral II. (Only Hall's first car had been front-engine rear-drive.) It qualified on the pole at the Los Angeles Times Grand Prix for the October 1963 Riverside raceway event and quit only when faulty electrics retired the car. Ford Motor Company unveiled its midengine GT40 Le Mans challenger in April 1963. Ferrari had first shown a midengine racing prototype in 1960, the 246SP; then it won Le Mans in June 1963 with its midengine 250P roadster.

In early 1962, Duntov had proposed a midengine-development project to Chevrolet's chief engineer Harry Barr. Once approved, he was delayed and distracted by the Grand Sports: Duntov finished the 1,500-pound, 400-horsepower all-wheel-drive midengine CERV II in early 1964. But teething problems and other struggles kept it from competing except internally.

Opposite, top: Just before the start of the Nassau Preliminary Tourist Trophy race on December 1, 1963, driver Augie Pabst walks past teammate Roger Penske in the 1963 Corvette Grand Sport no. 50. Pabst won (driving a Lola barely visible at far right), while Dr. Dick Thompson, driving the no. 80 Grand Sport, took second place. *GM Media Archive*

Opposite, bottom: The 1963 Grand Sports weighed about 2,000 pounds and their 377-cubic-inch engines developed around 550 horsepower, giving them the capability to nearly lift their front wheels on hard acceleration. Here, Roger Penske in no. 50 and Augie Pabst in no. 65 race up the front straight during the Governor's Trophy on December 6. They finished third and fourth, respectively. *GM Media Archive*

Below: It was a potent combination: Dick Moroso— "Tricky Dick," as the nickname above the door said—and heads and other engine treatments from Jim Minnick Racing Enterprises. Still other parts came from Crane and Hooker. No matter the venue, drag racers came to like the balance and weight transfer of the Sting Ray. *GM Media Archive*

Above: GM management made it clear to Zora Duntov that he was to destroy the Grand Sports. Instead, he successfully hid them, and in 1965 he loaned two roadsters, chassis numbers 001 and 002, to Roger Penske to race.
Randy Leffingwell © 2012

Right: Prior to the Penske loan, Anthony De Lorenzo, GM vice president of communication, got a call from his son asking if GM could send a car to a show at Purdue University where he was in school. Dad contacted Zora Duntov, got the no. 002 roadster painted "Bill Mitchell Blue," and trucked it to the show.
Randy Leffingwell © 2012

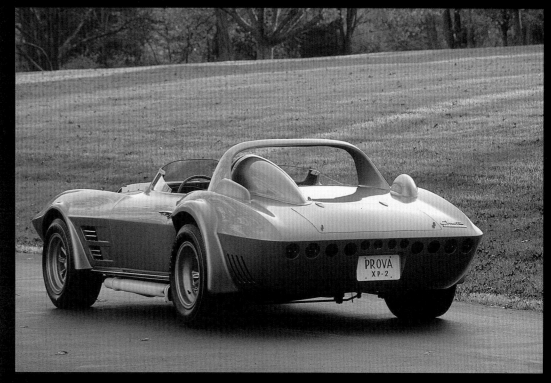

Above: **Zora Duntov wanted to win the 24 hours of Daytona, and to do that he created a special 427-cubic-inch engine labeled L88. The first one went into this car, which Dick Guldstrand and George Wintersteen drove to first place in the 1966 Daytona 24 Hours.**
Randy Leffingwell

For road courses and drag strips, Chevrolet's next potent weapon for the Corvette arrived in early 1966 with the "regular production option" code L88. This 427-cubic-inch-displacement engine developed 530 horsepower and 530 foot-pounds of torque. With Sunoco sponsorship and Roger Penske management, Dick Guldstrand introduced the car to competitors and racing fans alike at Daytona International Speedway on February 5 and 6. Despite a nighttime crash that removed the front end of the car and forced Guldstrand and his co-driver to continue the race with flashlights racer-taped to what remained of the front fenders, the red car no. 6 finished in 12th place overall, first in the over-3-liter GT class. It was the best-finishing front-engine car. Its strong performance generated a slowly building interest in the potential that the engine and car offered. For 1967, Chevrolet produced just 20 for sale, as a $947.90 option for the Corvette. For 1968, production quadrupled to 80 copies at the same price. In 1969, the company found 116 takers among drag racers and those in SCCA and international events.

For drag racers—and more for those campaigning Camaros in NHRA events—Chevrolet produced an all-aluminum-block version of the L88-coded ZL1. This engine emerged from Frank Winchell's R&D efforts. Because of his relationship with Fred Gibb Chevrolet in La Harpe, Illinois, Winchell funneled 69 of the engines to Gibb for installation in cars destined for NHRA Super Stock competition. Duntov was able to snare just a handful of the engines for Corvettes. Two were delivered in customer cars as a $4,718.35 option. He had one such engine in his development mule for a while, and there were three other engineering cars available on sign-out for testing and evaluation purposes. One of them, usually signed out to Corvette engineer Gibson Hufstader, ran the quarter mile in 10.9 seconds at 132 miles per hour.

L88 engines remained available as "crate motors" long after Chevrolet deleted them as regular production options on Corvettes and racers built and rebuilt them for competition through the 1970s. As Le Mans historian Tim Considine discovered, French rally driver Henri Greder got a 1968 Corvette with the L88 to drive at Le Mans. Qualifying 26th fastest out of 54 starters, Greder and co-driver Umberto Maglioli completed 53 laps before the engine let go. Greder returned in 1969, again starting in 26th position among the 45 qualifiers. After 196 laps, the transmission failed.

Perseverance and faith put Greder on the grid again in 1970, starting in 35th among 51 who began the race. Experiencing a replay of the previous year's gearbox problems, Greder and co-driver Jean-Paul Rouget took things easy, a wise decision with an ailing car in a race characterized by endless rain. They led the race in their class for 16 hours, but eventually a midengine Porsche 914/6 overtook them. Greder and Rouget completed 286 laps, yet owing to arcane regulations and formulas calculating performance against distance covered, while they finished the race, they were not classified.

Pacing the Racers

Corvette had survived its first 25 years. Inside GM and within the Chevrolet division, there had been serious discussions several times about letting the sports car disappear. Its earliest years were marked with more agonies of defeat than thrills of victory.

As it became clear that Chevrolet planned to manufacture a Corvette for model year 1978, however, a new round of serious discussions questioned how to celebrate this silver anniversary. Before he retired in 1975, Bill Mitchell suggested to Jerry Palmer, the Design staff's Corvette stylist, that Chevrolet should create a commemorative in Mitchell's favorite color, silver. Palmer put his own imprint on the idea; a red stripe beltline set off the silver upper body from the charcoal lower panels.

To help honor and celebrate Corvette's 25th year, Chevrolet public relations approached Indianapolis Motor Speedway management. They proposed the Speedway select the anniversary commemorative as its official pace car for the 1978 race. A short while later, they modified the proposal, inviting Speedway owner Tony Hulman and his board to determine a color scheme for the pace car. They devised the black-over-silver combination with the red beltline stripe.

It was Corvette's first run at the Speedway, and as Chevrolet wrestled with the question of producing a limited number of pace-car replicas, excitement among enthusiasts soared. Chevrolet announced the price: $13,653.21, and dealers began taking orders, sometimes tagging on 100

Right, top: Corvette's first four Indianapolis 500 pace cars pose in the infield garage area. From top clockwise, the cars were the yellow 1986 convertible, the dark purple-and-white 1995 convertible, the purple 1998 convertible, and the black-over-silver 1978 coupe.
GM Media Archive

Right, bottom: Before Chevrolet planners and Corvette designers even had completed the 1978 Indy 500 Pace Car decals for the car, outside vendors had developed a scale-model Go-Kart with their own logos. Local photographer Stan Cusumano documented the vehicles.
GM Media Archive

Opposite, top: To continue the endurance race pace car program, Chevrolet provided a Corvette hardtop to Daytona International Speedway for the 24-hour race on February 5 and 6, 2000. Corvette's C5-R won the event outright in 2001.
GM Media Archive

Opposite, bottom: To emphasize Corvette's return to the 24 Hours of Le Mans endurance race in France, Chevrolet provided the race organizer L'Automobile Club de l'Ouest, with pace and official cars for the 67th running of the event.
GM Media Archive

percent price markups. Then General Motors' legal department concluded Chevrolet had to manufacture one car for each of its 6,502 dealers. Exclusivity disappeared and some dealers still had unsold replicas in their showroom at Thanksgiving.

Pace cars have specific duties: Since 1974, the car has run two parade laps at 75 miles per hour and one pace lap at 90 miles per hour just before the start. During yellow flag sessions, the pace car runs between 110 and 120 miles per hour to keep racing tires hot enough to grip.

Corvette's placement as a pace car became a popular proposition for the Speedway and Chevrolet. The 1978 model inaugurated a relationship that expanded beyond Indy car events to include NASCAR and other series. Since 1978, Corvettes have undertaken official duties at the Indy 500 in 1986, 1995, 1998, 2002, and 2004 through 2008. In addition, Chevrolet has provided Corvettes as parade, official, and event cars for many of these races. The Corvette also paced each Brickyard 400 from 2006 through 2010 and at the Daytona 500 from 2005 through 2008. With Corvette's participation in American Le Mans Series (ALMS) endurance races, Chevrolet provided pace cars for the Daytona 24 Hours in 1999 and for the 24 Hours of Le Mans, France, in 1999 and 2000.

Owners and enthusiasts of Corvette Pace Cars and replicas have a useful and valuable resource available to them with the Pace Car Registry. This Internet site offers information and history at www.pacecarregistry.com.

For 1971, Greder, perhaps believing the fourth time had to be his, started 28th but failed to finish, once again due to engine woes. A second Corvette, also a French entry, lasted only slightly longer before its transmission surrendered. Greder was an eternal optimist, and he launched a fifth attempt in 1972, starting from 46th position on the grid and completing 235 laps before an accident took his car out of the race.

NART CORVETTE

One other Corvette did better in 1972. Painted Ferrari Racing Red as an entry from Ferrari's U.S. importer Luigi Chinetti (forced on him by tire supplier Goodyear and their racing director Leo Mehl), Dave Heinz and Bob Johnson started 51st out of 55 cars and finished 15th of 16 cars running at the end.

Henri Greder and his evergreen 1968 L88 succeeded on their sixth attempt in 1973. Starting from 37th position on the grid of 55 cars, Greder and co-driver Charmasson nursed their aging 1968 Sport Coupe around the Le Mans 8.48-mile circuit 304 times to finish 12th overall out of 12 finishers. However, they were the only "Grand Touring Over 5-Liter" car running at the end so they earned their class win. (To follow their saga on, they finished 18th in 1974, and then qualified 34th fastest but did not complete a single lap in 1975, after which Greder and the near-classic coupe retired. For years, Greder had been the sole competitor in a Corvette.)

In 1976, the assignment for Corvette representation at Le Mans fell to John Greenwood with his IMSA-class powerhouses. While Greenwood qualified ninth fastest, he completed just 29 laps. When a rear tire blew, it demolished

Opposite: No sooner had Duntov gotten his wish at Daytona than he sent another L88 off to be the first in Europe. Dana Chevrolet entered this 1967 coupe in the June 10–11, 1967, running of the 24 Hours of Le Mans. *GM Media Archive*

Left, top: Drivers Dick Guldstrand and Bob Bondurant gave it their best efforts, but the L88 engine in their 1967 L88 lasted just half the 24-hour distance. Small consolation: The no. 16 Ford GT did not finish either, although Porsche no. 41 went on to take fifth overall. *GM Media Archive*

Left, bottom: Henri Greder and Jean-Paul Rouget finished the 1970 running of the 24 Hours of Le Mans in sixth place overall in their 1970 L88. They completed 286 laps—2,393.5 miles—which put them in first place in "over 5,000cc Grand Touring" class. *GM Media Archive*

some bodywork, taking part of the fuel cell with it and giving co-driver Bernard Darniche a thrill ride. The resulting fuel leak sidelined the car emblazoned with a Spirit of Le Mans paint scheme.

In an effort to strengthen its bond with Daytona, Le Mans organizers in 1976 had invited IMSA to send two entries from its "All-American GT" category, and NASCAR to send two stock car racers as well. It was a grand experiment in French-American racing diplomacy and marked the first time Greenwood took on international competitors on the long French circuit.

Greenwood first raced as a teenager on the streets of his hometown, Detroit. He bought his first Corvette, a silver 1964 coupe, and immediately dropped an early 427 into it, modifying the frame rails to fit the new engine. Then he bought a new 1968 coupe. He installed an L88 in it the first night he had it. Driving schools followed; then came his SCCA licenses. He was building his business manufacturing racing engines. In 1969 and 1970, he ran a 1969 coupe that he converted to a roadster for 1970. He won A-production championships both years, earning B. F. Goodrich sponsorship that kept him racing through 1972 and 1973.

Through the late 1960s and early 1970s, Corvettes at the hands of one team or another won their classes at Daytona and Sebring. Often these class positions placed them in the top 10 overall on the heels of prototype Ferrari and Porsche sports racers.

Sensing the SCCA was catering to manufacturers, John Bishop and Bill France Jr. founded the International Motorsports Association (IMS) in 1969. Bishop, long a member of SCCA management, and France established IMSA to give privateers better representation in regulations making, promotion, and event management. Following a modest first year, IMSA expanded its horizons, introducing endurance racing to U.S. audiences. Greenwood liked what he saw. While IMSA had rules, too, its organization encouraged the kind of cars and racing Greenwood wanted to develop. Many competitors preferred what IMSA offered, while others remained loyal to SCCA, providing Corvette racers and enthusiasts more events and venues at which to enjoy their cars.

Through the 1960s and 1970s, Corvette's relatively short wheelbase with its engines set back in the chassis continued their appeal with drag racers. During the 1970s, competitors such as John Lingenfelter, Bernie Agaman, Paul Blevins, Tony Christian, and Don Coonce wracked up repeated NHRA national titles. Wheel-stander Lee Shepherd thrilled huge

Above: In mid-1971, B. F. Goodrich introduced a new series of street radials and, looking for a way to promote them among performance enthusiasts, contracted with John Greenwood to race two cars with the Lifesaver Radials as his competition tires for the 1972 season. Painted red, white, and blue, the very successful cars became known as the Stars and Stripes Corvettes. *GM Media Archive*

Opposite, top: In one of racing's typical quirks, Goodyear Tire and Rubber's effective racing manager Leo Mehl "convinced" U.S. Ferrari distributor Luigi Chinetti to enter a 1972 L88-powered Corvette along with their Italian cars at Le Mans. Painted Ferrari Red, with an NART Ferrari badge on each door, the car finished 15th overall. *GM Media Archive*

Opposite, bottom: John and Burt Greenwood were among America's most innovative and inventive race car builders and John was a fine driver as well. For 1976, the Le Mans organizers invited four American teams to compete and their "Spirit of Le Mans" provided race fans with thunderous noise and staggering speed. *Randy Leffingwell*

Above: Chevrolet debuted the C4 in Playboy Challenge Showroom Stock racing series at the 24 Hours of Nelson Ledges in Parkman, Ohio, on June 29, 1984. The car led for 9 of the 24 hours. *GM Media Archive*

Right: For all its aerodynamic enhancements, John Greenwood's "wide-body" Corvettes, including this, his first "tube frame" car, were easily recognizable to Corvette fans. The Greenwoods' cars raced for more than a decade with 750-plus-horsepower ZL1 engines that frequently were too strong for their transmissions. *GM Media Archive*

Above: Greenwood's racing and engineering successes earned him GM's respect. *Randy Leffingwell*

crowds with his Reher-Morrison Modified Production Stingray. In 1978, Tom McEwen, "the Mongoose," won the NHRA U.S. Nationals in his nitro-methane fueled Corvette funny car.

Acceleration in a quarter-mile was one measure of speed. Terminal velocity over a mile is another. With the arrival of the Sting Ray in 1963, and its descendants in 1968 and later, the seemingly slippery shape of the car has encouraged a number of attempts on the title "World's Fastest Corvette." In 1985, Juris Mindenbergs, of Redmond, Washington, bought a 1984 C4 and set out to learn how fast it would go. Four years of tinkering with a 502-cubic-inch 1,000-plus horsepower engine brought him answers: He recorded a two-way average of 266.45 miles per hour, including one run at 271.04 during the Bonneville Speed Trials in September.

SCORCHED EARTH

Through this same period of time, Corvette's new C4 began a scorched-earth campaign within an SCCA series sponsored by Playboy Enterprises. The Showroom Stock Endurance Series began in 1985. The organizers posted strict rules for cars in four classes. Porsche put up its new 944 coupe and Nissan offered its 300ZX turbo coupe among the most potent competitors. But Dave McLellan worked with Don Runkle, director of Chevrolet market planning, Herb Fischel, Chevrolet's racing programs manager, and Ralph Kramer, head of Chevrolet public relations, to provide technical support for any Corvette racer interested in the series. These races ran 3, 6, 12, or 24 hours, a challenge for a purpose-built racer let alone one derived from series production. Extensive testing with a team made up of Tommy Morrison, Jim Cook, and

Below: At Riverside International Raceway on April 27, 1986, the Hendricks Motorsports Corvette GTP competed in the six-hour Los Angeles Times Grand Prix. Involved in a crash, it did not finish. *GM Media Archive*

Opposite, top: One of the goals of the Corvette GTP program was to test enthusiast response to the idea of a turbocharged V-6 engine in production models. With decades of front-engine V-8s in their experience, it was difficult for fans to identify with the V-6 or the midengine. *GM Media Archive*

Opposite, bottom: Bobby Rahal drove the normally aspirated V-8-powered Hendrick Motorsports Corvette GTP to fifth overall in the 1988 season-ending event in Del Mar, California. Hendrick switched to the V-8 at the beginning of the season to improve reliability. *GM Media Archive*

Dick Gulstrand led to a series of rules-legal updates that Chevrolet circulated to all Corvette teams. Corvette won each of the six endurance races. As Dave McLellan explained in his book, *Corvette from the Inside*, "The competing Porsche and Nissan competition teams certainly didn't expect this outcome: They came back race after race, trying even harder. But so did we, and we were able to keep just ahead of the competition."

Escort replaced Playboy as major sponsor for 1986. The eight-race series was a near-carbon copy of 1985 despite Porsche campaigning its 944 Turbo to challenge the 300ZX Turbo and Corvette. The Corvette's four-wheel ABS proved to be its secret weapon. It was so new that one of the series participants organized anti-lock braking driver training classes to teach the racers how to get the most from the new system. It proved its worth at Portland when it began to rain shortly before the finish. Racing to a corner, the lead Porsche spun while the second-place Corvette braked smoothly and got around it. It never surrendered the lead after that, and Corvette went on to win every race in the second season as well.

Porsche and Nissan returned with ABS and more powerful engines for 1987. This encouraged Corvette to petition the rule makers to raise their own horsepower. Regulations allowed entrants to use production pieces from the coming year's cars; in some ways these "showroom stock" cars were customers' fantasies. Competition grew closer in 1987, but as before, Corvette came to each track more advanced than in the previous event. Kim Baker Racing, running yellow cars number 3 and number 4, won every race, took the series, and claimed the manufacturer's championship for Corvette for a third year in a row.

Worried that fans were bored with 36 straight Corvette victories, the SCCA barred the Corvette and the 944 Turbo from the series in 1988. Chevrolet proposed its own match-race series to SCCA management. Where previous showroom stock events had offered enthusiasts of several makes a chance to cheer or lament the performance of their favorites, the Corvette Challenge caught the imagination of even non-Corvette owners with extremely close racing. Held as supporting events alongside SCCA Trans-Am races, the Challenge routinely started 15 to 20 well-prepared Corvettes. Trans-Am series spectators cheered John Greenwood, Marshall Robbins, Jerry Hansen, and Greg Pickett in battles against Ford Mustangs, Mercury Capris, Nissans, Porsches, Audi Quattros, and even Camaros through the late 1980s.

A CORVETTE LIKE NO OTHER

Manufacturers often shifted from one series to another, one sanctioning body to another, as rules appeared that stifled their innovations or encouraged them. Starting in 1981, IMSA inaugurated a prototype GTP category in its popular Camel GT series. These midengine purpose-built sports racers came from Nissan, Jaguar, Porsche, Mazda, and others. Collaborating with Lola Cars International, Corvette's sleek midengine cars wore a thin fiberglass body that loosely resembled the production C4, created by design staffers Jerry Palmer and Randy Wittine (who had helped John Greenwood develop the wild bodies and aerodynamic forms that Greenwood wrapped around his running gear). For the GTP car, Chevrolet developed a twin-turbocharged V-6 derived from its production engines that created as much as 1,200 horsepower. The motive behind this combination was to test enthusiast reaction to this kind of engine package. The car debuted in late 1984 and competed sporadically in the 1985 season; teething problems common to any new racing car plagued the project, and development experiments sometimes tripped up progress through 1986 and 1987.

Some consistency arrived in 1988, accompanied by the switch to a normally aspirated 6-liter V-8, but performance and engineering challenges forced Chevrolet to end its support of the project after 1988. It had won just two races, at Road Atlanta and then at Palm Beach, both in April 1986. One team struggled with a car in 1989 but gained poor results. The Corvette GTP entered racing history only as a lower-case footnote.

Traditional front-engine/rear-drive Corvettes did much better. In the early 1990s, ZR1-derived coupes competing in IMSA GTO classes claimed victories and season titles. In one particular event however, a ZR1 raced an L98 against a clock around Firestone's test track in Texas. At the end of 24 hours, the ZR1 had set a dozen new speed records, including 175.885 miles-per-hour average speed for 24 hours.

That wasn't quite fast enough for Kim Baker who set his sights a bit higher in 1994. The Silver State Classic Challenge, founded in 1988, pitted a hundred or more racers against a 90-mile stretch of Nevada Highway 318. Having been part of the team that averaged 175-plus around the Firestone circle, Baker built an unlimited class ZR1, taking the car apart down to its last nut and bolt. Recognizing the speed potential—and for disaster with a crash on a closed but unprotected public road—he made countless safety improvements to the car and installed a more potent powerplant. Over the two-lane road from Hiko, Nevada, to Lund, he averaged 181 miles per hour and passed the finish line at 201 to win the event. In subsequent efforts, he won two additional closed-highway events in Nevada.

As the fifth-generation Corvette moved through the design and engineering processes, a group of engineers and managers met in early 1996 to contemplate the future. An IMSA offshoot group, Professional SportCar Racing, had announced its intention to stage a 10-hour endurance race, Petit Le Mans. Rumors that this inaugural race would lead to an American Le Mans series, ALMS, inspired Chevrolet to consider making the C5 a part of this plan. Production classes

Opposite: Second-season cars enjoyed more sponsorship, although individual teams had to find it. One big improvement for 1989 was a free-flow exhaust that made the cars sound as fast as they were. Bill Cooper's car no. 3 was the series champion. *Randy Leffingwell © 2012*

Below: Because it remained essentially a showroom stock series, the cars got a pair of matching competition seats, a roll cage, and a fire system. The stereo radio, air conditioning, and power windows continued to function, however.
Randy Leffingwell © 2012

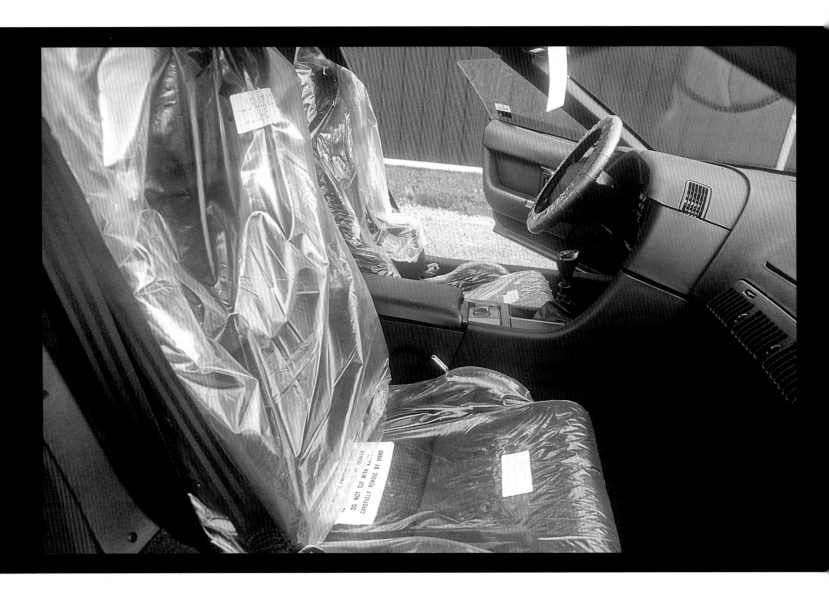

Back to Le Mans

Above: While the timing seems unlikely, it appears that Zora Duntov got the 1957 Corvette SS out one more time for a banked track test. The 1959 model full-size Chevrolets began to appear in racing in late 1958. *GM Media Archive*

Zora Arkus-Duntov, who had competed at Le Mans in the 1950s, racing Cadillac-powered Allards in 1952 and 1953, and in 1,100cc Porsches to class victories in 1954 and 1955, agreed to drive the 24-hour event one more time in 1982. Tyco Corporation, manufacturers of slot car racers and track systems, approached writers at *AutoWeek* magazine, hoping to generate a story to rekindle interest in slot cars. After dozens of phone calls and hundreds of hours of work, the magazine and Tyco staged the *24 Heures du Mans de Slot Car* at a hotel in Detroit over the Le Mans race weekend in France. Organizers insisted on veracity and Tyco's engineers responded, creating a Ferrari 512S, Porsche 917K, Ford GT40, and Corvette L88, each in 1/87th scale. Keeping to that proportion, the Mulsanne straight ran 247 feet long, through two ballrooms. The entire track covered more than 550 feet with four lanes. Tyco's technical director fabricated hundreds of custom-made curve sections.

Because Le Mans is a 24-hour race, Tyco installed working headlights in the cars, necessary because the hotel, in the spirit of the event, shut off the lights in the room at 10 p.m. An illuminated Erector-Set carousel churned through the night, interrupted only by the start of several fog machines that laid a thick cloud over the floor starting at 5 a.m. (The hotel, generous to a fault, drew the line at running the fire sprinklers to simulate the rains that frequently occur.) Each team had four drivers; Zora, ever a racer, drove his 1-hour sessions every four hours around the clock. Edsel Ford spent several sessions commanding the GT40. Corner workers from Detroit region SCCA stationed themselves at each corner for the entire 24 hours, patiently signaling, righting, and resetting the 1/87th-scale cars that flew off at the Mulsanne hairpin, or Tertre Route, or Maison Blanc. At 4 p.m. Sunday afternoon, SCCA officials flagged the race to a close. Zora had driven for the final hour and he brought his L88 home to victory. It marked Corvette's first overall win at Le Mans. The organizers presented the winning car to Zora, who tearfully accepted his trophy.

One of Zora's teammates, Daniel Charles Ross, had friends at ABC, which traditionally broadcasted motorsports. As the magazine staff planned the event, Ross mentioned it to Paul Page, who laughed and said coverage depended on what else was happening in the sports world at the time.

As it turned out, it was a slow fall sports season. The National Football League players were on strike and there was no Sunday, Monday, or holiday professional football. Page had hedged his bet, covering the race himself with a crew for the entire 24 hours. To everyone's amazement on the *ABC Wide World of Sports Thanksgiving Day Special*, Jim McKay introduced the event with a smile, calling it ABC's early Christmas gift to its viewers. It ran nearly 20 minutes on a desperately slow sports holiday.

Writer George Damon Levy, who was Duntov's longtime friend and his teammate through that long day, said that the white-and-red hardtop still was on Duntov's living room mantle when he died, at age 86, in 1996.

Above: Prematurely gray from an early age, it always was hard to guess Zora Duntov's age. He never was far from a cigarette. *GM Media Archive*

Right: When Zora Duntov couldn't run the entire Pikes Peak climb in October 1961 because of snow at the higher altitudes, he turned the session into a tire test. Technicians from Firestone and Goodyear struggled to find a tire to get the CERV I's power onto the ground. *GM Media Archive*

Above: Tommy Morrison entered two competition-prepared ZR1 coupes in the 1991 24 Hours of Daytona. The sister car, no. 92, finished 12th overall, while electrical problems and impact with another competitor slowed this car considerably. *Randy Leffingwell © 2012*

Right: Mercury Marine blueprinted the ZR1 engines and ported the cylinder heads. Output was rumored at 550 horsepower in a car using carbon-fiber bodywork to save 600 pounds over production models. *Randy Leffingwell © 2012*

for this new series required manufacturers to compete with precisely modified versions of their series production cars. GM motorsports manager Herb Fischel and racing team manager Doug Fehan planned to enter cars in the 1999 Daytona 24-hour race, giving them three years to introduce the new production model and revise it to complete such an event. Some 18 months before the planned debut of the cars in Las Vegas in November 1998, Chevrolet brought in two outside racing teams, Pratt and Miller based in Detroit and Riley and Scott from Indianapolis, to develop and campaign the cars. (Riley and Scott developed cars through 1999 but then left the project.)

Pratt and Miller stretched the wheelbase by a quarter inch from 104.5 to 104.7 inches and lengthened the body from 179.7 to 182.8 inches. They worked the production 364-cubic-inch block with bore and stroke of 4.125 by 3.42 inches to produce about 600 horsepower at 7,200 rpm.

C5-R

The 1999 Daytona debut delivered plenty of drama. Chevrolet ran two cars, known as the C5-R. One of these suffered a suspension problem that could not be resolved. Battling a team of Dodge Vipers entered by the French team ORECA, the second Corvette held the class lead until an oil leak dropped them to third in class at the finish. As the season continued, the Pratt and Miller team ran six of the nine events with the cars painted in silver-and-black GM Goodwrench colors. By the end of the season, they competed with 7-liter 427-cubic-inch aluminum-cast engines producing 590 horsepower. The engines were developed by Katech outside Detroit.

For 2000, Pratt and Miller introduced the new yellow paint scheme. The team joined the ALMS midseason and battled Vipers and Ford-powered Saleens with frustrating results. That changed at Texas Motor Speedway in September when chassis 003 won its class. It was the first class victory for the C5-R Corvettes. Both cars 003 and 004 raced the rest of the season.

Below: As Chevrolet prepared its role as official pace car for the 1999 24 Hours of Le Mans, it considered many paint schemes for the cars. One of the possibilities was this red-white-and-blue combination that would have been a hit in France where the national flag uses the same colors in three vertical bands. *GM Media Archive*

Pratt and Miller planned to campaign the entire ALMS season for 2001 and it started off well. At Daytona, chassis 003 won outright, first overall. This was a welcome victory because a Viper had taken first overall in 2000, just edging out 003. In 2001 the closest Viper followed nearly 450 miles behind, in 31st place. Corvette number 4, chassis 004, was a popular favorite with Daytona and NASCAR favorite father-and-son team Dale Earnhardt Sr. and Jr., and Andy Pilgrim and Kelly Collins sharing driving duties. They finished fourth overall, second in class. In Texas in September, 003 won class honors.

For Le Mans, Pratt and Miller switched car race numbers to 63 and 64, and the team revisited Corvette competition history 41 years after Briggs Cunningham's attempts. Drivers Ron Fellows, Scott Pruett, and Johnny O'Connell, in number 63, chassis 003, finished first in GTS class, completing 278 laps to take eighth overall. It was Corvette's first class triumph in France since 1960. Throughout the rest of the year, 003 served as the reliable workhorse, adding class victories at Sonoma, California; Portland, Oregon; Mosport, Ontario, Canada; and Mid-Ohio to its resumé. Chassis 004 claimed class honors at the season finale at Road Atlanta. Pratt and Miller accepted deposits from two teams to acquire C5-R models for their own efforts. Those cars ran Katech engines as well.

Sebring 2002 added another class success to Pratt and Miller's C5-R stable and so did Le Mans for a second year in a row, despite challenges from a team of Ferraris. Two new chassis began racing through the summer and into the fall, taking home seven more class victories.

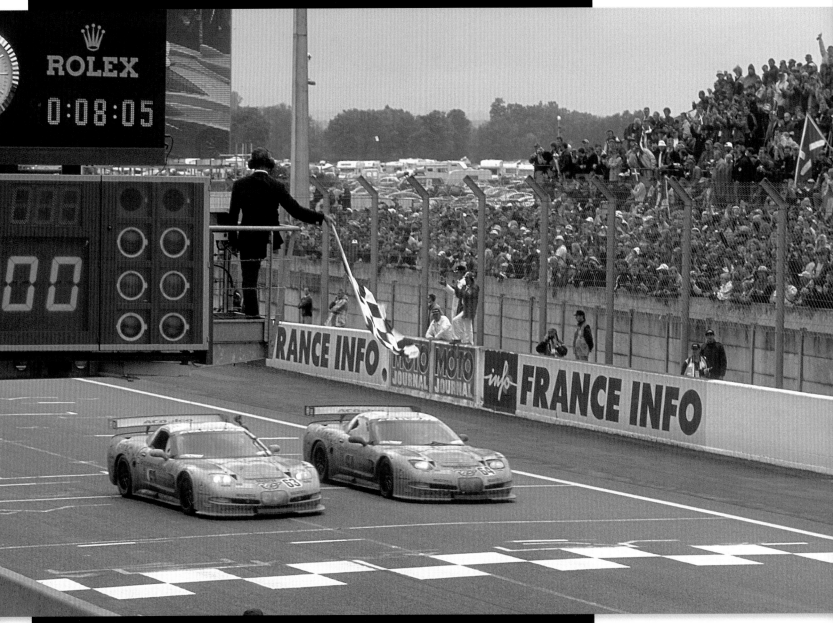

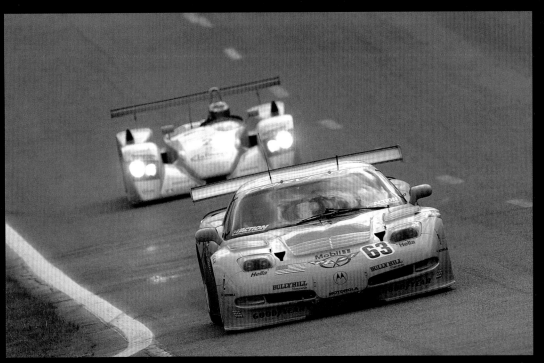

Above: Squadron finishes became popular among victorious teams during the late 1960s, and endurance race results were determined by distance traveled. Here, 2000 Le Mans GTS-class contestants no. 64, driven by Franck Freon, Andy Pilgrim, and Kelly Collins pace teammates, and no. 63, with Chris Kneifel, Ron Fellows, and Justin Bell sharing driving duties, cross the finish line in 10th and 11th place overall, third and fourth in GTS class.
GM Media Archive

Left: Ron Fellows played a hunch at the start of the 24 Hours of Le Mans in 2001 and argued with team manager Doug Fehan to start on intermediate rain tires. Soon it was pouring and C5-R no. 63 moved up many places, ultimately finishing eighth overall and first in GTS class.
GM Media Archive

Above: Most drivers hate the 24 Hours of Le Mans (and the 24-hour race at Daytona) because they are "boring" and "go on too long." Not only is the dark a problem, but at both events often there is hard rain or thick fog. *GM Media Archive*

Right: In 2002, in advance of Corvette's 50th Anniversary, Chevrolet sponsored a photo contest, inviting entries from around the world. German photographer Achim Hartman captured this custom 1965 coupe in a night drag race. *GM Media Archive*

Above: Ron Fellows, along with co-drivers Oliver Gavin and Johnny O'Connell, repeated their 2001 GTS class win again in 2002, finishing 11th overall and first in GTS. In 24 hours they completed 335 laps to cover 2,832.1 miles. *GM Media Archive*

Pratt and Miller went to Le Mans 2003 with high hopes but realistic expectations. It was, after all, the 50th anniversary of the Corvette. The Ferraris again challenged them but Corvette's own vehicle ailments forced the team to settle for second and third in class. Le Mans in 2004 read like a litany of bad luck for team Corvette, this time swatting away the nuisance of six separate Ferrari entries devoted to beating them. Accidents and spins slowed the Corvettes, but late hour mechanical ills slowed the Ferraris. Corvettes took first and second in GTS class. Through six years of running C5-R models, Corvette won five ALMS class championships and earned equal honors for the team drivers.

C6.R

ALMS season 2005 introduced a new car, the C6.R, and a new racing classification, GT1. It brought intensified competition from a new Aston Martin DBR9 and a squadron of new Ferrari 575s. The season opener at Sebring made for 12 long hours punctuated by accidents to both Corvettes in the eighth hour; they settled for second and third in class behind an Aston Martin.

Corvettes won their class at Road Atlanta in April and Mid-Ohio in May as a tune-up before Le Mans in June. There the competition was intense. The two Corvettes chased two Aston Martins for 23 hours. Then one Aston ran out of fuel almost in sight of the pits, and the other retired with a leaking radiator. There is an old axiom in endurance racing: To win you have to finish. The Corvettes ended the race in one-two order in their class.

The last half of 2005 reminded historians of Showroom Stock races; the two C6.Rs won a record 10 of 11 races. No great accomplishment goes unpunished, however, especially in racing. Sanctioning bodies have the power to limit horsepower through "restrictor plates" beneath fuel-injector plenums or to add weight to slow a car. Or they can do both. Every racing director, whether manufacturer or event promoter, understood there were—and are—three purposes to racing: prove engineering, sell cars, and entertain the paying customers.

Above: German photographer Achim Hartman mounted a camera on the nose of this custom 1965 drag-racing coupe and ran it past the lights to claim another prize in Corvette's worldwide photo contest in 2002, a year before its 50th Anniversary.
GM Media Archive

Above: This was the final GTS win for the C5-R at Le Mans in 2004. Car no. 64, with Oliver Gavin, Olivier Beretta, and Jan Magnussen driving, finished sixth overall and first in GTS. They completed 345 laps covering 2,916.6 miles. *GM Media Archive*

ALMS rule makers introduced a series of adjustments they called "performance balancing," a euphemism for power limitations and weight additions. They applied these to the too-successful Corvettes. Ironically, it turned out that tire choice—Michelins on the Corvettes versus Pirellis on the Aston Martins—had the most to do with who won. The Pirellis lost their grip more quickly. According to Corvette historian Jerry Burton, "Frustrations mounted in the Corvette camp as the Corvettes began to lose races they would have won handily before the sanctions. Despite being beneficiaries, the Aston Martin camp wasn't much happier with the situation and both sides began to question whether they would return to the series in 2007."

At season end, Corvette engineering was the real winner. The C6.R took Corvette's sixth consecutive series class championship. They earned their third straight GT1 victory at Le Mans. In France, the only surviving Aston Martin finished five laps back, second in class.

ALMS season 2007 painted a different picture altogether. Rule makers agreed to provide competitors with a longer warning before restrictions changed their cars. At Sebring, a single privately entered Aston Martin—the only Aston entered—gave them a run but settled for third place behind the two Corvettes. The next few months were odd. There was no competition in GT1. The rest of the Aston Martins and every other competitor in GT1 waited until Le Mans to show their hand. There, a dozen competitors lined up: six Astons, two Ford-powered Saleen coupes, a single Ferrari 550, and three private entry Corvettes.

Car number 64 retired early with a broken driveshaft, leaving number 63 to persevere. Through the night it crept up on the strongest factory-entry Aston. Then the safety car appeared Sunday afternoon to manage the pace through a heavy downpour. That sealed their fate: Aston Martin first GT1, Corvette second. Back in the United States, Corvette quickly made amends, sweeping every other ALMS meeting and taking its seventh manufacturer's title in a row in GT1.

Some victories force even the combatants to take stock. Race year 2008 proved an exact repeat of the previous year. Corvettes had no competition through the ALMS season in the United States and came in second place behind the same Aston Martin entrant at Le Mans. The next year, after the 2009 C6.R took the GT1 class win at Le Mans, Corvette shifted gears. Choosing to campaign a ZR1-derived, normally aspirated, 5.8-liter V-8 allowed Corvette's reclassification into the hotly competitive GT2 class. It was a courageous move. But it was one that proved to be a nightmare for the dream Corvette team: following Le Mans, they earned only one other class victory in 2009.

ALMS season 2010 proved something of a replay of 2009—Corvettes took a single class victory only at the end of the season, at the Petit Le Mans event at Road Atlanta. Vigorous competition from BMW, Porsche, and Ferrari limited the Corvette effort to seasonal fourth place, in that order. In France, the Ford-powered Saleen won GT1. Corvette was second, followed by an Aston Martin.

The 2011 ALMS season challenged Corvette racing again. The cars once more found strong competition from BMW, Porsche, and Ferrari, with nagging challenges from Jaguar. Corvette took class wins at Mosport and recorded podium finishes at Sebring, Long Beach, Mid-Ohio, and Baltimore. Drivers Oliver Gavin and Jan Magnussen claimed second place in season driver championships. At Le Mans in June, Corvette, racing in a new category called LM GTE Pro, finished in the top spot, first in class, eleventh overall, at the end of 24 hours. Drivers Olivier Beretta, Tommy Milner, and Antonio Garcia shared the victory. Corvette's nearest competitor, Ferrari, finished two slots down. The ten finishers ahead were exclusively racing prototypes.

The 2012 season began strong with podium finishes in the first three events, a second and third at Sebring, a class win in ALMS GT at Long Beach, and a first and second at Laguna Seca. The new GTE Pro class at Le Mans in June stacked tough competition and tougher challenges against the Corvettes, and they finished fifth and sixth in class. Back in the United States, podium finishes characterized six of the remaining seven events with class wins at Mid-Ohio and Virginia International Raceway (VIR). The VIR victory also cinched driver championships for Oliver Gavin and Tommy Milner driving car number 4, as well as the ALMS GT Manufacturer Championship for Corvette.

Corvette number 4 took the GT class win at Sebring in March 2013. At Laguna, its teammate car number 3 won the class at Laguna. Success at Le Mans again proved elusive as the Europeans kept the Americans clearly in their sights for the entire 24 hours, the two Corvettes finishing fourth and seventh in class. As in 2012, podium finishes occurred in all but one of the remaining races as Corvettes came in second at Lime Rock, won their class at Mosport, Baltimore, and Austin, and finished third at Virginia. The season-ending endurance 1,000-miles-or-10-hours event at Road Atlanta saw Corvettes finish in sixth and tenth. At VIR, Corvette again claimed the ALMS GT team championship; however, the driver's title came only at the end of the Road Atlanta long run when Antonio Garcia and Jan Magnussen in number 3 took the honors.

For the 2014 season, Corvette Racing debuted its new C7.R model, developed hand-in-hand with the production seventh-generation Z06 model (see next chapter), which pulled many engineering and design features from the C6.R's highly successful previous generation of racers. In addition for 2014, two previous series—American Le Mans Series (ALMS) and Grand-Am Rolex Sport Car Series—merged under new sponsorship as the Tudor United SportsCar Championship, under the Tudor watch company. Corvette started its season with the 24-hour endurance classic at Daytona, where electrical gremlins sidelined one of the cars while number 4 finished fifth in class. A two-hour run at Sebring in March proved equally frustrating as Corvette finished sixth and eighth, but those memories quickly disappeared at Long Beach with a class win and a third. Corvette took the class again at Laguna, and then Corvette Racing packed up and shipped the team to France for the 24 Hours of Le Mans in mid-June. At that race, teammates Antonio Garcia, Jan Magnussen, and Jordan Taylor, driving the number 73 C7.R, finished second in GTE Pro class, completing 338 laps or 2,862.5 miles over the 24 hours. Two weeks later, at Watkins Glen on June 29, Garcia and Magnussen took the GT Le Mans class victory in car number 3, while the DP Corvettes took third and fourth overall. Then at Mosport, near Toronto, Canada, on July 13, the two C7.R cars and a pair of Corvette DP Prototypes fought a tough seventh race of the season. Corvette DP number 90, the Spirit of Daytona entry co-driven by Richard Westbrook and Michael Valiante, finished second overall, while number 5, the Action Express car with Christian Fittipaldi and João Barbosa sharing driving duties, followed two places back. In sixth overall, Magnussen and Garcia took GT Le Mans honors.

In late July, Corvette celebrated its first Indianapolis win as Fittipaldi and Barbosa took the DP number 5 prototype across the finish line first overall in the Brick Yard Grand Prix. It was a strong show for the Corvette DPs with the Spirit of Daytona Entry, number 90, driven by Westbrook and Valiante, finishing third. Car number 10, the Wayne Taylor Racing prototype, crossed the line in fourth overall with driving duties shared between Taylor's sons Ricky and Jordan. The Tudor series provided sports car and prototype racing fans very close and exciting races through 2014.

5 RADICAL RESTYLING

THE SEVENTH GENERATION

Discussions of Chevrolet's seventh-generation Corvette began in 2007. It was rather unfortunate timing for its parents, which had to endure the enormous financial crisis of 2008 and 2009, followed by General Motors' bankruptcy from June 2009 through December 2013, when the U.S. Treasury recovered $39 billion of its $51 billion investment in the automaker through assets sales. This bailout saved more than 1.2 million jobs in the reorganized corporation. By this time, the seventh generation, which had debuted in January 2013, was available to the public.

In the earliest planning sessions, discussions had included evolving the Corvette from its traditional front engine/rear drive to a mid-engine configuration, but as time passed, development costs prohibited this change. The 2013 Corvette used a 455-horsepower 6.2-liter V-8 with the buyer's choice of seven-speed manual or six-speed automatic transmission. An innovative cylinder-deactivation system gave the sports car the fuel economy of a compact and praises from owners who, in less frugal moments, discovered acceleration from 0 to 60 miles per hour in just 3.8 seconds. Sophisticated independent suspension delivered true sports car handling.

Early critics harped on the car's rear-end styling, critical of its resemblance to the popular and newly reintroduced Camaro. Overall, the new Corvette's traditional curvilinear forms became sharp angles, creases, and numerous new surfaces to catch the observer's eye. Its resemblance to the attractive (and considerably more expensive) Ferrari 458 surely was no accident. In fact, its designers have admitted that its more radical restyling was intended to attract younger observers (and hopefully buyers) than the car's traditional audience. Whereas cynics had characterized the sixth-generation C5 replacement as a C5.5, no one gave the C7 anything less than full marks for engineering and styling. The interior received as much attention as the outside appearance, introducing an innovative twin-cockpit concept that separated and emphasized the equal but different pleasures of driving and riding.

Above: **Menacing is a good word to describe the stance of the Z06.** *Photo © 2020, courtesy GM Media Archives*

For 2014, the C7 with its removable roof panel also offered a full convertible model. Premiere Editions were available, the popular Z51 Performance Package returned, and the 3LT Interior Package appeared. At the annual SEMA show, Chevrolet also unveiled the Gran Turismo Concept, commemorating the Sony PlayStation game console's fifteenth anniversary.

Model year 2015 brought engineering and performance innovations and improvements. Chevrolet replaced its six-speed automatic transmission with a new optional eight-speed automatic, improving performance and fuel economy. The Z06 returned, with tweaks to the basic 6.2-liter engine that boosted output from the basic 455 horsepower/460 foot-pounds of torque to 650 horsepower and 650 foot-pounds, available as either a coupe or a convertible.

Great drives are what the Corvette has been about, certainly since engineers such as Zora Arkus-Duntov got their hands on the cars in the 1950s. But starting with the 2015 models, Corvette engineers and product planners provided owners a way to take home a souvenir of the drive that wasn't just a T-shirt or a moving violation citation. The new Performance Data Recorder incorporated a high-definition video camera, telemetry recorder, and Track, Sport, Performance, and Touring modes, all writable onto an SD card with its dedicated loading slot in the glove box. Although the feature targeted Corvette track-day devotees particularly, more than a few owners confessed to improving cornering speeds on the daily commute to work.

In addition to carrying over the 3LT Interior Package, Chevrolet introduced Stingray Atlantic Design and Pacific Design packages, reflecting how Corvette planners viewed East and West Coast customers: the Atlantic was a luxurious GT convertible while the Pacific was a track-day-oriented performance coupe. In 2015, the C7.R emerged, too, from Pratt and Miller to battle Ferraris, Aston Martins, Porsches, and the GT Le Mans series in North America and Europe. For those enamored with Corvette's racing efforts, the company offered the Z06 CR.7 Edition as a 500-example homage to the international series race cars.

In contrast, model year 2016 was more about a shuffling of exterior colors and interior packages, with no engineering or performance changes. Interior trim designations added levels 3LT and LZ, each increasing the proportions of carbon fiber, leather, and "sueded microfiber" in the cabin. As one sharp-eyed observer noted, "The higher the number, the more you get, and the more you pay."

Above: Chevrolet assembled 550 Premiere Edition convertibles, each with the six-speed automatic transmission as standard equipment. *Photos © 2020, courtesy GM Media Archives*

Left: The 3LT interior, the limited-production Atlantic Edition, made for a delightful open sports car. *Photo © 2020, courtesy GM Media Archives*

HOW DO YOU TOP A STINGRAY?

Corvette Stingray convertible 3LT in Blade Silver Metallic with available Z51 Performance Package and Atlantic Design Package.

Above: **Take a black car, put it in a black studio, and add light. The result: stunning.**
Photo © 2020, courtesy GM Media Archives

The legendary Corvette Grand Sport returned for 2017. Stylistically, it was a masterful blend of Z06, Z51, and Stingray body styling and bits but with notable wheel, tire, and brake upgrades. Michelin Pilot Super Sport tires rode on new Grand Sports wheels on 19x10s in the front and 20x12s at the rear. Brembo brake rotors and calipers fit inside the new bigger wheels, and all this connected the chassis to the ground through Corvette's Magnetic Ride Control system with an electronic limited-slip rear differential. Engine adjustments delivered 460 horsepower with dry-sump lubrication. The seven-speed manual transmission provided an electronic Revs Match capability to turn every driver into a heel-and-toe-downshifting master. If the Grand Sport was not exclusive enough, Chevrolet offered the Z15 Heritage Package and a Z25 Collector Edition, though with 1,000 manufactured, collectability may be a relative concept.

Model year 2018 continued the base Stingray as well as the Z06 and Grand Sport models. And it reintroduced Corvette's ultimate achiever, the ZR1. Specific engine tunes boosted output to 755 horsepower and 715 foot-pounds of torque. The ZL1 version included the rev-matching seven-speed manual or eight-speed automatic transmissions and significantly more carbon-fiber bodywork as well as an elevated full body-width rear wing.

The production schedule for 2018 was startlingly brief—June and July followed by a three-month plant shutdown until November when manufacture resumed. The factory was hardly idle, however, as Chevrolet used the time to reorganize the facility well in advance of starting assembly of the successor C8. Late-production C7s benefited from the relocated paint shops and body final-assembly areas. More disappointing to enthusiasts, Bowling Green plant management discontinued all factory tours for more than 18 months. Because of the shutdown, sales numbers for 2018 looked grim: just 9,686 cars (only 16 cars more than 1959 with its 9,670 production). But, as has been the case since 1954, rumors of the Corvette's demise were greatly exaggerated.

Above and left: When the covers came off the ZR1 coupe at the Los Angeles Auto Show, the crowd of professionally trained, jaded, blasé automotive journalists erupted into loud applause and approval. For those who believe cars are only sporty if they are convertibles, Chevrolet had one of those too. *Photos © 2020, courtesy GM Media Archives*

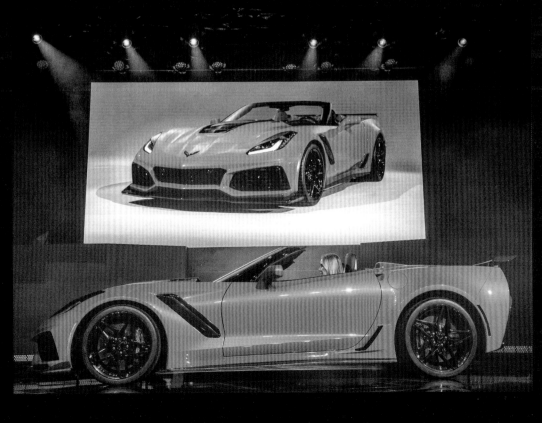

Top and above: The C7.R won the GTE-Pro Class at the 24 Hours of Le Mans with Oliver Gavin, Tommy Milner, and Jordan Taylor sharing driving duties. The 2,475-pound race car (including driver, fluids, and fuel) ran Chevrolet's LT 5.5-liter V8 developing 491 horsepower at 6,000 rpm. *Photos by Richard Prince © 2020. Courtesy of Prince and GM Media Archives*

To commemorate Corvette's 65th year—2018—product planners released a Z30 Edition, also known as the Carbon 65, in convertible and coupe form with plenty of carbon fiber on either Grand Sport or Z06 platforms. And to celebrate the whole point of the Corvette, product planners released an end-of-series Drivers Edition Corvette Grand Sport, available in four color schemes selected by the CR.7 team drivers.

The Bowling Green plant shut down in mid-November 2019 after assembling the final C7s. Chevrolet public relations announced that C8 production was to begin in February 2020 with training for existing and new employees starting when the plant reopened in early December 2019.

Above: **The Corvette Carbon 65 Edition boasts a fender-top graphic, a door logo, and carbon fiber everywhere else.** *Photo © 2020, courtesy GM Media Archives*

THE 2020 STINGRAY

THE EIGHTH GENERATION

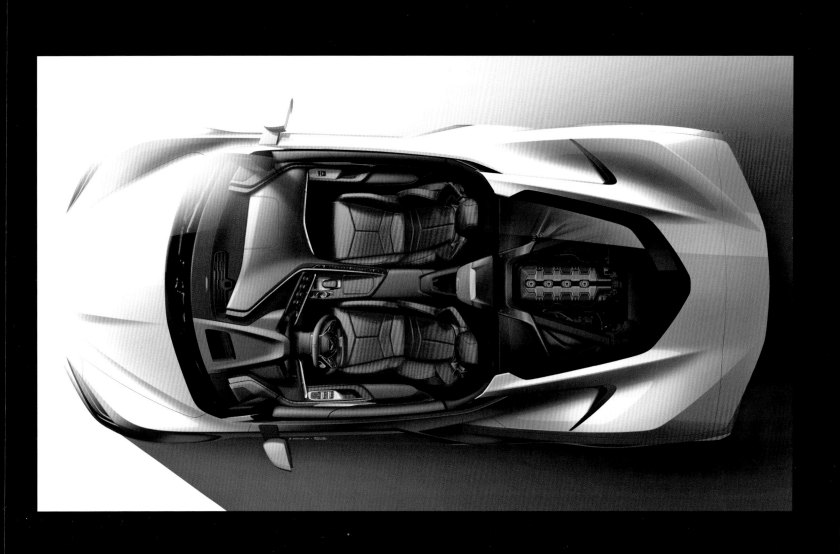

Executive chief engineer Tadge Juechter explained the Corvette's long-anticipated shift from a front- to mid-engine design by returning to the 1960s and one man: "Zora Arkus-Duntov, the man who put Corvette on the map, was mainly focused on engineering and nothing else. He lived in a time when the elite racing classes were changing, shifting from engines in front to engines placed behind the driver." For Duntov, a racer himself, building a mid-engine Corvette became his career-long obsession.

Juechter recognized potential limitations in bringing this long-cherished concept into full—and exclusive—production. It's not as though Chevrolet authorized two C8s, one with the front engine owners were so familiar with and another mid-engine option.

"We knew we could 'do' a mid-engine car," Juechter acknowledged, "but our biggest question was, 'Is it going to be something that you can live with? Will it have a reasonable amount of luggage storage? Will it be loud—you have an engine inches from you?'" According to *Car & Driver*'s Rich Ceppos, "Extensive acoustic insulation has made the C8 not only quieter by three decibels at 70 mph than the C7, but just plain quiet. This kind of dynamic bandwidth is almost unheard of in the mid-engine exotic realm. Can a car that looks this angry actually be too refined?" Its angry looks, described by many as more Ferrari than Chevrolet, entered design history books as one of the final accomplishments of chief stylist Tom Peters, who retired in the spring of 2019 following design approval.

Ceppos took a new C8 and an identically spec'd C7 to Grattan Raceway Park, a 2.2-mile circuit in Grand Rapids, Michigan, to determine whether Corvette's experiment had worked. "Mid-engine sports cars, due to their superior weight distribution, should lap a racetrack quicker than a front-engined car," he wrote. At the end of the dozen-lap test,

the C8 posted times that were 0.9 seconds quicker over the 2.2 miles. A nearly one-second improvement is something race teams spend tens of thousands of dollars and countless track hours in testing to achieve. In a theoretical one-hour race at Gratan, the C8 completed 41.81 laps, compared to 41.38 for the C7. Victory by half a lap over second place is a huge margin.

Chevrolet unveiled the coupe on July 18, 2019, many months before the first customer deliveries. The coupe features a lift-off roof panel familiar to C7 owners that stores in the rear trunk in lieu of two golf bags. The front trunk accommodates a standard airline roll-aboard overhead bag. Through clever design, packaging, and engineering, the new Corvette offers a retractable hardtop as its convertible, first seen on October 2, 2019. The raise-or-lower operation takes just 12 seconds and is possible while the car is traveling up to 30 miles per hour. The hardware, including six electric motors to lift, relocate, and fold the top, adds 77 pounds to the total weight of the car. The elevated headrests remain, preserving the profile of the coupe, yet airflow around the occupants is pure convertible. The top storage sacrifices no space from the car's other storages areas.

Car interiors—especially those at the highest end of manufacturer lineups—have all too often disappointed buyers and owners. Budgets go to engineering and to exterior design. The engineering certainly benefits the owners with safe, satisfying, and even thrilling driving capabilities. The exteriors are the seductresses, inspiring some to open their checkbooks and even greater numbers to envy those who can. But then ownership becomes a kind of betrayal: onlookers follow your progress with their eyes, while inside you endure seating as uncomfortable as bus station waiting-room chairs, while plastic switchgear, common to your car and every other one in the car maker's lineup, including those cheapest penalty-box economy-class rentals, tune the audio and operate windows and wipers.

Chevrolet turned an important corner—and stretched budgets for better quality and feel in soft goods and hard surfaces—with their approach to the C7, which featured a divided cockpit concept. The C8, with its "Driver-Centric Cockpit," reinforced its concern for those matters and pressed forward its attention to details. "The expectation for what that car has is set so high by the exterior," acknowledged Tristan Murphy, lead interior designer.

Above: The many-faceted bodywork Corvette introduced with the seventh-generation models in 2014 takes another step because of the requirements for engine breathing and cooling with its engine amidships. *Photo © 2020, courtesy GM Media Archives*

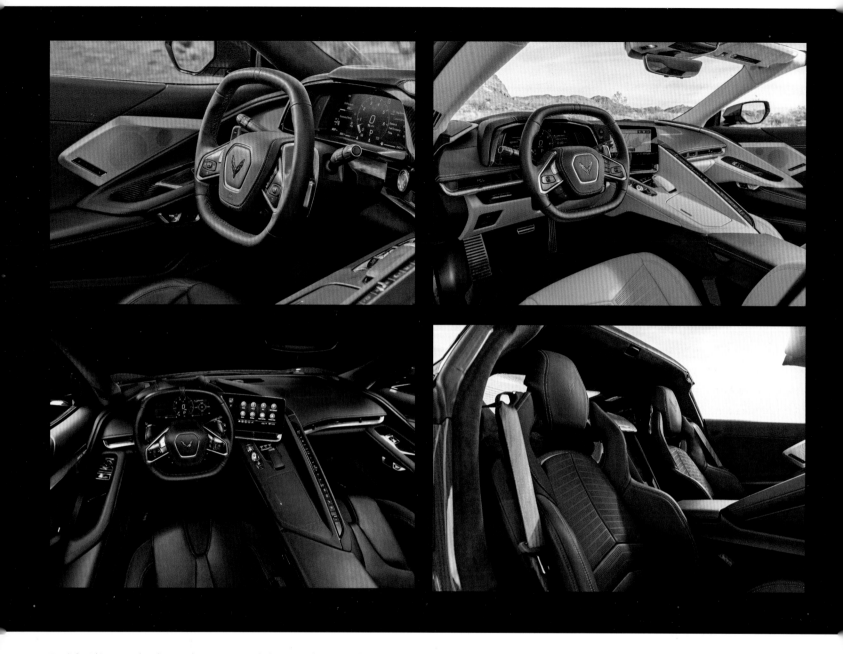

Top left: A bit unusual and somewhat controversial, the squared steering wheel is a matter of function. With the car's low cowl, forward vision was improved, but a round wheel blocked the view, hence the top and bottom arcs designers refer to as "the flats." *Photo © 2020, courtesy GM Media Archives*

Bottom left: The instrument cluster, with countless options for programming and information display, is another reason for the unusual steering wheel because it provides increased visibility. Audio entertainment, navigation, and communication with the outside world are linked through the large "infotainment" screen at center. *Photo © 2020, courtesy GM Media Archives*

Top right: Tristan Murphy created the highly personalized "Driver-Centric Cockpit" for the eighth-generation Corvette. There are some controls the passenger cannot even reach but are natural and comfortable for the driver. *Photo © 2020, courtesy GM Media Archives*

Bottom right: Three levels of interior trim—1LT, 2LT, and 3LT—offer seats that range from the GT1 comfortable seat to the race-track secure "Competition Sport" seat. *Photo © 2020, courtesy GM Media Archives*

"Sitting in the car, the controls literally wrap around you in all directions," Juechter explained. At the same time, mounting the engine behind the cockpit enabled exterior designers to push the front deck lid lower and gave interior designers an opportunity for significantly improved forward visibility. "We had these great open sight lines," Murphy emphasized, "compared to what you had with a front engine. So we wanted to make sure the [steering] wasn't obscuring it in any way." This led to a design decision that brought one of the few criticisms of the car: its square wheel. "Now we have 'flats' on the bottom and on the top, creating a roughly rectangular opening that gives you a perfect view of the wide-screen configurable display," Juechter added.

Corvette again offered the car in three trim levels, designated 1, 2, and 3LT. Model product planners aimed the 1LT at driving and performance purists, with the lightest weight and fewest excesses. For example, the 1LT audio system was a Bose 10-speaker configuration. The 2LT added four speakers among other upgrades that also included a "front curb view camera" option to protect the nose and wheels from curb strikes. Chevrolet priced the 1LT at $59,995 for the coupe and $67,495 for the convertible—the model traditionally selected by some 50 percent of Corvette buyers. The 2LT prices were set at $67,295 and $74,295; the 3LT started at $71,945 for the coupe and $78,945 for the convertible.

There were three seats available: the Mulan-leather upholstered GT1, standard in 1LT and 2LT models; the Napa leather–wrapped GT2 seat, optional in 2LT and standard in 3LT models; and the Competition Sport Seat, with deeper bolsters for greater cornering support.

Power for the C8 came from its new aluminum-block dry-sump 6.2-liter LT2 V-8 that, with the $5,000 Z51 Performance Package or the performance exhaust option, delivers 495 horsepower at 6,450 rpm and 470 foot-pounds of torque at 5150 rpm. Mid-engine placement revised the 50/50 weight balance Juechter and his engineers achieved with the C7 and gave the new car 60.6 percent on the rear tires. Chevrolet stated that in the Z51 configuration, acceleration from a standstill to 60 miles per hour took just 2.9 seconds, the quarter mile required only 11.2 seconds at 122 miles per hour, and the car's top speed was published at 194 miles per hour.

The car used an eight-speed double-clutch Tremec transmission (the only one offered). Sales of manual gearboxes onboard C7s dwindled to just 20 percent and doomed the seven-speed. On the C8, drivers would select park, reverse, drive, and "manual" functions by pushbuttons inset into the center console; paddles behind the steering wheel took care of individual gear changes. To further enhance handling, the optional $1,895 Magnetic Ride Control system introduced on the 50th Anniversary C5 is in Generation 4.0 on the C8, with suspension input reaction times as brief as 10 to 15 milliseconds. Driver Mode Selection allowed distinctions beyond the usual Tour, Sport, Track, and Weather, which were preset. My-Mode and Z-Mode allow owners to customize settings: My-Mode became a regular-use setting, say for those participating regularly in track days at the same circuit. This could be "keyed up," that is, set into the system so it engaged with each key-start. Z-Mode was single use—a new route from work offers curves and hills—but was not automatically engaged on engine start. The car rode on 19-inch front wheels and 20-inch rears, fitted with Michelin Pilot Sport tires. Four-piston Brembo ventilated brakes handle stopping.

Above: The heart of the new C8 is its 6.2-liter (1.6 gallon) LT2 V-8. With the Z51 Performance Package, the engine produces 495 horsepower at 6,450 rpm and 470 pound-feet of torque at 5,150 rpm. *Photo © 2020, courtesy GM Media Archives*

Above: **The best way to see the entire shape of the new C8 is to have two of them! The rear roofline of the convertible sacrifices the engine view, which is a wonderful feature of these coupes.**
Photo © 2020, courtesy GM Media Archives

As expected, the Enhanced Navigation system offered a three-dimensional view. Bluetooth pairing was as simple as placing the phone above the audio volume button to pair the two, and 4G LTE WiFi was available. A $1,495 front-lift suspension option elevated the nose of the car 2 inches to clear driveways and curbs and was GPS programmable. The Performance Data Recorder (PDR) from the C7 received a video upgrade from 720 pixels to 1080 pixels to enhance visual memory. A Valet Mode on the PDR let owners record the behavior of those trusted with driving the car.

"This new Stingray is the car for a new generation," interior designer Murphy stated, revealing that this Corvette was aimed equally at those who had driven them—or at least wished they had—through several generations, as well as at those who had Italian mid-engine supercar posters on their walls as kids. The new car's deeply carved, multifaceted exterior skin extended ideas introduced with the C7 into the realm of international ultraperformance sports car design. "People are going to see it and say, 'Oh my gosh, that's the car I have to have!'" Murphy added. "You open the door, climb in, and think, 'This thing feels like a Corvette.' But it feels like no Corvette you've ever been in before."

As Ceppos hinted in his *Car & Driver* story, "This is but the opening salvo in Chevy's supercar revolution." Beyond declaring, "This is by far the best Corvette interior ever," he noted that equipping a 1LT with the Z51 and FE4 magnetic dampers led to a sticker price of "only $66,890. This is nothing less than the democratization of the exotic car." But there is more to come: For its racing purposes, Chevrolet developed a 5.5-liter dual-overhead camshaft 32-valve V-8 using a flat-plane crankshaft. For homologation purposes, it must be available to customers with something like 600 horsepower on offer. As the Z06, it was destined for twin-turbos. A hybrid, developing 1,000 combined horsepower, is in the pipeline.

Chevrolet announced creation of the C8.R during the C8 convertible introduction, the first complete redesign of Corvette's racer since the 1999 C5.R. This new edition—mid-engine, naturally—made use of that new Chevrolet 5.5-liter twin-cam four-valve-per-cylinder normally aspirated V-8, developing 500 horsepower and 480 foot-pounds of torque with appropriate restrictors in place. The compact six-speed Xtrac sequential manual transmission left room to fit an airflow diffuser in back; this could be adjusted for individual tracks.

Mark Kent, Corvette's director of motorsports, made clear that the C8.R shares about one hundred really large parts with its series production sibling. Corvette chief engineer Ed Piatek explained that, with the convertible in mind from the start, his engineers developed the C8 with additional stiffness from the tunnel structure through the center of the body. The C8 platform was aluminum, its body made of SMC composites. "It was important for us to develop the new race car alongside the production car, so that each product could properly take advantage of the new architecture."

Two C8.Rs debuted at the Rolex 24 race at Daytona International Speedway January 25–26, 2020. Car number 3, with Antonio Garcia, Jordan Taylor, and Nicky Catsburg co-driving, qualified 13th fastest overall and fastest in GT Le Mans (GTLM) for the pole position in its class. The second team car (number 4), with Tommy Milner, Marcel Fässler, and Oliver Gavin, was 17th fastest and 5th quickest in class. Seven cars started in their class, including two Porsches, two BMWs, and a Ferrari. Antonio Garcia drove the number 3 across the finish line in 4th place in GTLM class, 16th overall, and a single lap behind the class winner. This was a fine performance for a racing debut 24 hours in length. The car completed 785 laps of the 3.56-mile Speedway Sports Car Course, covering 2,794.6 miles at an average speed of 116.4 miles per hour.

Below: The new C8 sits on a 107.2-inch (2.7 m) wheelbase to support its 182.3-inch (4.6 m) overall length. The coupe stands 48.6 inches (1.2 m) tall and weighs 3,366 pounds dry, just 80 pounds more than its predecessor. *Photo © 2020, courtesy GM Media Archives*

Below: The new Corvette has been called "a supercar for the rest of us," "the most significant car of the year," and "the Car of the Year" for 2020. Some have described its front view as "angry," but perhaps that's just the reaction of competing carmakers stunned by its $60,000 price. *Photo © 2020, courtesy GM Media Archives*

Series production was due to start in February 2020 following delays caused when UAW workers struck General Motors for 40 days in September and October 2019.

Ceppos, in *Car & Driver*, concluded, "It's clear the new C8 isn't just a better Corvette but a supercar for the rest of us." His American colleagues agreed, and opportunities for praise from British, Australian, and Japanese publications were likely, as Chevrolet planned to offer not only left-hand-drive C8s but also right-hand-drive versions for the first time. *Road & Track* writer Jason Cammisa summed up the new Stingray: "The C8 Corvette is, without question, the most significant car of the year." *Motor Trend* magazine concurred, naming it the Car of the Year 2020.

INDEX

255